# Thirteen
# *Sizzling*
# *Confessions*
# *and...*
# CRIMES OF
# THE HEART

Leisure Entertainment Service Co., Inc.
(LESCO Distribution Group)
And
Dorchester Media LLC.

For Paul J. Gross,
a man who turned good ideas
into great things. Sorely missed
and deeply loved by family and
friends

Leisure Entertainment Service Co., Inc. (LESCO Distribution Group)
65 Richard Road Ivyland, PA 18974   www.leisureent.com

Published by special arrangement with Dorchester Media, LLC.

Printed in the United States of America.

A Special LESCO Edition

FIRST TIME IN PAPERBACK

Dorchester Media is
a consumer magazine publisher.

Our Women's Romance Group of
eight titles includes the world's
largest and best selling women's
romance magazine, *True Story*.
*True Story* has a great history
(1919) and heritage and continues to
touch the heart, mind and soul of
readers by sharing everyday
experiences of romantic life.

In addition to *True Story*, sister
publications include *True Confessions*,
*True Romance*, and *True Love*.
Special collector magazines from
the substantial archive include
*True Story Remember When*.

For more information on all of
Dorchester Media publications, write
to Publisher, Dorchester Media,
333 Seventh Avenue, 11th Floor,
New York, N.Y. 10001.

We hope you enjoy the book.

# Table Of Contents

This book consists of true stories. Names, characters, places and incidents were changed. Any resemblance to actual events, locales, or persons, living or dead, is entirely coincidental.

An *Original* Publication of Dorchester Media, LLC.

ISBN:
First LESCO Edition Printing: February 2006
1-60016-010-7
Printed in the U.S.A.

Leisure Entertainment Service Co., Inc.
(LESCO Distribution Group)
65 Richard Road Ivyland, PA 18974
www.leisureent.com

# THIRTEEN
# SIZZLING
# CONFESSIONS
# AND CRIMES
# OF THE HEART

# FATAL OBSESSION

My memories of high school seemed especially sweet when I had been out of school for fifteen years. The bad times were forgotten and the good times magnified. My first date, prom night, and my first love, were all memories that held a special place in my heart. At a class reunion, all those memories are taken out and lovingly examined, and I wanted my reunion to be no exception.

When Teddy called a few weeks before our fifteen-year class reunion, I tumbled back in time. Teddy was a bad boy, the type parents don't trust and teenage girls can't seem to resist. His good looks, rebellious toughness, and the reason for his arrival in our town set him apart from the rest of us. When he was fifteen, Teddy came to live with his aunt and uncle to recover from a knife wound. The fight had almost killed him, but his brush with death hadn't tamed him a bit. As soon as he had healed, he went looking for the toughest boy in school, which happened to be my boyfriend, Clint Sharpe.

They met under the bridge at the south of town late one night, and although both emerged bruised and bloody, neither could claim victory. Teddy never forgot that he was unable to beat Clint, and he hated him for the rest of his life.

Because Clint and Teddy were enemies, I wasn't interested in associating with Teddy at all. But fate intervened. My brother, Curtis, and Teddy had become best friends, and although Teddy was supposed to be living with his aunt and uncle, he actually stayed at our house more often.

I liked Clint a great deal and I gave him my total loyalty. When Teddy began to pay more attention to me than necessary, I just ignored him. It was an uncomfortable situation.

Unfortunately, Teddy could not be ignored. Even our teachers, who disapproved of him, found themselves under his spell. With little effort he was an excellent student. And often there were times when he would recite from memory—Shakespeare, Emily Dickinson, or Charles Dickens. Students, as well as teachers were mesmerized. He was fascinating—a tough guy who had the potential to be anything he desired.

One weekend when Clint was out of town, I accepted a ride home from Teddy. It never occurred to me that Clint might consider it a betrayal, or that Teddy would embellish the facts. But that was exactly what happened. Clint cruelly dumped me and broke my heart. And despite the fact that he had caused our breakup, Teddy never forgave Clint for his treatment of me.

Gradually, Teddy slipped into my life and before long he had my head spinning with his kisses, poetry, and conversation that was always interesting, because of the vast amount of information he had stored in his mind.

Then another man came into my life and changed my destiny forever. . . .

My husband, Robert, has always insisted that he married me to win a five-dollar bet, made on the night we met. He and his friend saw me from across the room and Robert bet that he would marry me, even though he didn't know my name.

Unable to choose between Teddy and Robert, I began to see both of them. I saw Teddy after school and on Saturdays. Because Robert was from the next town, I saw him on Sunday evenings. It was an arrangement that suited me, and neither boy knew about the other. Then my brother, Curtis, decided to throw a wrench in the works and arrange for both of them to arrive on the same day, at almost the same time.

Teddy left in anger, and when he had gone Robert gave me an ultimatum. I could marry him in August or he would walk out the door and never come back. I decided to marry him. Teddy begged me not to marry Robert, and so did my parents because they wanted me to wait, but I married Robert anyway. And despite the hardships of a teenage marriage, I never regretted my decision. Robert and I have had the kind of passionate, perfect love that most people only dream about.

After a month I was pregnant with the first of our four children, and I was engrossed in a life that was hard, but full of love and laughter.

Teddy joined the Army, and I only saw him once before he left. He told me he would always love me.

The next time I heard from him was the day he called about our class reunion. We talked for quite a while, reminiscing about the things we'd done, the people we'd known, and catching up on what our old friends were doing. When he hung up I didn't expect to hear from him again, although I assumed I would see him at our reunion.

When he called again, to find out more information on the reunion, I thought nothing of it. But the third time he called I knew the reunion was just an excuse. He began the conversation by telling me that he had never gotten over me and still loved me. I was surprised, but flattered.

He told me that he had been married and that he had gotten a divorce, one of the main reasons being that he had named his daughter after me. After he told his wife, she found life with an old love between them intolerable, and she left him. I felt awful about that, but I told him I was happily married and in love with my life and my family. I thought that would be the end of it.

But it was far from over. When I told him he shouldn't call me anymore, he became angry. He ignored me and kept on talking.

"Do you know what I do for a living?" he asked.

"No," I replied, never dreaming that his reply would start a sequence of events that even now seems like a horrible nightmare.

"I'm a hit man," he said.

I laughed, thinking it was a joke, and thinking he was possibly a bit crazy.

"You don't believe me? Do you want me to prove it?" he asked.

I stopped laughing. His voice had turned cold and

hard, and suddenly I had the awful feeling that he was telling the truth.

"I can prove it—I can send someone to visit you, or tell you the name I go by. Of course, that would be the end of it for you and your family," he said.

"No, no! Please don't tell me anything," I begged. "I don't want to know anything else. I believe you."

I was too stunned to do much more than listen for the next few minutes as he continued to talk. When I came to my senses, I told him not to call me again and I hung up the phone. When it rang a few minutes later, I didn't answer it, and then I didn't answer the phone for the rest of the day.

"Don't ever hang up on me again," he screamed as soon as I answered the phone the next day. "If you do, I'll have Robert killed—you won't know when until it's too late. Maybe one day he'll answer the door and someone will just blow him away. Or maybe he'll have an accident; maybe one of the children will have an accident."

"Oh, no, please don't hurt Robert or my kids," I pleaded. I felt an overwhelming terror. I didn't want to talk to him, but I had to. I had to keep him happy so he wouldn't hurt my family. That was all I could think about, and all I cared about. I don't even know what we talked about, because I blocked it out.

When he finally hung up, I began to think more clearly. I wavered between disbelief and terror, trying to convince myself that this couldn't be happening to me. Things like this just don't happen in a small town like ours.

The phone calls that followed convinced me that he was really telling the truth. I also realized that he was having me watched. I never could figure out how he did it, but he began to mention clothing I had worn, places I had been, and people I had spoken to. He knew things he shouldn't have known.

I was too frightened of the consequences to tell Robert or contact the police. The constant threats kept me in a sort of limbo. I was afraid to leave the house for fear of being watched and I was afraid to stay home for fear that he would call, or worse, show up on my doorstep.

At one point Teddy questioned me about Clint Sharpe, wanting to know where he lived. The fact that Clint had gone into law enforcement grated on his nerves. It was just one more reason for him to hate Clint—one more reason to want him dead. I refused to tell him anything. I pretended I knew nothing, and hoped he wouldn't have time to check. I knew Teddy was busy taking care of business because it was sometimes several days or a week between calls. He never told me any names, and every time he tried to tell me details I would plead with him not to. I think he enjoyed that.

The whole business made me sick. I had lost thirty-five pounds since Teddy began calling me and I was very nervous and upset. I worried constantly that one of my children would just disappear, that Robert would have an accident, or that Teddy would come to my home and force me to leave with him.

Then one day he called and told me he was getting out of the business. He couldn't take any more. He had killed his best friend—he hadn't wanted to do it, but when it came down to it, it was either his friend or his own life. I felt sick and didn't want to listen to any more, but he seemed to need to talk about his friend. I did my best to tune out what he was saying, but it made me feel very sick.

After that, his phone calls were less frequent because the organization was after him. He had to keep moving.

He called me from many places, but I never knew exactly where he was, and I begged him never to tell me. For a short while I was even able to believe that it was over, because he didn't call for several weeks. But it turned out he had been staying with his sister, recovering from a gunshot wound. He was still on the run, but they were always just one step behind him. All I hoped was that he would stay far from me and my family.

When vacation time rolled around, I was thrilled to get away. I could relax for a while, knowing that my family was safe with me and that Teddy wouldn't know where to find us. But time seemed to fly by and soon we were back home.

Teddy was furious that I had been gone and began making more threats to get me scared. He wanted me to come stay with him, but I didn't want to go. I played along with him, because he would get so angry when I balked or wouldn't pretend to agree with him. Every time he threatened me, I hoped that they would catch up with him and put an end to my nightmare.

Then came the day I will never forget as long as I live. It was a few weeks after we got home from vacation and Robert came home unexpectedly early. One look at his face told me that something awful had happened.

The FBI had called him and told him a foolish story. They told him I was planning to run off with another man, a man wanted for a lot of crimes. They also told him if I continued to have contact with the fugitive I would become an accomplice. They made it sound like I wanted to run off with Teddy and was willingly conspiring to get rid of Robert.

Robert was angry, enraged, and in shock. He couldn't understand how I could have kept something like this from him. I told Robert the real story of how Teddy had threatened him and the children, how Teddy seemed to know everything I did, and how frightened I was. And I promised that I would never keep a secret from him again. He knew that I had only done what I felt I had to do to protect our family. We discussed everything about the situation, and decided to comply with the FBI.

The FBI called me that evening. The agent told me they had traced me through phone calls Teddy had made from an old house he had lived in. They said that there was also a tap on our phone and if they could get to Teddy first they might be able to save him. They also said that continued contact with Teddy would make me an accomplice. I had to hang up on him the next time he called.

"If you've got my phone tapped then you knew why I went along with what he said. You also knew he was threatening my family," I said to the agent.

"Yes, we know."

They knew the truth of the situation and yet they had given my husband the impression that I was a willing participant! I was outraged that the FBI would do this to me.

If this situation taught me anything, it was that there are a lot of cruel, insensitive people in the world—and sometimes they're supposed to be the good guys.

"If I hang up or just tell him not to call me any-more, he'll threaten my family and he'll keep calling back," I said.

"You can tell him what we've told you. If he calls after that, just hang up."

After the FBI called, I was a basket case. I was scared Teddy would call again. And I was scared of what might happen to my family if he got angry.

When Teddy finally called again, I told him exact-ly what the FBI had told me—to never call again. I could tell he was frightened when he told me that he understood, and that he wouldn't be calling me again. He was certain the end was near.

In the weeks that followed, Robert and I were both worried. As a protective measure we never went to my class reunion. We tried not to go out much. When we did go out, we always had to be cautious. A couple of times we were pretty fright-ened when men we didn't know, and whose cloth-ing immediately made them look out of place, were tailing us. I don't know if they were good guys or bad guys—it doesn't matter. Either way we aged a lot during that time. It took us a long time to get over the fear that someone could just walk in and start shooting.

For several months after this, our phone was tapped and there were always policemen driving by our house or following me around if I went shopping in the nearest city. I don't know if they were there to protect me or make sure I didn't meet Teddy.

The FBI never called again and neither did Teddy. A few months ago his cousin told me Teddy was killed in a car accident. I don't know if it was an accident, a murder, or an FBI plan to hide him, and I don't want to know. Because, even now, when I'm all alone in the house and the phone rings, a knot of terror wells up inside of me. And even though I know it can't be Teddy, sometimes, I just let it ring. . . .    THE END

# FORBIDDEN PASSION AND LUST

I saw Eric get out of his car and prayed: Please, God, let me love him the way I love my other brothers, nothing more. But then I caught sight of his familiar features, the laughing eyes that always made my heart beat faster, and I knew the old feeling was still there.

"Hello, Laura." He kissed me, and I felt the same intense emotions as I always had.

"Hi, Eric." I hadn't wanted to come home because I knew he'd be there, but I'd had to. Phillip, who had raised me and whom I'd come to look on as my father, had had an accident and needed care.

I hadn't seen Eric in years. But I still wanted him. I hated myself for it; he was engaged now, though his fiancé wasn't with him. Why couldn't I let go of the impossible situation and find ordinary happiness?

I kept busy all day, trying to keep my mind off him, hoping he wouldn't notice the color in my cheeks, the stammer in my voice when he was near. But as soon as Phillip was asleep and we were alone he pulled me toward him in front of the big fireplace where we'd played as kids.

His touch made my spine tingle. "Laura," he said, "it's still the same for me, too. What are we going to do?"

"I don't know." I clung to him, shivering and miserable. I wanted him to kiss me, wanted to abandon myself to the rising passion I felt. Yet I knew it was wrong. I'd never known what to do about Eric, from that long-ago day when the attraction had first begun. We'd had a long history of struggling with our desires. We'd been raised as brother and sister for thirteen unlucky years, had fought our own natures. I was tired of fighting.

How had my life become so tangled? It had started long ago, when I'd lost my real parents. My mother had died in childbirth. My father had to work extra hours to provide for me. One day when I was four he'd been driving, exhausted, along the highway and had been killed in an accident.

The loss of my parents left me with terrible scars. As I was growing up, I kept thinking that they'd both died, directly or indirectly, because I'd been born.

I went to live with my father's best friend, Phillip, his wife, Lois, and their five sons. Phillip and my dad had been in the Marines together, and had stayed friends afterward.

It must have been a struggle for Phillip and Lois to take me in—money was tight. Phillip was the owner of a boat that took tourists out fishing. During the hard winters he did odd jobs when he could find them.

But Phillip wanted me, and at first Lois did, too. She couldn't have any more children, and since they had only boys, she wanted a girl. She was hoping for someone who would help her clean house and cook; the boys worked with their father on the boat. But I disappointed her from the first. I hated being indoors, disliked her fussy ways, and wanted to be just like her sons, especially Eric, whom I idolized on sight. At supper I'd listen to his stories about the boat and then ask why I couldn't go on the boat like Eric. Phillip would laugh and think it was cute, but Lois always said sternly, "You're a girl. You don't belong on the boat." She disapproved of everything about me from the beginning. It only confirmed my feeling that there was something wrong with me.

When I was eight, Eric helped me make my first trip on the boat. Two of his brothers had come down with chicken pox in the middle of the tourist season. I'd been carrying their meals to them, while Lois complained I wasn't quick enough. When a third brother took sick, Phillip asked, "How'll I manage without a crew?"

"How about Laura?" Eric suggested.

Lois argued against my going but, for once, she lost.

Whenever I could, I'd be with Eric. From the very first, he was my hero, my god. His brothers were mean and made fun of me, calling me an orphan. Throughout my childhood that was my nickname. When Eric wasn't around, Kurt, the oldest, would yell, "Hey, Orphan, get me a drink of water. Hurry up, Orphan!" When Eric was there, they were careful of me. Even though he was the youngest, he was braver and smarter than they were. They all respected him.

# FORBIDDEN PASSION AND LUST

He was only two years older than me, but Eric was my protector. He'd walk me to school, make sure none of his brothers hurt me, and carry my books. He helped me with lessons and showed me how to do my homework.

Sometimes when he was around I'd catch Lois giving me a funny look. She was jealous of anyone who went near him. Eric was her favorite, and she had plans for him.

"You'll marry a rich girl, Eric," she'd say, glaring at me through narrowed eyes. "Someone who deserves you. And you'll get ahead in this world. You won't end up in a little nothing town, like your father."

She wanted him to live in a big city when she grew up. But Eric loved the shore. He seemed happiest when we were on the boat, breezes blowing our hair, or walking along the quiet shore together chasing gulls. "See those houses?" he'd say, pointing to the expensive homes facing the sea. "Someday I'm going to own one." And I'd dream with him the way children do.

"I'll live there with you Eric," I'd say. "I'll keep house for you."

Our best times were when we were little, before our bodies started developing. Once we began to mature, we were in danger, though we didn't know it then. We were caught in a trap that would hold us for years. . . .

I grew into a shy young woman, with hair I thought was too stringy, very few curves, and no confidence at all. I had nothing to say to anyone but Eric. When I was with him I felt smart and pretty. Otherwise I was all elbows and stammering hesitation. Once, when I was dressing for a school dance, he caught me looking in the mirror, telling my reflection how ugly I was.

"Don't, Laura," he said in a low voice, touching my hair. "You're beautiful."

Suddenly strangely excited, I walked away from him, my cheeks blazing. For some odd reason everything had changed and I felt beautiful—hadn't Eric said I was?

Lois had seen the whole thing and that night, before I left, she took me aside. "Don't get any ideas about your brother Eric," she told me.

"What do you mean?"

"Just remember, he's off-limits."

I was puzzled by what she'd said and soon forgot it. What I couldn't forget was Eric's touch, how wonderful it made me feel, and how alive. I danced with some of the boys at school but all I could think of was Eric. I wished I were home, with him. I loved to listen to him talk or walk with him to our private place, at the water, and sit with him there saying nothing.

I was the most miserable teenager in the world. If I wasn't with Eric, I was thinking about him, which was just as bad. I'd never paid much attention to my body when we were together, but now I was always careful to cover myself up when he was near. I even wore a bra under my bathrobe so that my growing curves wouldn't be at all visible. And Eric also seemed extra careful not to expose an inch of himself to me. He always buttoned his shirt. We'd been skinny dipping just a year ago, but now neither of us ever suggested it.

Periodically Lois warned me as she had the night

of the dance.

"I saw you making eyes at Eric, Laura," she'd say.

"Lois, you're wrong—"

"Just remember, I'm watching you."

She never let me forget that Eric and I had different lives ahead. He was going to college. She'd planned for it, scrimped and saved for his education. He was going to be a lawyer, settling in a big city.

The summer I turned sixteen she left for two weeks to take care of her sister in Detroit. It was a sad time for me as it was for Eric. In less than a month he'd leave for school. By unspoken agreement we were together all the time, working on the boat or in the house. The weather was unbearably hot. At night I'd wander out to get a breath of air. One evening Eric walked with me and we started aimlessly toward the water, half a mile inland along a deserted path. When we got there it was so peaceful and silent neither of us said anything. We sat near each other, careful not to touch.

"No one knows this place," Eric whispered.

"It's ours, private," I agreed.

Suddenly he turned and kissed me, full on the lips in a way I'd never been kissed before. For the first time I felt the fire start, the burning awareness I was to know so well over the next years. I returned the kiss, savoring the sweetness of his mouth.

"I don't want to go away, Laura. I don't want to leave you."

"But you have to—what about college?"

"I can go to a local school."

He pulled me toward him, more fiercely this time, and kissed me hungrily, held me close. I loved the

24

sensations racing through my body—every sense was heightened. After minutes had gone by I began to tremble, afraid of something I couldn't name. I stood abruptly. "Come on, we'd better go.

We left without any further discussion; he didn't try to convince me to stay. The next night, when I was through with my chores, he was waiting for me. Without a word we headed for the shore again. When we got there we picked up where we'd left off, tasting, touching, venturing further bit by wonderful bit. It seemed natural to be giving pleasure to Eric, to be seeking pleasure from him. There wasn't anyone in the world I was closer to.

For two weeks, while Lois was away, we continued to explore. One night during that time we became lovers. The physical act grew out of what we felt for one another. Though I was only sixteen, I felt as mature as any woman. I knew that I wanted only Eric, to be with him and share the rest of our lives together.

I lay in his arms on that last night, so long ago, and told him, "Your mother's coming home tomorrow."

"We'll have to tell her," he said. "I want to marry you."

My heart thrilled at his words but I remembered Lois's warnings over the years. "I'm worried, Eric. Your mother's not going to like this. She thinks of us as brother and sister."

He kissed the tip of my nose. "So does everyone else. We'll just have to tell them our plans, right?"

That made sense. After all, there was no blood between us—we'd been born to different sets of parents. Why was I afraid?

Lois came home the following night and never took her sharp eyes off me and Eric. In a few hours she was giving us suspicious looks—in some funny way she'd guessed our secret. She sent Eric on a long errand in town and called me into her room for a serious talk. Phillip sat near her, looking uncomfortable.

"Laura," she said, eyeing me coldly, "what have you and Eric been up to while I was away?"

"I—well—nothing," I began to stammer, and couldn't finish.

"You've made a mess of things. He's your brother."

"Yes, but only—" I began.

"Your real brother." She looked over at Phillip, who was holding a match to his pipe with shaking fingers. "A long time ago, while your father was in the war, Phillip spent a few nights with your mother. Nine months later you were born."

I stared. If the house had washed into the sea at that moment I couldn't have been more shocked. "But that can't be! I—"

"That's why Phillip was so willing to take you in. You're half his."

"No! It isn't true. . . ." Tears ran down my cheeks and I couldn't finish.

Phillip said to her softly, "Lois, maybe we shouldn't—"

"You stay out of this. I'll handle it." She turned back to me. "You have only yourself to blame, Laura. I warned you."

"But I love him!"

"Your brother? To love him that way is disgusting! You make me sick."

For minutes I cried hysterically. When I looked up and became aware of anything besides my tears I could see Phillip biting his lip, looking at me pityingly. He seemed to want to say something, but kept glancing at Lois fearfully.

I felt so ashamed. If I could have found a way to get rid of my body, I would have. I'd had relations with my own brother and I'd enjoyed it.

"Does Eric know he's half my brother?" I asked finally.

"No," Lois said. "He has a great career ahead of him. He'd never forgive himself for what he'd done."

That was true. He'd feel as terrible as I did now.

And yet ashamed as I was, I knew that I still wanted him. How awful I must have been to know I'd sinned and still wanted to do it again and again! I couldn't help myself. "Lois," I cried, "I still love him!"

"You're young. Once he goes away, you'll forget. It won't be the same."

"But what about until then?" I asked forlornly.

"You can go to my sister's tonight. I'll help you pack and tell her it was an emergency."

That's just what she did. I left the house so fast that I was gone before Eric returned.

The minute I walked into Lois's sister's house the phone rang. It was Eric, wanting to know what had happened. "You left in a hurry," he said.

"It was an emergency."

"You sound funny, Laura."

I didn't answer.

"Laura," he whispered, "I love you."

All I could do was cry, letting the tears splash noiselessly onto the receiver. In the silence I could hear his puzzlement. "I'm going to come down on

27

the weekend," he began.

"Don't, Eric! I won't be here."

"What's wrong? Tell me."

But I couldn't. Somehow the old feelings had come back, that I was no good. I'd ruined my parents' lives, had disappointed Lois, and now I'd wreck Eric's life if he didn't stay away.

I lied about my age and got a job as a practical nurse, working in a home where they wanted live-in help. I didn't tell Lois or Phillip where I was. I didn't want Eric to find out. The work was hard, but I welcomed it. I was too tired to think about Eric except at night, when I tossed restlessly in bed, unable to sleep. *Where is he? Does he still care about me?* I'd wonder.

In a month I moved onto another patient. By then I called Lois to let her know where I was and what I was doing. I told myself she'd be worried, but actually I was dying for news of Eric. Lois said he'd gone away to college. "He loves it there. He's doing very well."

He'd forgotten me. It was a blow—I couldn't forget him, no matter how hard I tried. But if he'd managed to get me off his mind and move on with his life, I was glad.

I didn't go home for Christmas. Eric would be there and I didn't want to start things up again.

A year passed. Every time I spoke to Lois she said Eric was fine, had adjusted well to school, and was making friends. It was time for me to think about my own life.

I'd been hired to care for a young man recovering from minor surgery, Mark Crater. He was the best-looking man I'd ever seen. And he was attracted to me, and as soon as he was well enough we started dating. He was always handsomely dressed and liked to bring me flowers. He took me to the finest restaurants, bought me jewelry, and told me how lovely I looked. He was a banker. When I asked where he worked, he said he worked for his father's bank.

I was hungry for his sweet talk. After a month I thought I was in love. We became engaged. When we made love I felt cool and in control. It wasn't the animal longing I'd had for Eric, the fire that threatened to consume me, but that passion was something I was ashamed of, something I wanted to forget.

When Christmas came again I decided to go home and introduce Mark to Lois and Phillip. I felt confident enough to face Eric again. If he'd forgotten about us, I could, too.

Eric had grown up; there was a new, manly look in his eye that spoke of pain and experience. Had that come from our breakup? I still felt pulled toward him but reminded myself that I was engaged now.

He and Mark didn't get along well at all. In spite of two years of college, Eric was still honest and open. Mark was a city guy, much more poised and sure of himself.

Eric and I weren't alone until after Christmas dinner. Lois had an emergency dental appointment and Phillip offered to show Mark the boat. Eric was all set to go with them but at the last minute he backed out and stayed behind.

As soon as we were alone Eric put his arms around me and kissed me. "I've been dying to do that," he whispered. The old heat started at the pit of my stomach. "See," he said. "You still care. Otherwise you couldn't kiss me that way."

"I—I thought you'd forgotten me."

"Forgotten you? I'll never forget. Why did you run away? What happened?"

"Look, Eric, it's all over. Whatever my reasons were, I'm engaged now," I said firmly.

"I don't think much of your choice," he commented hastily.

"Why, because he's a successful businessman and you're still at school?" The minute I said it I was sorry. I could tell that I'd hurt him, but I couldn't get the words back.

"He's too smooth, Laura. He'll hurt you."

"You're just jealous! You're acting like a little boy!" A muscle twitched in Eric's cheek. "Was I too childish for you? Is that why you didn't wait for me?"

I couldn't answer; I couldn't tell him the truth. Though it was icy cold, I grabbed my coat and ran outside to escape his anger. When Mark came back, I told him I wasn't feeling well and we went home right away.

Eric was right about Mark, as he was about so many things, but it took me years to discover it. Mark and I were married in the spring, and slowly I learned that he was a compulsive gambler, whose only pleasure was betting on horses. He was lucky during the first few years of our marriage. Then his father fired him and we began to live off my earnings. Soon I discovered he was taking money from my purse. He denied it, but I knew he was lying. Other things disappeared—jewelry, family heirlooms. He was stealing whatever was light enough to lift, and selling it. I confronted him and he said he'd stop gambling. He'd get a regular job, he promised.

I never told Lois the truth when I phoned her. I hadn't been back home in three years, not since that Christmas when I'd seen Eric. I didn't want to take a chance on another confrontation, especially now when my own life was such a mess. But I stayed in touch with Lois, since the need to know how Eric was, was almost a physical ache at times.

Eric was the only bright spot in her life. Especially since she was getting sicker with the cancer she'd been fighting. He was graduating soon, at the top of his class.

I missed him all the time. I'd lie awake in my lonely bed—Mark was out most nights playing cards—and dream that by some miracle Eric was next to me, that I'd wake up in his arms, touching him, holding him close.

I'd always thought that time would make me forget him, but it wasn't working out that way. Even though he was far away, he was the only person in the world that really mattered. I started saving for his graduation present, an expensive set of law books. I squirreled away nickels, dimes, and dollars, hiding them under a loose board near the corner of the carpet so that they'd be safe from Mark. I did without small luxuries, skimped on meals and clothing, so that I could add to my savings. Soon I had eight hundred dollars. I kept thinking of Eric's dear face, how pleased he'd be when he opened my present.

One autumn night Philip called me, Lois had passed away. It was a shock; I hadn't realized she was that sick. I threw some clothes into a suitcase and left a note for Mark before I went. He was out with friends at the track. All his promises of finding a job had turned out to be empty. My eye fell on the corner where I had hidden the money for Eric's present and wondered if I should take it with me. But I knew it wasn't safe to travel with that much cash. If Mark hadn't found it before, he probably wouldn't find it ever.

I found myself hungry to see Eric. Lois was gone now. Why shouldn't I tell him the terrible secret I'd lived with all those years? At least he'd know that I hadn't just run out on him. I wanted to share other things with him, too—my disappointment in Mark, how my marriage was on the rocks. I would tell him all my troubles, confide in him, and he'd listen, as he always had, in his steady, thoughtful way. He'd help me untangle my life.

But I was due for another shock. When I walked into the house where I'd grown up, there was a young woman at his side. She was a beautiful girl, soft and gentle, with kind eyes and a warm smile. "Eric has told me so much about you," she said as she took my hand. Her name was Becky, and she was everything I'd always wanted to be and never could.

Eric looked at me to see how I was taking it. I swallowed and forced a smile to my lips. "I'm so glad to meet you," I said.

During the funeral and afterward, I kept busy to avoid thinking about the deep, hurting pain I felt. When it was too much to bear I slipped out of the house and ran toward the beach, walking along the edge of the shore. A shadow fell across my path and I looked up to see Eric. I'd planned to tell him about my ruined marriage, and ask his advice, but I couldn't open my mouth.

"Mark didn't come with you?" he asked.

"No. He couldn't get away."

"Are you happy, Laura?" he asked gently.

I didn't even hesitate. "Sure. When are you and Becky going to take the plunge?"

He looked away. "Not for a while." And then, as if to explain, he said, "I'm going to work in her father's law firm in New York."

"Whatever happened to your dream of living here, in one of those big houses?" I asked impulsively.

He seemed angry now, a deep frown creasing his forehead. "All kids have dreams," he said coldly. "Fantasies that have nothing to do with real life." He added bitterly, "That's growing up—giving up your dreams."

I couldn't stand the sound of his despair and thought I was going to cry. "I'd better get back," I said. "I'll miss my bus."

I did cry, all through the long bus trip back home. Once there, new losses awaited me. The money I'd saved for Eric's gift was gone, and so was Mark. He hadn't even bothered replacing the carpet over my hiding place.

It was the final pain I would suffer at his hands. In the morning I found an attorney and began divorce proceedings, explaining that I had no money but that I'd pay the fee slowly out of my earnings. It took a year—the most bitter year of my life—but I was finally free.

And then the full misery of my life sank in on me. I had my freedom but I didn't want to do anything with it. I wasn't interested in men—the one man I wanted was involved with someone else, and even if he hadn't been, he was unavailable to me. I thought of suicide, but a natural desire to stay alive kept me going. I was twenty-two, with no prospects of romance. I could see myself in ten years, or twenty—the kind of person who took care of others, who was available when someone needed help, sacrificing and dependable. Everyone's aunt. Aunt Laura.

I stayed in touch with Phillip and once in awhile, when I was sure Eric and Becky weren't going to be there, I'd go home for a weekend. But it was always painful. Everywhere I looked, I'd see Eric, and remember his touch, his smile. Then I'd realize that he was with Becky, holding her, whispering to her, and I'd feel an ache as sharp as a knife.

Phillip told me Eric was planning to become engaged.

"Pretty little thing, isn't she. And rich, too." He looked at me carefully. "Just what his mother would have wanted for him."

I couldn't even speak.

In August I was surprised by a call from Phillip—he very rarely phoned me. But he'd been hurt on the boat and the doctor wanted him to spend time in bed. He asked if I could come and take care of him. I hesitated, thinking that if Phillip had been hurt, Eric and Becky would come to visit and I'd never be able to bear that.

"I'll pay you," Phillip offered as he waited for my answer, so I laughed and said don't be silly, of course I'd help out.

And so I'd gone home, knowing Eric would show up, and dreading the moment. Yet Becky wasn't with him when he came and in my secret heart I was glad she'd stayed away.

We kissed hungrily in front of the fireplace and I knew that I was too weak to fight the driving desire I still felt for Eric. I prayed for some kind of answer.

"It's still the same, isn't it, Laura?" Eric asked. "What are we going to do?"

"I don't know. I don't really care what happens to me," I whispered.

"Don't talk that way! You're important to me," he insisted.

I felt weak and confused. "It's wrong for you to hold me this way, Eric. You have a fiancée now."

"I'm not sure I do. I told Becky I'd let her know about us after I saw you."

I felt a surge of excitement. "Why? I thought—"

"Can't you see, honey? I still love you. I've never stopped."

I pulled out of his arms. "Eric, I think you should know, there can't ever be anything between us. We're really brother and sister. Literally. Lois told me the truth years ago. It seems my mother had a little fling with Phillip."

Eric was staring at me through narrowed eyes, listening as I spilled the secret I'd carried for so many years. Then he spoke finally. "That's a lie, Laura. I can prove it."

Eric took me by the shoulders and held me at arm's length. "Is that why you ran away?" he demanded. "Why didn't you tell me years ago? Do you realize how you made me suffer?"

I said in a low voice, "I suffered, too, Eric."

"But it never had to be!"

He released me and ran toward the closet where Phillip kept his box that held important papers. He twisted the key and pulled out a bunch of envelopes, each tied with a violet ribbon. "Look!" he said.

They were letters that had been sent to Lois years ago. There were dozens of them. Phillip had written to his wife every day.

"He was the one in the war, honey. He talks about your father—how lucky your dad was to have escaped having to go. Phillip couldn't have been your father—it wasn't physically possible!"

He tugged at my wrist, pulled me into the bedroom where Phillip slept. "Let's hear the truth from Dad."

Gently, he woke his father, and explained what he wanted to know. The old man turned his head away on the pillow so that we wouldn't see his tears. "Forgive me," he finally said. "I lied. I was too weak to go against Lois's wishes."

As Eric forgave his father, a peace and radiance were born inside me, a serenity I'd never known before. Eric and I left the room together knowing we'd be joined together for the rest of our lives.

Eric went to tell Becky of his decision. We were married a week later, as soon as Phillip was well enough to appear in church.

We spent our honeymoon at the shore, revisiting scenes of our childhood and talking together, catching up on years of silence. Lying on the warm sand one day, I leaned back into his arms and asked, "You don't really like New York, do you?"

"No. I want to settle here, that's always been my dream." He smiled that endearing, familiar smile and asked, "If I buy one of those big places at the shore, will you keep house for me?"

"I told you I would, remember?"

And that's what we did. Of course we didn't start there—we rented a small home and Eric opened a law office in town. His practice grew during the years that I was busy raising our two daughters, and by the time our son arrived, six years after our marriage, we were able to afford the place we'd always dreamed of. It overlooks the old house we grew up in, where Phillip still lives and where we visit, bringing his grandchildren to see him.

The view of the beach is breathtaking. Sometimes at dusk the light plays tricks with my eyes. I think I see Eric and myself as children, running along the shore chasing gulls. But then I realize that the children are really ours, born of the love that Eric and I had shared all our lives. The love that was my destiny. . . .

THE END

# DATING IS
# MURDER

I liked Eric Runyon a lot. He hadn't exactly said he loved me, but I'd felt he cared. So why hadn't sex worked for us?

I huddled in bed, the white sheet pulled over my nude body, watching Eric as he dressed. The answer to my question was simple. We weren't the same kind of people. He was smooth and gentle. He had lovely manners and treated me like a lady. But I was no lady. I looked like I belonged in jeans, hanging on to the back of a motorcycle, which is exactly what most of my boyfriends had driven.

Eric had his back to me, pulling on his jeans. He's modest, I realized, shaking my head. I'd never known a modest man before. It was a curious thing that made me want to cry.

Eric turned around slowly. "It wasn't very good for you, was it?" he asked.

"No, it wasn't," I admitted with a small shake of my head. I'd tried, and he'd tried, but the more desperate and grasping we became, the worse it had been.

"I'm sorry, Patty."

"Don't apologize," I said. "It doesn't matter."

A look of pain passed over his face. Then his eyes dulled and his face became passive. "I'll step out so you can dress," he offered.

"Thank you," I whispered, my head down.

When I was finished dressing, I walked out into the living room, where Eric was slumped in an easy chair.

He jumped up quickly when I walked in, his eyes seeking mine. I looked away. I wasn't good enough for a man like him. It just wasn't going to work. "Good-bye, Eric," I said.

He made a gesture toward me. "Patty, wait."

"For what?"

He shrugged helplessly. "I don't want just to let you walk out," he said awkwardly. "I must have done something wrong. I'm to blame."

I sighed. "No, Eric. We're just wrong together." I'd been fooling myself. I could never hope to have a man like Eric. Before he could protest any further, I left.

Eric was a salesman at the car dealership where I worked. He was a sweet, solemn guy, terribly honest in spite of what you hear about car salesmen. I liked him from the beginning. We'd had three very pleasant dates together, and tonight I had wanted to please him. I'd wanted us to be in love and talk of marriage and a family. Had I been kidding myself! My eyes burned with unshed tears. Well, I wouldn't cry. I never cried. Girls like me made it on their own.

I started driving down the highway, then glanced at my gas gauge. It was sitting on empty. I always bought my gas at the station across the street from the dealership, so I cut over one block.

Bud Merrick came ambling out of the station. "Hi, babe," he greeted me. "Out sort of late, aren't you?"

I shrugged. Bud was the type I knew how to handle. "I need some gas," I said, getting out. I leaned against the pump while Bud filled my tank. All the time his eyes were on me, speculating.

Bud was a big bear of a man, standing over six feet tall. His shirt was open and his shirt sleeves were rolled up to show off his muscular arms. Something in me twisted, and a little chill darted up my spine.

"Hey, wanna go grab a beer?" he asked as he screwed the gas cap back on. "I was just getting ready to close up."

"Why not?" I replied. I sure didn't want to go home and brood. I paid him and waited while he closed.

He came out and jumped into my car. "I'll leave my bike here," he said. "I've been working on her. I'm taking her out to enter the desert rally in a couple of weeks."

He directed me to a small bar called The Danger Zone a couple of blocks away. It was Friday night and the place was rocking. All I had to do was step inside with Bud and everything in me eased out and relaxed. This was it, where I belonged. Only a couple of dim lights glowed alongside beer signs. A jukebox blared out country music and two guys struggled to shoot pool without poking the other customers. A bowling machine rang bells and flashed lights as someone threw a strike.

As Bud and I edged through the crowd he casually let his hand brush across my body. We made it to the bar where he ordered draft beers. Jammed so close together, I became acutely aware of his body. His hand grazed my thigh and a wave of warm longing passed over me. I knew Bud would give me what Eric hadn't. Satisfaction.

Bud spotted some biker friends, so we edged through to a back booth. They crowded together and we sat down with them. Bud was wedged in so tightly against me I could barely breathe. "Hey, stud," a guy named Sid addressed Bud. "New girl, huh?"

"Yeah," Bud drawled lazily, giving me a long look. "The stud's got a new girl. Guys, this is Patty." There were more names and murmurs exchanged and Bud began to massage my inner thigh and knee. I sat quietly, not really listening to them talk. With the things Bud's hand was doing to me, I couldn't think of anything but my longing. I felt secure with Bud. There wasn't anything phony about him. He was earthy, and honest about what he wanted from me.

I'd learned a long time ago that there were two kinds of men, the real men and the phonies. I was raised by my brothers after my pop died. My mom had taken off years before with a bartender and we never heard from her. My brothers, Jim and Mike, raised me like I was another boy, putting me to work beside them in the small garage they ran. By the time I was fourteen, I knew a lot about cars, men, and sex.

I was ready for the real thing when Peter Bradshaw came along. He was eighteen and hung around the garage a lot. He treated me like a girl instead of a kid. I fell in love with him quickly and easily.

# DATING IS MURDER

Peter was big and dark, his hands rough and cal-
loused. The first time we made love I was scared
and it hurt. The second time, I melted under Peter
as if I were coming apart at the seams. Sex had
found me and I had found sex. Jim and Mike and all
the rest were right—sex made the world go around.
It was like riding the tail of a comet. It was the ulti-
mate thrill, the only way you could truly be close to
another person.

Peter loved me in his way for almost a year. He
cared enough to see that I was on the Pill and he
treated me like a woman. With Peter, I grew up.

Sure, he hit me a few times, but it was only
because he was jealous, because he cared so
much. Every time he hit me, he was sorry afterward.
He'd cup my face in his hands and beg me not to
cry. "I didn't mean it, baby. Honest, I didn't. I love
you."

I'd have forgiven him anything in the name of
love. Peter was it, my world. Until he joined the
Army. He wasn't much of a letter writer and neither
was I. But I was so lonely, I thought I was surely
going to die.

Then when I started my junior year in high school,
one of the smoothest guys in school noticed me. I
fell, hard. John was the senior class president. I
learned about his kind in the hardest way possible.
He'd take me out parking for sex, but he wouldn't
take me to a school dance. He and the others like
him were all alike. They would never introduce you
to their family or their friends. I got hurt twice that
way before I got smart and stayed away from that
kind.

After that, I stuck with my own kind of guys. At

43

least they weren't ashamed of me. There was Sam Walker. I was seventeen and I loved him so much. He was big, and brawny enough to be a wrestler. He had thick hair and he took me everywhere he went on the back of his motorcycle. Everyone knew I was Sam's girl.

I had some silly dreams about us. I was out of high school and working as a waitress and I was starting to think about getting married and having a couple of kids. But Sam wasn't thinking that way. When I started talking about marriage, he took off for Arizona. For a long time I hoped he'd come back, but he didn't.

Then my brother Mike blew everyone's mind by getting married. That meant Jim and I had to move out of Mike's place and find a house of our own.

Some of the pain over losing Sam began to fade. I wanted to change. I wanted a new way of life, something different. Mike gave me money and I bought myself some new clothes and got the job at the car dealership. I knew that somewhere there had to be another kind of guy.

After meeting Eric Runyon, I'd dared to think he could be that man. For a long time all we did was talk in the office when we were both free. Mornings he would bring me a cup of coffee, and in the afternoons he'd buy me sodas from the machine. Eric finally asked me out for dinner and a movie, and on our second date we went to a concert.

It was like being in another world when I was with him. He opened doors for me, and worried about if I was comfortable. His kisses were sweet and tender, like nothing I'd ever known before. Tonight had been our third date. He'd cooked us an Italian dinner from scratch, and when he finally took me in his arms, I was feverish with desire. I wrapped myself around him, responding to him with everything I had in me. I wanted it to be good and special with Eric Runyon. In a daze, we undressed each other and moved to the bedroom. We kissed and caressed, but somehow it wasn't working. He was too gentle.

Sam used to talk all the time when we made love. Some of the words hadn't been very nice, but they had been raw and real. After awhile, Eric finally made it, but I didn't, and he knew it.

So now I sat in a bar with Bud Merrick.

Bud squeezed my knee. "Wanna dance?"

"Sure," I answered and slid out of the crowded booth. We edged around the pool table to the tiny space in back where a few couples moved to the sounds of the western music. Bud yanked me close, his big chest pressed against me.

"You're really hot, baby," he said. "I've been looking at you for a long time."

I smiled up at him. He rubbed up against me seductively and I went hot all over, burning with desire. His hand strayed downward and made hot little circles over the small of my back. "Let's you and me get out of here," he whispered in my ear.

"Let's," I agreed with a nod, unable to say any more.

We went to my apartment. I slipped into the bathroom and took off most of my clothes, and when I came out Bud was on the bed, lying stark naked, a beer can in his hand. My knees buckled underneath me as a flood of passion washed over me. Bud flashed a lopsided grin. "Come on, baby. Come to Papa."

I took a deep breath and moved slowly toward him, stopping at the side of the bed. He rose up and stripped off my bra. Then his hands moved over me.

"Please!" I cried out as a dart of pain shot through me.

"Don't you like it?" he asked.

God help me, but I liked it. I was dizzy with need. Bud buried his face in my breasts. A spasm shook my body as his hands worked over me—hard, seeking hands that made me throb. When I couldn't stand it any longer I crumpled on the bed. The sex act was hard and brutal, and totally satisfying. When he finished, I was so drained I couldn't move.

Bud yawned and sat up. "That was good, baby."

"Yes," I said. "You're good, Bud. Very good."

He grinned broadly, then reached over and grabbed me again.

"You're—hurting me," I gasped, trying to pull away.

"And you like it!" He leaned over and kissed me on the mouth.

"Stop it!" I pulled my mouth away from his. I didn't like wet, smeary kisses.

I yanked the covers up over me and huddled underneath them. We'd had sex for pleasure. It was what we'd both wanted. Raw and good, with no promises. So why did I feel like crying?

Bud's hand slipped under the covers and pinched me—hard!

"You—!" I came straight up and flung a hand at his face, but he caught my arm in a tight grip and grinned, showing crooked teeth.

Animal-like, I leaped at him. He laughed and caught me and we tumbled off the bed, half-fighting, half-loving. Then we started again. I lost all sense of time and space. It was mean. It was brutal. It was fast. I was consumed by time. I threw back my head and let soft whimpering sounds slip through my lips. At the height a small scream of pleasure jerked from me.

Bud finished with a solid grunt of satisfaction. We faced each other, both covered with sweat and breathing hard.

"Good God!" Bud exclaimed, staring down at me. "Baby, you and me are something else!"

"Go away," I said through bruised lips. "Go away, Bud."

"Huh?" He looked stunned.

"I don't let men sleep in my bed all night. Go away."

He seemed taken aback. "I'll walk back to the station and get my bike," he said. "You don't have to drive me."

"Thanks," I muttered harshly. I didn't like him. And yet, the things he had done to me. Oh, God, the way he'd made me feel!

"I'll be back," he told me, then left without another word.

I got into bed again and buried my face in my pillow. I began to cry. Softly at first, then harder. Sometime later I fell into an exhausted sleep.

The next morning I felt bruised, and a little ill. I didn't want to move from the bed. But it was Saturday, a big day for car dealers. I pulled myself up and got dressed. I found a small bruise on my chin. I didn't know how I got it, but I covered it with makeup as best I could.

I went to work, though my body was stiff and

aching. Dana Moore, my boss, popped into my cubbyhole for a minute. "Patty, you look a little pale," she remarked. "Do you feel all right?"

I shrugged, unable to meet her eyes. "A little achy," I said. "Maybe I'm coming down with the flu."

"Well, you take care of yourself. And go home if you need to. You know, we think you're special around here."

"Thank you," I said, and then got very busy. I had to blink hard against a mist of tears.

Eleven in the morning arrived all too quickly. The nearer it got to the time Eric usually came in with the coffee, the more nervous I became. But surely he'd stay away today. *He must hate me,* I thought.

Shortly after eleven, the door opened. It was Eric. "I brought your coffee," he said.

I gestured helplessly toward the desk. He set the cup down, and then moved toward me. I got up from the chair and went to a file cabinet. "Patty," he said, "I tried to call you last night."

"Oh?" I felt so confused and bewildered by the conflicting emotions rushing through me. I didn't know whether to laugh or cry.

"I couldn't get an answer," he went on, pressing me.

"I didn't answer the phone last night," I replied.

"Patty." He came up behind me, and I stiffened. When he seemed about to touch me, I turned around and moved away from him again. "Patty, we can work things out. So last night wasn't all fireworks and heaven. Maybe we tried too soon. We should have waited."

"Why?" I asked him bluntly, flinging my hair back from my face. No other guy had ever wanted to wait.

48

Eric gave me a long puzzled look. "So we'd have had more time to get to know each other."

I shrugged. "We don't have anything in common, Eric."

"Funny, I thought we did. I thought we liked each other," he said, the pain showing plainly in his voice. Then he walked out of the room.

*Oh, Eric,* I thought. I wanted to run after him, but I didn't. I rubbed the back of my hand angrily against my eyes. I was not going to cry.

It was my bad luck to be in the showroom when Bud came ambling over from the station. The garage where he worked did the cleaning on the engines of the used cars we took in, so it wasn't unusual for him to be around. A wide grin spread across his face at the sight of me. "Hi, baby!" He handed me some papers and I took them. "Don't you have any sweet words for the old stud?"

"You stupid lug!" I hissed at him. "Keep your mouth shut!"

"Hey!" He just grinned, taunting me. Just then, Eric came out of a booth with a customer, his eyes fastened on Bud and me. Shame flooded over me as Bud chose that moment to reach out and brush a tendril of hair back from my face. "I want to see you again," he said softly.

"We can't talk here," I told him, silently begging him to go away.

"We'll talk later," Bud said, chucking my chin with the back of his fist. But he certainly didn't have talking in mind.

My face burning, I took the papers in to Dana. When I came back out, Eric was waiting for me.

"Listen," he said. "You aren't mixed up with Bud,

are you?"

I shrugged.

"Patty, he's bad news. He's got such a bad reputation."

"It's none of your business," I snapped, trying to turn away before my tears started falling.

He touched my arm gently, holding me back. "I suppose it isn't any of my business," he said softly. "Except I do care about you, Patty."

Something inside me burst. I wanted a man like him, but I'd never be able to have one. Choking back a sob, I pulled from him and ran for the safety of the ladies' room.

So I became Bud's girl. I went back to wearing jeans and old shirts when I wasn't at work. I'd often meet Bud at ten when he closed the station and we'd drift down to the bar for a few beers, or we'd just go straight to his place or mine to make love.

It was wild and savage. In a lot of ways it was fun, being Bud's girl. He was proud of me. Sometimes he'd take me around to different bars and announce, "Hey, people—look what I've got. Ain't she something?" Then he'd whack me on the behind.

"Cut it out!" I'd yelp, then whack him right back. He'd roar and the whole place would laugh.

I could do some things better than most men. Like shooting pool. My brother had taught me years ago. Sometimes I could run the whole table on Bud. "I'll get you for that!" he'd warn me. "I'll get you!" And he would, later in bed.

Then one Saturday night, Bud had more than beer to drink. We were in a booth with some jokers who were putting together the next motorcycle rally, and Bud was taking slugs out of a bottle wrapped in a brown paper bag. Casually he draped one arm over my shoulder and let his hand dangle down over my breast. I shrugged, trying to move his arm, while two guys opposite us watched intently. One of them began to grin and Bud saw it.

"Some body, huh?" he asked. His hand snaked down lower.

"Bud!" I flung his arm away and jumped out of the booth.

He grabbed my arm and yanked me back down. "I didn't say you could leave."

"Get your hands off me!" I yelled, but Bud's grip tightened. A little thrill darted through me. I felt my blood beginning to warm at the sight of his face. He grinned, but it wasn't humorous. It held a kind of controlled animal fury. He was bigger and stronger. I quieted and sat there, shaking slightly. I was scared, yet excited. The combination put me on a high.

"Now, you be good," Bud warned me. "And I'll take care of you later. These dudes and I have some things to discuss."

I sat there, feeling almost demure and little-girlish. I kept my head down and stayed quiet and later, in Bud's room, we had sex like wild animals.

Afterward I got so sick I ran for the bathroom and threw up. Bud was waiting when I came out. "You okay, honey?" he asked. His voice was unusually soft, and there was a look of genuine concern in his eyes.

"I don't know," I whispered. "What are we, Bud?"

"Just two people who need each other," he answered. He put his arms around me and we stood there holding each other for a long time.

His tenderness left me feeling more confused than the primitive sex we'd had. He drove me home, asking repeatedly if I was all right. We made plans for the upcoming rally and I went to bed alone.

I drifted off into a torment of sleep and dreamed of Eric Runyon. I woke up shaking and drenched with sweat. I couldn't remember any part of the dream except Eric's face, his accusing eyes.

Sunday I hung around the station while Bud worked on his cycle. I felt almost tender toward him. It was a little like being with my brothers as I fetched and carried tools for him. He was hopping up his cycle as much as he could for the rally races.

Meanwhile, Eric and I had reached a sort of truce at work. We remained polite to each other when we happened to come into contact. Otherwise, we carefully avoided each other. That's why I was so stunned when he asked me out for Saturday night.

"I can't," I told him. "I already have a date."

"With Bud Merrick?" he asked.

"As a matter of fact, yes," I said, holding my head high.

"You're too good for him, Patty."

I frowned, feeling suddenly angry. "How would you know? Why do you keep hanging around me?"

He turned his head slightly to one side. "Don't you know, Patty? I see a little girl in you, a little girl who needs someone to take care of her."

"I should laugh in your face," I hooted, running my hands down over my body. "I'm not exactly built like a kid."

"The little girl is inside of you, Patty. She has many unfulfilled dreams fighting to get out."

I deliberately sneered at him, but my hands were shaking. He was coming too close to the truth. I had to destroy that little girl inside me. Her dreams were unrealistic. They were schoolgirl dreams. I was a woman.

"If you ever need me," Eric offered.

"I won't," I replied flippantly, then turned and walked away from him.

On Saturday Bud picked me up at noon, and we headed out to the country for the dirt races. There were no stands out there, but the various raceways had been marked off. Some short, just for speed. Others were long, over rough terrain that required plenty of skill to stay upright. There was a big truck set up with loudspeakers attached. The racers paid their entry fees and drew their starting places. The races started at two.

I found some friends of Bud's who had their girl-friends and wives with them, and we made a place for ourselves under a large tree. Some had brought food and there was a vendor selling from a truck. We ate and drank cold beer and talked about bikes and other rallies.

Bud had entered three events—a hill climb, a short dash, and a ten-mile endurance run. He came in second in the endurance run, and he was furious. Stomping like a wild man, he flung his helmet to the ground.

The big high point was to be a midnight hill climb. That one worried me. It was dangerous enough in the daytime, but downright stupid at night. Bud spent the evening drinking quite heavily, and as midnight neared I began to get apprehensive. He could kill himself out there. I pulled at his arm.

"Honey, let's go home," I suggested. "I can drive."

"You think I can't?" he asked.

"I don't like it out here."

He shook my arm loose. "I'm gonna make that hill climb. I can do it. I can win this one."

"Honey, please," I begged, deliberately rubbing up against him. "We don't need racing thrills. We have our own."

His face brightened, making me think for a moment I had won. Then his hand flew out and grabbed my wrist. "Come on," he said. "We'll have a quickie."

"No, Bud!" I cried, but he was already pulling me toward a stand of trees. I stumbled over a rock and almost fell. He jerked me to my feet. Then we were back in the trees, but people were still only a few feet away from us. "I won't do it!" I hissed. "Not out here!"

"You'll do anything I tell you!" he barked, breathing his beer breath in my face.

"I will not!" I jerked free of him.

He came at me like a bull, hitting me hard, and we both went down on the rocky earth. My fingers scratched at his face and he gave a loud grunt. "You'll regret that!" He grabbed my flailing arm and pinned me down. "Stay still!" he ordered.

"No, no!" I cried. It was important, so important, to me that I not be raped. It was the one injury my soul could not bear. No man had ever done that to me.

I twisted underneath him, but he just grinned as he straddled me. When he loosened his grip on me with one arm to unzip his trousers, I took advantage, coming up from the ground with all my

54

strength right into his chest.

He grunted. Then before I could move, I saw his fist coming at me. I ducked to one side, but it was too late. It caught the side of my head and sent me flying.

He hit me again across the face, making red lights explode inside my head. I felt his foot nudging me. He moved me, then became still as the loudspeakers blared for the racers to line up for the hill climb.

"You stay here," he ordered me. "Right here. Don't move until I get back. I'll show you what a stud I am."

Then he was up and moving away, his feet crunching against the pebbles. I sat up slowly. Everything seemed so far away. The loudspeaker was going on and on. Floodlights were turned onto the hillside. There were raw dirt paths where others had been before.

I got to my feet, but the pounding inside my head nearly sent me back to the ground. I found a tree and steadied myself against it. There was something sick in me. Something terribly sick to make me want men like Bud. Rough, crude men who spoke four-letter words and knocked their women around.

I took a deep breath and let it out slowly. I had to escape from Bud now—or it might be too late. I might be trapped for life. I eased out of the trees and down to the road, where I found a pickup that was loaded with two bikes. The guys in it were getting ready to leave.

"Could I hitch a ride?" I asked.

"You okay?" one of them asked.

"I will be," I vowed. "I will be." Once and for all, I had to break away. I had to free myself totally from this kind of life.

The two guys were kind. When we got back to the highway, I found out they were going one way and I the other, but they were good enough to drive me to a truck stop and let me out there.

I had some change in my pocket, but nothing else. Stumbling into an outside telephone booth, I put in a call to Eric.

I prayed as the phone rang.

Finally a sleepy voice answered. "Hello?"

"Eric, I need you," I said simply. "Can you come for me?"

"Where are you?" he asked. I told him and we hung up.

I went to find a rest room and cleaned myself up as best I could. Then I went back outside and found a small bench that faced the highway. I sat there to wait for Eric.

I'd wanted a new life. But I hadn't freed myself of my old ways. I needed help, maybe a lot of it, to break my old patterns. But for the sake of my self-respect I had to make the break now.

Maybe Eric could help me, maybe he couldn't. But whatever lay ahead for us, I knew I'd be a better person for knowing him. I had to let the little girl in me take over and follow her dreams—they were the right dreams, the good and decent ones. THE END

# MY EX STOLE
# OUR CHILDREN

My story could be any mother's. I was divorced and had custody of our two kids. Our divorce had been bitter, but I knew my ex-husband did love the kids. I had to let him see them because it wouldn't be fair to the kids, who loved him, not to let him. I should have known better though than to trust him to take them out for an entire weekend. But how was I to know I might never see them again?

My ex-husband, Michael, and I had joint custody of our children, but he only saw them on occasional weekends. "Daddy's coming! Daddy!" I heard the excited cries of Brianna and Susie from the yard where I'd sent them to play, while I packed their bags that Friday. I saw them running toward the front gate just as Michael's car pulled up. A minute later he came in with them trailing after him, looking exactly like the typical daddy—the perfect picture of fatherly devotion. It was a picture I might have daydreamed a long time ago. But pictures can lie.

*Let me forget,* I prayed. *Help me to stop being angry and critical and suspicious. Let me somehow remember the good times and forget the bad. Surely there had been some good times. When the babies were born—when we bought a house—the times Michael promised things were going to be different. The times when I'd been vulnerable and trusting, instead of disillusioned, the way I'd become.*

That's what Michael had done to me. He'd mixed up my mind and destroyed my self-confidence. His instability had made me doubt my own stability. He'd say things that would really upset me, and then when I'd finally react, he'd raise his eyebrows innocently and pretend to be shocked.

"I don't know what's getting into you lately, Karen," he'd say in an insinuating tone. "You're not acting normal. You're always reading something into every little thing I say." He'd also tell me I'd said things I knew I hadn't said. He tried to make me think I was losing my mind, which I knew I wasn't. I knew what I'd said and I hadn't said. Furthermore, I didn't have that problem with anyone else. Just Michael.

Since our divorce I'd hoped he'd change, that he'd find happiness and security so he wouldn't have to push other people down in order to feel good about himself. That he'd get over his need to be abusive. That he'd somehow become a whole, happy person and not be angry any longer for no apparent reason.

"How are the little elves?" he piped in that falsetto tone that always irritated me—the patronizing voice he often used to talk down to the children. I just wished he could see them as real people with needs and feelings, not as animated characters created for his own private amusement when he felt so inclined.

I didn't doubt that Michael loved the children or that he had loved me. But a lot of different feelings are called love. Michael's love was self-centered and self-serving. It could be turned on and off at will, or swing suddenly from extreme indulgence to shocking hostility. It didn't include concern or caring or even responsibility, but was expressed in extravagant ways, like buying luxuries the kids didn't really need, while neglecting basic necessities. It was not consistent.

He took the pleasure and took all the glory, while leaving the thankless drudgery to someone else. Already Brianna was saying Daddy always bought nice presents, and Mommy only bought boring things like socks and pajamas. Kids don't get excited about socks and pajamas. They expect them—and they have a right to expect them. But I resented constantly having to play the heavy to Michael's free-and easy role.

*I do need a break,* I admitted to myself. *I really do have an attitude problem. I need this weekend alone. Michael always said I had a bad attitude.* Maybe he was right. But I still couldn't help feeling resentful that all the responsibility fell on my shoulders, while Michael got off easy, except for paying child support, and he couldn't even manage to do that.

I was thankful for my children and I loved them. But sometimes I felt victimized by that love. At times, I thought it would be nice not to have all the responsibility—to be able to sleep late on weekends or have more freedom and less worry, not to mention a little peace and quiet occasionally.

"Let's hurry now," Michael said. "Grandma's invited us for supper, and tomorrow we're going to the zoo. How about that, kids? Want to see the lions and the tigers?" Then, with a glance at me, he added, "I hope they haven't been fed."

*Kids aren't fed, Michael. Animals are fed,* I thought. *Kids eat.* I reminded myself not to be cranky. After all, I was getting a few days' break. Brianna and Susie stared up at their father, their eyes shining at the thought of wild animals and cotton candy and peanuts for the elephants.

"They should be hungry. They haven't eaten since lunch." I spoke softly, not showing my irritation. "Susie has had a cold. I packed cough medicine and also sweaters in case the weather cools. By the way, how about the check?" Michael was late again with his support check, and he'd promised to bring it with him.

"I'll have it when we get back," he lied. "I have to collect some money a guy owes me." It was an old story. Michael would have the money if he could find the guy and if the guy had the money and if the guy would pay. And that translated into a slim chance of getting any money.

But Michael never personally suffered from the inconvenience of not having any cash. He was wearing designer jeans, soft leather shoes, and a gold nugget on a chain. It said a lot about his priorities. The least he could have done was to go home and stop adding insult to injury.

"I'm hungry," Karen announced in her high voice,

clutching her pink rabbit, Doc. "I need a hamburger." Susie's favorite expression was "I need," and she'd learned how to use it to get what she wanted. Brianna gave her a superior look and told her they were going to eat at Grandma's.

"Did you pack toys?" Michael asked as he set their bags by the door. I hadn't, of course. I didn't think they'd need toys just for the weekend. It sounded like they were going to have a busy weekend without toys.

But Michael was persistent. Looking annoyed, he gathered up some of their playthings. Then he asked for extra clothes, and some blankets for the car in case they got sleepy. Karen took Doc, and Brianna clutched her treasured, raggedy old bear.

Michael never had seemed that concerned about their needs before and I was pleased he was showing an awareness, so I didn't mind repacking. I was often uneasy about the children when they were away, convinced that no one took care of them as well as I did. Sometimes they came home dirty, and several times they'd even become sick from getting chilled or not eating right. But they loved to go, and I enjoyed having some time to myself.

"Good-bye, sweethearts," I said, stooping to hug them for a brief moment. I'd looked forward to the weekend, but now I suddenly didn't want them to go. Later, I wondered if that had been some sort of premonition.

Susie raised her face and gave me a moist kiss, while Brianna circled me with strong little arms and buried her nose in my neck. Michael showed his impatience, pointedly glancing at his watch and tapping his foot.

# MY EX STOLE OUR CHILDREN

"Be good for Grandma and have fun at the zoo," I said. "And don't forget to say your prayers." I stood, watching after them as they followed their father down the sidewalk to the car. "And brush your teeth," I yelled after them. "I love you!" They waved to me out of the window until the car disappeared around the corner and out of sight.

It was a nice weekend—pleasant and productive. I cleaned closets and did the kids' room over, hanging bright new curtains. I stuck cute teddy bear decals on their furniture and painted the shelves and the toy box. But I couldn't bring myself to take down the crayon drawings. There was love and joy in every colored line. Instead, I made a bulletin board out of burlap for their pictures. Later, those childish scribbles would tear my heart out—I'd treasure them, because they would be all I had left. . . .

Evan called on Saturday to see if I wanted to go out to eat. He'd been out of town on a business trip and he'd gotten back late because his flight was delayed.

I'd met Evan Muir about a year after my divorce in a therapy group. He was a widower with a young daughter, and I was attracted to him right away. It turned out we enjoyed many of the same things and my children got along well with his little girl, Lea.

Evan was so unlike all the other men I'd met— pleasant, relaxed, and easy to be with—and he didn't play silly games. After living with a walking time bomb, it was nice to meet someone sane and predictable, who could show appreciation instead of constantly making demands or being moody and irritable. I'd liked Evan from the beginning, but I knew I could never choose him, or any other man, ahead of my children, and I'd been honest enough to tell him so. But Evan didn't seem to see a problem.

"You worry too much, Karen," he'd said. "You need to just relax and let things work out." He liked kids, too. Especially Brianna and Susie. And not just because they were mine. Furthermore, he realized that children's needs couldn't just be put on the back burner, and in fact, they often had to come first. He saw that as a fact of life that mature adults should be able to handle.

"I don't want to go out to eat," I said. I really wanted to finish the children's room. I hadn't done my hair, and I had paint under my fingernails. So Evan offered to bring over some steaks and we'd eat in. He said he was tired, too, but he wanted to help with my decorating project. That was how Evan always was—easy to get along with.

In an hour he showed up, dressed in jeans and a sweatshirt, and bringing a cute clown picture for the kids' room. We had a casual, relaxed dinner. He moved the furniture for me, and then took a nap on the couch while I finished up.

By Sunday afternoon I was finished and tired. I soaked in the tub and scrubbed the paint off, then read and watched the clock until the time came for Michael to bring the children home. I didn't bother to cook, settling instead for leftovers. The children would have eaten. Later, I'd fix them a snack while they told me all about their weekend at Grandma's and their trip to the zoo.

Many times in the coming months, I would be reminded how we take so many things for granted—simple things like bedtime snacks and story-time and prayers, laughter and fun, often not realizing that these daily activities are the fabric of our lives, the things that cherished memories are made of. And memories would be all I had for the next three months, because my children didn't come home that night. They were kidnapped by their father. By the time I realized what was going on, they were thousands of miles away.

It was nearly midnight, and I became frantic. Michael was supposed to bring the children back by seven, and although I hadn't ever held him to the exact minute, I certainly didn't expect him to keep them out until all hours. After all, they were still small and they got tired.

Impatiently, I watched the hands of the clock creep past seven and eight, then nine and ten. After eleven o'clock came and there'd been no sign of them, I gave in and called Michael's mother, having put it off as long as I could.

I'd never been able to get close to Linette Payton. She was from the South, but not like most of the wonderful southern people I'd known. To her, northerners were under suspicion because of the Civil War, although it had happened over a hundred years ago. Michael's father had died of a heart attack not long after they'd moved here. Mrs. Payton had always wanted Michael to marry a girl from their hometown, so she'd never liked me.

"Hello?" Linette Payton answered in a familiar, honeyed drawl that always sounded rehearsed. She could get more mileage out of a simple hello than anyone else I'd ever known. Silently, I reprimanded myself for being annoyed. After all, she was my children's grandmother. I wanted them to respect her, and I really tried to set a good example. But she did get to me at times.

"Hello, Linette, this is Karen. I'm sorry to bother you," I said, trying to keep my voice from shattering, "but Michael hasn't returned with the children. It's so late and I'm worried."

Linette didn't seem the least bit upset. "Now, Karen, you just relax," she drawled in the breathy, scolding, little girl voice I'd learned to associate with insincerity. "Maybe he's run into traffic or possibly even decided to stay the night somewhere since he doesn't work Monday. No need to fuss. I'm sure they'll be along."

*I'm not fussing,* I thought. *I'm scared. And I have a right to be concerned about my children.* "But he should have called by now," I protested, fighting the impulse to scream at her. "And besides, he's supposed to bring them back at seven. That's the agreement."

"Now, Karen, Michael hasn't seen those babies for nearly a month," she said reproachfully. "And it just isn't right for you to be so hard on him. He misses them. After all, they need their daddy, too. They're with you every single day. Goodness, a person can't always operate on schedule, you know."

I hated it when she talked down to me as though I were a child. And I hated her talking about Michael as though he were still her little boy, even if he did act like one. Furthermore, she had no right to tell me not to worry about my own children. She'd made a permanent baby of her son, and that had been our problem from the start.

"Well, could you tell me what time he left your house?" I asked, rudely ignoring her words of admonition.

"My house?" she repeated. "Michael hasn't been here, Karen. I haven't seen him. Was he going to drop by, do you think?"

"He didn't bring the children there Friday night?" I asked. "Didn't he take them to the zoo Saturday?"

"Gracious, Karen, I wasn't even here Friday night. I spent three days with my sister and didn't get home until this evening. I haven't seen Michael for two weeks, although he did call me last Sunday."

So Michael hadn't taken the children to their grandmother's at all. He'd lied. Weakly I dropped the phone into the cradle without saying good-bye to her.

But where were my children? Where on earth did he take them if he hadn't gone to his mother's? And why wasn't he back here with them?

Suddenly, a fear began to form in my mind as I remembered the extra clothes, the blankets, and toys. . . . Michael had never intended to take the children to his mother's. And he'd never planned to bring them back home again. That's why he'd wanted the extra clothing and blankets and toys. My children had been stolen by their father!

Frantically, I called the police. I was told in a polite way that they could do nothing for twenty-four hours, and that in most cases there was only a delay or a change in plans and no cause for alarm. I screamed at the robotlike voice of the officer that my children had already been gone for over twenty-four hours. Seemingly oblivious to my distress, he told me in the same even, polite voice to call back the next day if they didn't turn up.

Helpless with rage and fear, I slammed the phone down, then darted from room to room trying to decide what to do next. I finally sank down in a chair and wrapped my arms around myself, rocking numbly back and forth, trying to stop the shaking.

I slept fitfully, emotionally drained, but tense from shock and stress. Even before I was fully awake the next morning, I sensed something was very wrong. The house seemed empty and cold and deathly still. My head pounded from tension and fatigue, and inside me there was an awful emptiness. I couldn't possibly go to work. I'd never be able to concentrate, and besides, I needed to stay near the phone in case there was some word.

I called the office, glad I had some sick leave saved. Then I called the day-care center and told them the children wouldn't be there until later in the day, wanting to believe they'd be home by noon, but knowing with a certain dread that they wouldn't. Finally, when I couldn't stand it any longer, I called the car dealership where Michael worked and was told he had resigned the week before, saying he was moving out of state. He had given no forwarding address and no one knew his whereabouts.

That did it. My worst fears had been confirmed, and I knew my children were gone. There was not even a glimmer of hope left. He had kidnapped them. Was that what he'd meant when he'd said on the day of our divorce that he'd make me sorry, that he'd get even with me if it was the last thing he ever did? If so, he'd done a good job. He'd hurt me in the worst way possible, in the only way that really mattered.

I'd often said I didn't know why I'd ever married Michael, but that wasn't true. I did know. I married Michael because I was tired of being single and because I was not thinking clearly. I was swept off my feet by his smooth, charming act and I was determined to land him before someone else did, because, even then, I knew he didn't go unnoticed by women. I thought he was a real catch, and I even thought I loved him, not knowing what love was. And so I married him without really knowing him.

Michael was the most charming man I had ever met. And he was the coldest and most calculating. Michael was a taker, not a giver. That was the way his mama raised him and the only way he knew how to be. He never really loved anyone. He didn't know how—he just knew how to need people and how to use them. Our courtship and marriage were grown-up versions of playing house, with no depth and no foundation. Michael was selfish, cruel, inhuman, and demanding—a suspicious, paranoid person with a vile temper and an unforgiving spirit; a person who devastated me emotionally and belittled me until I could hardly speak without stammering. For five years I was abused physically and emotionally and nearly destroyed, then discarded like a broken toy.

And when I say broken, that's exactly what I mean, because Michael Payton broke my spirit and my will, robbing me of my self-confidence. He tried to make me doubt my own sanity. Finally, he left me to fend for myself and the children, while he took off with a younger woman who soon walked out on him, probably because he abused her, too.

He'd wanted to come back; he'd promised he'd be different. But, by then, I was sick of his promises, and I'd learned that I could make it on my own and I didn't have to live like that. So I went ahead with the divorce.

Michael was furious. "You'll be sorry," he'd said the day the divorce was final. "I'll make you sorry, if it's the last thing I do!" Years later, a psychologist would say that Michael had a personality disorder, and was the manipulative type. That didn't mean he was unfriendly; he wasn't. He was very charming, but his charm was pathological. He couldn't adapt to society because he was coldhearted and manipulative. He could only abuse other people.

And Michael had gotten his revenge—the worst kind. He took my children far away and told them I didn't want them anymore; he'd said he'd find them a new mommy. He disguised himself—took an assumed name and grew a beard and wore contact lenses. He totally changed the way he looked. He'd left the state probably within an hour after he'd picked up Brianna and Susie. Later, I found out that he'd arranged to sell his car right after he'd left my house, and bought another one, so he couldn't be traced.

It was useless to try to sleep. Wrapped in a blanket in a chair by the phone, I trembled with fear, too scared to even cry. I got up and wandered into the children's bedroom and smelled the crayons and new paint. I couldn't stand the bedroom without Brianna and Susie. I felt so empty, so alone, and so consumed by panic and dread, I thought I'd die.

But the agony was only beginning. Days went by, then weeks, with no word of Michael or the children. The police finally got involved after twenty-four hours, but there were no leads. A police detective came to the house and gathered information for his search—photographs, handwriting samples, and

Michael's Social Security number.

The detective told me that Michael would probably use an alias, but that was not usually effective in eluding the police. He wanted to know all about Michael's background—his habits, whether he'd ever used an assumed name. I told him everything I knew, but it didn't seem like enough to do any good. I was forced to admit that I really hadn't known that much about Michael when I'd married him and still didn't really know him that well seven years later. Michael was a man of many faces, and no one could get to know him because he didn't want to know himself.

After three weeks I was becoming really discouraged. Then, early one morning the phone rang, and I was stunned to hear Michael's voice. He sounded far away, although I knew people don't always sound far away when it's long distance. It could have been a bad connection. Or it could have been Michael muffling the phone.

"The kids are fine," he said. "They have everything they need. I'll let you talk to them sometime later on. Just don't try to find us, because you can't." Then a click.

I tried to say something, but it was too late. I dropped the phone into the cradle and stood numbly, hearing his words echo over and over in my mind. And then I beat my fists against the phone and screamed out my desperation.

Brianna and Susie. Little angels' faces, chubby fingers, sturdy bodies. Brianna and Susie, gone. My little ones, maybe gone forever. I couldn't go on living without them. I couldn't. They were my life.

"We'll find them, Karen," my dad said, pacing

nervously while holding a cup of coffee, which he never touched. "There are ways we didn't have just a few years ago—and there are computers that can transfer information rapidly. And I know people who may be able to help."

I felt almost as bad for my dad as I did for myself. Daddy was a strong, gentle man who always told me whatever I did, good or bad, would come back to me in the end. What goes around comes around, he always said. Daddy really believed that, and he always tried to do the right thing. I guess a lot of people would consider my dad weak, but that's because they didn't understand him.

Daddy hadn't wanted me to marry Michael, and he'd tried hard on our wedding day not to show his concern. He thought I was rushing too fast, that I should wait. He was right, but I didn't realize it at the time.

I'd always tried to do the right thing because that was the way I was brought up. And somehow, I couldn't help wondering why this was happening to me. I hadn't hurt anyone, but I was being hurt in a terrible way. Why did the innocent always have to suffer, while the others ran over them and came out on top?

"All I can tell you, Karen," Daddy said, "is we all reap what we sow, sooner or later. I believe that. You've just got to have faith in yourself and realize that what Michael has done will eventually work against him."

They sounded like empty words. And no words could console me. I wanted my children. There was no comfort in anything else. *Dear God,* I prayed, *help me find them. Give me strength and patience and faith, and don't let me lose my mind.*

I remembered how Michael had often scoffed at my prayers and ridiculed me for teaching the children theirs. "Get serious, Karen," he'd say in an irritated voice. "I don't want my kids to grow up to be fanatics. Don't tell me you really believe that praying to a God you can't see does any more good than going out there in the yard and praying to that apple tree!"

"I've never prayed to an apple tree, Michael," I said, not wanting to argue and make him angry. Michael had a nasty temper and he never gave up until he won a point. He had a talent for putting me on the defensive and turning my words against me, bombarding me in his fast-talking way, until I couldn't even think.

I could just see Michael, wherever he was—smiling smugly, confident that he could outwit me, the police, and even God, himself. But I used every resource at my disposal, and never stopped until my children were found and returned. And even though it seemed hopeless, I believed that somehow my prayers would help. At least they made me feel better when the waves of sick panic swept over me and I couldn't eat or sleep or even sit still. They kept me from going completely out of my mind when I didn't know what to do.

"Come home with us, Karen," my mom said. "Don't stay alone. Pack some things and lock up this place."

My mom had always tried to see some good in Michael. Of course, he'd worked his phony charm on her, too, and she'd been hurt and bewildered by the person he turned out to be because she had accepted him as a son. So she hurt with me, wanting her grandchildren home safe.

"Mother, I can't leave," I begged. "I have to stay by the phone. Maybe I'll hear something. Maybe Michael will call again and let me talk to them." Tears sprang to my eyes at the thought, and my voice cracked and broke. Mother and Daddy reluctantly left without me, their faces lined with worry and despair.

Bad news always travels fast. Soon the phone calls started coming in. It was hard to tell people what happened, and painful to be the object of pity and curiosity. But most everyone was helpful and kind. There were a few inevitable crank calls, but we were told by the police to expect them. We had to listen to everyone. Someone might know something; someone could have seen the children somewhere. I wanted to take every single call myself, talk to each person.

I had called my boss. My sick leave would soon run out, and I didn't see how I could go back to work, although I really needed the money. I couldn't bear the thought of losing my job. I had to support us. Even if I didn't find my children, I still had to support myself. But I couldn't stand to think they wouldn't be found. I flung the thought away like the vile thing it was.

In a few days my boss, Mr. Sanford, called me. "Karen, don't worry about a thing," he said. "We all want to help in any way we can. I've arranged a paid leave of absence for you, and we're getting some temporary help. Just take care and let us know if there's anything we can do from this end."

When I tried to express my thanks, he only mumbled and told me to try not to worry; the children were certain to be found. He made me promise to keep him informed.

Everyone was kind. People brought food and sent cards and letters of encouragement, offering all kinds of help. A few even sent money, crumpled bills enclosed in awkwardly worded notes of kindness and concern. A local service organization offered a reward for anyone giving information that would help locate the children. It was reassuring to know I wasn't alone. It was only through the help and caring of others that I survived the agony.

I don't know what I could have done without Evan. He was so supportive, so determined to help, and so frustrated, because he didn't know where to start. He told me where he could be reached while he was traveling, and spent hours with me when he was in town on weekends, sometimes bringing his own little girl, Lea, to be with me.

"If only I had a clue," he'd say, his head bowed and clasped between his hands. "I'd get on a plane right now if I knew which way to go. People can't just drop out of sight. There's got to be a lead somewhere—someone who knows something, if we can just find that person."

He checked the post office for a forwarding address and found none. He went to the phone company and to the utilities, but Michael had left no forwarding address. He even went to the place where Michael had worked, but no one seemed to know anything. We were at a dead end, and the pain and frustration were unbearable.

Finally, the police tapped my phone. But when Michael called again it was to my parents' number.

He probably suspected a phone tap. "The kids are fine," he said to my mother, just as he'd said to me. "Don't worry and don't try to find us."

The newspapers had picked up the story, and I was contacted by the host of a popular radio talk show in our area, who let me go on the air and make a plea for information leading to the return of my kids. I arranged to meet him at the station for a taping session.

"Don't be nervous," he said. "Just identify yourself and tell the audience about the children, giving a description of each one. Then ask for information that might help locate them. We're taping this, so if it doesn't come out right, we can edit it or do a retake. Just relax and try to be calm."

I did fine until I had to give my children's names and describe them. Then, as I pictured each little face in my mind, I lost control and couldn't speak, choked by tears of grief and frustration. The host took over for me, reading from my notes and making an appeal for the public's help. "Perfect!" he said, ushering me out of the studio. "We'll edit out any rough spots and run it right away. It may bring in a few crank calls, but maybe it will do some good. Let's get some coffee."

The only calls were from people who hoped to be paid for their information, and I'd already been warned not to talk to them. I was told to refer them to the police detectives. Anyone who had real information would probably not want money, but would be eager to help. But we didn't hear from any of them.

Winter came, bringing with it a coldness that matched the empty chill in my heart. Christmas was coming, but there was no yuletide spirit for me. I didn't see how I'd ever get through the holidays. I wished I could go to sleep and wake up when it was all over.

Then one day a call came from a hairdresser named Crystal Wynne in a coastal town nearly a thousand miles away. She had picked up the talk show on the shortwave radio in her beauty parlor. She was certain she'd seen Michael and the children in late summer in the shop where she worked. She said she had cut Michael's hair, and also Brianna's, and had given Susie a shampoo and trimmed her bangs. She thought she remembered Michael saying he was on his way to Arkansas. She didn't see what kind of car he was driving.

I thanked her and took her phone number, asking her to call me back if she remembered anything else. And then I took the information to the police. Within hours word went out to officials and broadcast stations in Arkansas. Days went by with no results, and finally weeks. It had seemed like a good lead, but I waited helplessly while it fizzled out. Another dead end came and went.

Maybe Michael had lied to Crystal Wynne in an attempt to cover his trail. Or maybe it hadn't been Michael after all, but someone else with children who resembled mine. In any event, a police interview with Crystal turned up no other information. My hopes were shattered.

Mother and Daddy offered to close up their house and stay with me, but I felt I would do better alone. I had to stay strong and resist the temptation to become helpless and dependent. I had to keep fighting. And I needed privacy for my grief. I couldn't bear to have them see my pain—they had their own. I wanted them to think I was strong and brave, and I didn't want them to worry about me. Mother tucked some cash into my purse before they left, although I'd told her I didn't need money. She needed to feel she was doing something, and I didn't protest. I'd give it back later.

I put on an act for Evan, so he'd see how strong I was and not worry. But he saw right through it, holding me and letting me cry out my pain and frustration. It was all right to let Evan see my feelings because I didn't have to protect him. He was safe—not as emotionally involved as my parents were. Or at least that's what I thought at the time.

"We'll find them, Karen," he always reassured me. "We'll just keep trying. It isn't as though they've been kidnapped by a stranger. We know Michael has them and they're safe, and that means a lot. He'll at least take care of them until we can find them and get them back here where they belong."

*If we ever find them,* I thought dejectedly. They could be anywhere. Michael had vanished without a clue. He could change his identity, use an assumed name—and how would we ever know? Michael had no intention of being found and he was devious enough to cover his tracks. The children were so young—in a few years they wouldn't even remember me, or even where they'd lived before. Everything seemed hopeless to me.

Then early one cold afternoon in February there was a knock at the door. A thin, young woman in a worn coat smiled nervously when I answered. She clutched her purse with an anxious, hopeful expression and blinked tentatively against the biting wind.

"Hello, Mrs. Payton?" she asked, clearing her throat awkwardly.

"Yes. What can I do for you?" I replied.

"My name is Heidi Duff. I'm—I was a friend of Mike's. I really need to find him. Do you know where he is?"

Mike? Michael had never been known as Mike. "Michael Payton?" I asked, puzzled.

She nodded, looking confused.

"I'm afraid not. What do you need him for?"

She looked down, embarrassed. "He owes me some money. He borrowed a thousand dollars, then he left while I was out looking for a job, and I haven't heard from him since. It was all the money I had—my savings. And he also was wearing my gold nugget on a chain. It was from my sister, and I'd like to have it back."

The woman was not the type who would attract much attention from men, and I was surprised she'd known Michael. He liked good-looking women—it was part of his ego problem—and this woman was not really very attractive. She was shy and she did-n't know how to dress, but it was evident she'd tried to look her best. She looked as though she worked hard and worried too much. She was definitely not Michael's type. Looking past her to the street, I saw an old car parked there that had seen better days.

The word victim was written all over Heidi Duff. She had been victimized by life—and evidently by Michael. My heart went out to her. Suddenly, I was angry at Michael for taking advantage of us. I invited her in out of the cold and asked her to sit down. She perched tensely on the edge of a chair and refused coffee with a nervous, uncomfortable shrug.

"But why did you lend Michael money?" I asked her pointedly, never doubting that she would tell the truth. That woman was not a conniver. She was too simple and straightforward.

She swallowed, and then took a deep breath. "I've asked myself that." She sighed. "I met Mike at the lounge where I worked. We started seeing each other, then he moved in with me. Not long after that I lost my job, but I had some money saved. Mike said we could go away together. He said he was getting his kids and needed help with them. He said he couldn't take the little girl into rest rooms and needed a woman along. He also needed cash. I gave him all the money I had, and then he just disappeared. I found out he'd quit his job and left town—without me."

So Michael had planned all along to take the children, even trying to arrange for someone to help take care of them. And he'd taken advantage of this poor young woman—used her just as he'd used everyone else, and finally dumped her. I could easily believe it. That was his style.

"Heidi, do you ever read the newspapers or listen to the radio?" I asked her.

"Not much. I work all the time. I have two jobs now. Usually I just watch television." Her eyes widened significantly. "Why? Has something been in the news about Mike?" Her frank stare told me she was not pretending.

"Heidi, let me ask you this," I said. "Where did you and Michael plan to go?"

"Michael? Oh—Mike." She smiled, embarrassed. "He said I should call him Mike. We were going to Arkansas. But I guess he decided to take off without me, and I'll probably never see my money again. I never thought he'd do that."

"How did you find me?" I asked her. "Did Michael tell you where I live?"

"Yes. He said you'd probably get married again and the kids would only be in your way. I thought you were a terrible person not to want your own children, and I felt sorry for him. He was always talking about getting his kids and going to Arkansas. He asked me if I wanted to go along, and then he moved in with me. He said we'd go just as soon as he saved some more money. But when he disappeared, I knew he'd lied."

"Listen to me, Heidi," I said. "Michael is wanted by the police. He has kidnapped my children. They've been gone for six months without a trace. Why did you wait so long?"

Her eyes again grew large in her thin face. "I thought he would contact me." She paused for a moment and stared at the floor, then looked up guiltily. "And I was ashamed," she added. "I didn't want to admit that I got involved with Mike and that he ran out on me. I didn't want my family to know. My parents wouldn't approve of what I did. But I just can't afford to lose a thousand dollars. It's all the money I had in the world, and it took me two years to save it. And I'd like to get my jewelry back before it ends up in a pawnshop. I know he has it." Sighing in desperation, she stared at the floor, twisting a handkerchief, and then she raised her mournful eyes at me. "But I guess you're worse off than me. He only took my money, but he took your children."

I wanted to shake her, make her stop talking, so I could ask her more questions. I remembered the gold nugget I'd seen on a chain around Michael's neck. There was no doubt it was hers—he'd never had one before that day. "Listen, Heidi," I interrupted. "I'll get your money back. I don't have it right now, but I'll get it. Just give me your address and phone number and don't worry. I'll try to get your jewelry, too. Just try to remember—where was Michael headed?"

"To Arkansas," she said. "A place called Lost Caves or something like that. He had a job lined up there."

So maybe Michael was in Arkansas! I shoved a pencil and a scrap of paper at her and waited while she wrote her address. I was barely able to control myself until she left, so I could call the police and tell them what I'd found out. Digging in my purse, I found the money my parents had given me and shoved it at her.

"Take this," I insisted. "It's not much—three hundred dollars. I'll get you the rest just as soon as I can. I promise. You've helped me a lot. Just consider yourself lucky to be rid of Michael."

Her eyes widened at the sight of the money. It was evident she was not accustomed to seeing large amounts of cash. I felt sorry for her and hoped her future would be better. And I was thankful for what she'd done for me. The money wasn't important to me—only my children mattered.

"I can't take your money," she said. "You've got enough trouble already; he's the one who owes it to me, not you."

"Take it," I insisted. "And I'll get you the rest. What you've done is worth much more than that for me. Because of what you've told me, I may now be

81

able to find my children. I'll be in touch with you. And thank you, Heidi. I'm sorry you got stung."

As soon as she left, I called the police. Within minutes a bulletin went out to Lost Caves, Arkansas. Meanwhile, I made a quick call to Evan, thankful he was in town, and then waited by the phone for the rest of the day. At last I had an idea where my children were, and it seemed possible I'd soon have them back home again. I had hope.

Evan had just walked through the door that evening when the phone rang. A man asked to speak to me. I identified myself, stammering in my excitement, and waiting breathlessly for his next words.

"Mrs. Payton, this is Detective Roger Elliot. The police in Lost Caves, Arkansas, have your children in protective custody and you can pick them up. How soon can you get there?"

My children! The police had found my children!

"I'll be on the next flight out!" I told him, not realizing I was shouting. "Oh, thank you. Thank you, dear God. Thank you, sir. Call them back and tell them their mommy is coming!"

And I was, with Evan. He insisted on going with me, even buying our tickets. I didn't even change my clothes. I took just enough time to pack a small bag with a change of clothing for the children. I didn't call my parents. I'd have the kids home again by the time I heard from Mom and Dad. They'd be so happy. Evan and I jumped into his car and raced to the airport, barely catching the next flight out.

It was really a short trip by plane, but it seemed like the longest journey of my life. I was so impatient. I could hardly believe it—my children had been found at last! But nagging little doubts assailed my mind. What if it turned out they weren't mine, but someone else's? What if there was a mistake? Although I knew there was no way that could happen, I wouldn't really be sure until I held them in my arms again. I leaned forward in my seat, as though I could, by my own effort, make the plane get there sooner.

Brianna and Susie were being held at the police station where they'd been entertained by a police matron and several officers who'd enjoyed catering to their every wish. They'd had hamburgers, shakes, and popcorn; someone had bought them teddy bears. They were exhausted by the time we arrived, and were sleeping next to their new toys. They'd grown so much in six months and changed so much. Their little faces were beaded with perspiration and they looked so beautiful as they slept side by side, totally oblivious to all the excitement.

The police said they'd been found at a day-care center on a tip from a baby-sitter who'd heard about their disappearance on a news broadcast. Later they'd been picked up by the police when their identity was established from photographs.

Michael had used a false name to register them. At a car dealership in Lost Caves that afternoon, a salesman had responded to the name Mike Payton, and walked right into the arms of the police. But Michael was the least of my worries. I had found my little ones, and when they woke up they were safe in my arms once again.

"Mommy!" they screamed as they woke from sleep and sat up, staring at me as though they couldn't believe their eyes. I hugged them to me, kissing them again and again, and the officers smiled and blinked and cleared their throats awkwardly.

"We couldn't find you," Brianna said, her words tumbling out. "You got lost and we couldn't find you. We needed you. We cried for you. We don't like the other mommy. She makes us go to bed and she yells."

Evidently, Michael hadn't wasted any time finding a replacement for Heidi. I was horrified at the thought of another woman yelling at my children and forcing them to go to bed, so she could be alone with Michael. I was furious with him for allowing it. But I'd found them, and they were safe. That's all that really mattered to me.

"We're going home, my darlings," I said, holding them tightly. "Mommy has been looking everywhere for you. I'll never let you get away from me again. I've made your bedroom all pretty, and it's just waiting for you."

But it was several nights before they would sleep in their own room. I kept them right next to me in bed, holding them until they were sound asleep, grateful for their squirming, wriggling little bodies beside me. I didn't let them out of my sight for days.

We had a wonderful family celebration with my parents, and of course, Evan and Lea. And the press came, and the radio and press people, and the police officers who'd helped us. Friends and neighbors, and even strangers, stopped by to share our victory and express their joy that the children were safely home.

On the plane going home Susie had stirred in my arms and looked up at Evan with sleepy, adoring eyes as he held Brianna. "Evan, can you be my daddy now, please?" she asked him, a serious look on her little face. "I need another daddy."

"I'll certainly think about it, honey," Evan said, smiling at her and patting her chubby leg, then giving me a sidelong glance, one eyebrow raised in a familiar questioning look.

"And so will I," I whispered, smiling up at him and leaning my head on his warm, comfortable shoulder.

Evan had been as terrified by the children's disappearance as I was. I didn't realize until our crisis, how much he had come to care for us and how much we needed him. I don't think he'd realized it either, but the whole frightening experience drew us closer in a way that nothing else but time could have.

"I always knew it was a package deal, Karen," he said. "And I kept coming back, didn't I? I couldn't love you if you weren't the kind of mother you are, and without the kids that wouldn't be possible. I love them, too."

Evan cared for people, even children, just for themselves and not for anything they could do for him. He was patient and loving, loyal and responsible. And I was ready for that. Through my ordeal I had come to realize how special he really was and how much I depended on him.

And I knew that what we give out really does come back to us eventually. Our prayers don't go unheard. Even bad things can work for our good sometimes. Because Michael took advantage of Heidi, it was possible for Michael to be traced through her information, and my children were found. And if I hadn't been willing to put aside my own grief and listen to an unfortunate woman and care about her problem, I would never have found out where my children were. My prayers were answered. No one can deny that.

Heidi's jewelry was returned to her and I gladly gave her the rest of her money, even though I had to use my own money. I owed her much more than I could ever repay. And I think Heidi learned a lesson about men she'll never forget.

Michael had to face criminal charges. He's on probation now and won't cause us any more trouble. There is a restraining order so he can't see the children, and he has to pay his child support on time as a condition of his probation.

But our terror is over. We're trying to forget the past and face the future with joy, thankful each day for the little things we've so often taken for granted. Sometimes I just hold the little faces of my children between my hands and look at them until they squirm and ask, "Why are you staring, Mommy?"

And I reply, "Because I've got to make up for all the days I didn't see you."

It's hard for one parent to have to do the job of both. I'm only human, and I've often felt it's not fair. It will be easier when Evan and I are married. We'll go live with Evan and Lea. I know we'll have a happy home. And just having my children home and knowing they are safe is worth everything.     THE END

# THE THINGS I HAD TO DO FOR LOVE

I guess Webster was just like any other small town. There were the haves and the have-nots, and my family was one of the have-nots.

Everyone knew my mother, Elaine McCall. She worked at Lou's Café tending bar, and after hours she did her "socializing." My dad was in construction, on the road, and he wasn't home too much. When he was, and when he and my mother were in the house together, there was always violent quarreling—arguments with never-ending threats and accusations. Dad would leave, slamming the door behind him, and Mother would shrug her shoulders and say he shouldn't get so shook up. And all the time I'd think: *Why can't they be like other parents?*

I had one good friend, Lori Kramer. We were almost in the same situation, only her mother worked cleaning houses for rich people and her dad was in and out of detoxification centers for drinking. Lori baby-sat for the Speers family, and when she was old enough, she got a job at the Pine Cone Inn, owned by the Speerses. She got me a job there, too. That's how Bruce Callier and I started dating. He was two years older than I was and his dad owned the big lumberyard on the highway. Bruce was home from college and he always came out to eat, dance, and drink a little.

Usually Mr. Speers took Lori and me home, but Mrs. Speers got sick one night so Mr. Speers asked Bruce if he'd mind giving us a lift back to town. Bruce shrugged and said he'd be glad to give us a ride.

Well, Lori lived north of town so he dropped her off first, and then he came on down Main. I said he should just leave me off at the corner of Third, but he said he wouldn't do that since it was after midnight and raining besides. He kept his eyes on the road ahead and said, "I know where you live and I know who you are and you don't have to apologize to me. I remember seeing you in high school." He glanced at me. "You were cute then but now you're really pretty."

I was so surprised, I couldn't think of anything to say.

"Look, how about you and me going to a movie or something?" he said, pulling up to the curb.

I opened the door. "You want to take me out?" I asked.

His eyes met mine. "I do. Honest. Do you work Friday nights?"

"No, Friday is usually my night off," I said.

"That's what I thought. I'll pick you up here about seven. Oh, and dress casually."

He left. I turned to walk into the house, not caring about getting drenched in the rain. I was feeling excited and scared and didn't want to go inside.

Dad was home. He was sitting in the living room. "You're as bad as your mother, staying out all night," he said, staring at me sullenly.

"I wasn't out. I was working. Mr. Speers asked a friend of his to give me a ride home."

"Well, your mother is out in high-class company. She's with George Callier. Seems she's moving up in the world."

The name sent shock waves through me. "Not George Callier!" I said. "He wouldn't date Mother. You know that."

Dad stood up, eyes glaring. "Well, he would. I saw him pick her up in the alley. He was driving that pickup truck they use at the lumberyard; your mother turned and laughed at me."

I went to my room upstairs. I didn't want the magic of the ride home to disappear like every other good thing that ever happened in my life. Bruce's dad wouldn't date my mother! Important Mr. Callier wouldn't stoop to date Elaine McCall. Why, he wouldn't even look at me when the people he went around with came out to the inn. He'd order his drinks and walk away or not look at me at all.

I was so tired, but I pushed the bed next to the window and lay down, waiting to see if the pickup truck brought Mother home. And sure enough, around three, the pickup came down the dark, narrow road of the alley and Mother got out, stumbled to the house, and came in. I knew the scene so well. The shouting downstairs that carried up, Mother's hair disheveled, makeup smeared, and clothes wrinkled and sometimes torn. Then she'd stumble into bed and fall into a deep sleep.

Well, Dad was shouting his usual threats again. But this time he said he meant it—he was going to divorce her and start over. She said for him to go ahead. I remember her laughing and taunting him that now she was dating a man who was a real somebody and that Dad was jealous. And then there was silence. . . .

The next day, the sun was shining brightly and when I came downstairs, Dad was drinking coffee. He was standing at the window, staring outside. He turned to me and said, "I am going to divorce your mother. I've had it. Anyway, I've met someone nice and I want to marry her. I want to move to the city and make a life for myself."

I couldn't blame him, but it did hurt. I thought about how it would be with Dad never coming home again, and it cut me up inside. But I said nothing. I didn't even ask: What about me? I guess I knew.

I'd be staying there. So I poured some coffee, made a piece of toast, ate it, and left.

When I got home that afternoon, Mother was just getting up. She roamed around the house in her robe and made a few phone calls. One was to Hank Brown, a guy she dated. She told him she was feeling under the weather and that she'd see him the next night. Then she made another call and told that person she'd be seeing him at the same time and same place. Then she looked at me and said, "No man is ever going to own me. I go where it's best for me."

My stomach churned sickly because I knew what she meant. She had ruined my life and I hated her for it.

"Dad is really going to divorce you and marry

somebody else!" I said. I waited for a reaction, but all she did was look at me.

"Well, what do I care?" she said finally. "He's never done anything that I'd miss him for—just so he keeps the money coming in for the house."

Around nine that night, Mother got all dressed up and went out the back door, saying, "If anyone calls, tell them I'm feeling too sick to talk."

I watched some television for a while, talked to Lori on the phone, and then went up to bed. Sometime later, I heard pounding at the back door. I went down and saw it was Hank. He was calling my mother's name.

"She's not here, Hank. Mother is out," I said.

Hank was a big man, over six feet tall and strong. He shoved the strength of his body against the door and broke in. He stomped through the house to Mother's room, saw the empty bed, and roared, "Where is she?"

My throat was tight and I swallowed hard. "I don't know. I never know where she is. You know that," I said.

He sat down on the bed, looked around, and then threw a vase to the floor. Then he grabbed me and roughly pressed his lips against mine. "She owes me," he said. "I paid her, but I guess you'll do."

I screamed and cried and pleaded, but he kept kissing me and pawing at me. With one swift motion, he tore my nightgown off, and then set me down on the bed. He started to unbuckle his belt and I jumped up and ran downstairs to the basement. I bolted the two heavy locks on the door and hid behind the furnace. I heard him pounding on the door and calling my name, but I just closed my eyes and prayed.

After what seemed like hours, I heard a door slam and a car drive away. I looked out the basement window to be sure Hank was gone, and then I fell to the floor and sobbed.

The pickup truck brought Mother home later that night. The moonlight was bright so there was no mistaking that she was with George Callier.

I met Mother at the door, my whole body trembling. "Hank was here," I said. "Do you know what he tried to do to me?"

Her eyes widened, but not out of concern for me. "You didn't tell him who I was with, did you, Beth?" she asked.

I just gave her a look of disgust and went back upstairs.

I was sick all the next day. At eight o'clock, I called Lori and asked her to meet me at the corner. We walked uptown. I was going to tell her about Hank, but I couldn't. I was too ashamed, so I told her about Mother and George Callier. Lori said it wasn't my fault and that I should just forget it and go out with Bruce.

I felt better when I was with Lori, but when I was alone I was scared. The nightmares of Hank kept racing through my mind over and over again. I cringed when I thought about his dirty, grubby hands touching me, his body pinning me down.

When I got my paycheck from Mr. Speers, I went downtown and bought a skirt and blouse to wear Friday night. On Friday, I was sure Bruce wouldn't turn up, but at seven o'clock sharp his car came around the corner and pulled up in front of our house.

# THE THINGS I HAD TO DO FOR LOVE

I ran out to meet him. I didn't want him to come in.

Bruce looked at me and smiled, walked me around to the side of his car, and opened the door. He put his hand on my shoulder and said, "You look nice."

It was awkward being with Bruce. I kept wishing we'd get to the movie theater—wishing we'd get inside in the dark so I wouldn't have to make conversation. When we did get there, he put his arm around me. I was so nervous, I don't remember what the movie was about.

Afterward, we went for ice-cream sundaes. Bruce talked about college and the lumberyard and his old friends who were home for the summer. He also talked about their cabin up north and fishing and golfing and going to Florida before the fall semester started.

Later, Bruce drove me around the city, then out past the airport to a dark country road. It was getting late and I was getting a little apprehensive. I finally told him that we had better get back to town, and he sort of laughed and said, "I suppose your mother waits up." The words cut through me and I looked away. He reached out for me and said, "Look, I'm sorry. That was a low blow."

I wanted to say: *Does your mother wait up for your father?* But of course I wouldn't cut him down that way.

We were parked in front of my house, which was on Oak Lane. It was one of the oldest blocks in Webster and the most run-down. It was a dark, tree-lined street; no one had ever bothered to complain that we didn't have a streetlight. Anyway, Bruce put his arm around me and I wanted to get away. I wanted him and I didn't.

"One kiss? Just one?" he asked, coming toward me. Then his lips were on mine—warm, soft, tender.

Suddenly, I pulled away and got out of the car.

"I've got to get in," I said. "Thanks for the movie and everything."

Bruce looked angry. "You're no fun," he said. "No fun at all." He started his car and sped off.

I walked slowly to the house. So that dream was over. Hot tears burned down my face.

Mother was home—in bed with someone, probably. The house smelled of beer, and giggling came from her room. I took my shoes off and tiptoed up the stairs to bed. I pushed the dresser against the door.

Lori's mother gave us a ride to work the next afternoon and left us off at the road that wound around the golf course and led to the inn. I saw Bruce walking with someone. He saw Lori and me and he waved. I just nodded, but my heart did flip-flops.

Later, he came to the dining room and ordered a steak. He grabbed my arm. "About last night—I'm sorry," he said. "I acted like a jerk."

My cheeks were flaming, but I tried being nonchalant. "It doesn't matter, really," I said.

I went to the kitchen and I felt his eyes on my back.

Millie Munson was cooking and she motioned for me to come over to the grill. "I see Bruce is hitting on you," she said. "He tried that last year with Jane Sawyer. He dated her off and on all summer. Jane even had an abortion—not that I know it was Bruce's kid, but she had one. Of course, Bruce went back to school and Jane moved away. So don't let him fool you. He just wants a summer fling and you're too nice a kid to get hurt."

I looked at Bruce through the serving window. He was enjoying a drink, looking relaxed and casual—like he had no worries.

After work Bruce was waiting for me in the parking lot. Mr. Speers was walking with Lori and Judy Probst and me—he was taking us all home. Bruce got out of his car and called my name. "Beth? I'll give you a ride home."

Lori looked at me.

"Thanks, but no thanks," I said.

Bruce walked toward us. "Oh, come on," he said. "I just want to talk to you. We'll go straight to your house, okay?"

Mr. Speers started his car; Lori and Judy were already inside. I hesitated, and Bruce touched my arm gently. I said I was going to ride home with Bruce and they left.

He drove right to my house like he had promised. Then he turned on the radio and played soft music. He turned to me and said, "Listen, I feel bad about the other night, I really do. I thought I'd date you once and forget you, but you're on my mind all the time."

I looked away. Did he expect me to believe that? "Sure," I said sarcastically. "I'm so special."

"Listen," he said angrily, "I could date any girl in this town. But I want to see you. I don't want to date anyone else—not all summer."

I looked at him. "What about Jane Sawyer?"

He looked sort of strange. "Yeah, I went with Jane for a while," he said. "She was a nice girl. But Jane was dating some man from the city at the same time. She thought they were getting married, but she learned he already was married. Then she had some bad luck and moved. But not because of me, because of him." He took my hand. "So now that I've cleared my past, do you suppose I could take you out again? Would you give me a second chance?"

I agreed to see him again—because I was attracted to him and because he was the only guy who ever paid any attention to me, and because he was like the man of my dreams.

After that, Bruce took me home often and on my night off he'd take me out to the city for dinner and a movie or something. Lori sort of shut me out; Bruce said she was jealous. I don't know if that was it, but a couple of times when I called her, she kind of cut it short. She never called me. One night she didn't come to work and Millie said that Lori was seeing a married man. Then she added that it was kind of like the situation I was getting myself into. I didn't want to ask what she meant, but finally I turned around and faced her, saying, "What is that supposed to mean?"

Millie slapped a hamburger on the grill and only glanced at me. "That means that you are both being used, and if you can't see it for yourselves, telling you won't help."

My mouth was dry, my throat tense and tight. "I have a lot of fun with Bruce. He's very nice to me. Why couldn't he care for me? Am I that bad?" I asked.

Millie put her arm around me. "Listen, I don't want to hurt you, but if Bruce really cared about you he'd take you home, introduce you to his family as his girl. He'd take you out in Webster—not out of town like you're someone to hide." She sighed. "Why can't you see it? And Lori thinks this character she's seeing is going to get a divorce next year. Well, why next year? Why not now? Look, the two of you are sweet girls. You could get away from here, move to the city, and make a whole new life. I don't see why you stick around where you're sunk before you start, before you give yourself a chance."

What Millie said really hurt. I couldn't wait for Lori to return to work so we could talk it over. I wanted us to be the friends that we used to be—sharing heartaches and disappointments, and building dreams of moving away and starting over.

But Lori didn't come back to the inn, so I went over to her house the next day. Her mother came to the door and seemed relieved to see me. She was going to work, she said, but I should go on into Lori's room and visit with her—try to cheer her up.

When Lori saw me, she turned away and started to cry. "I wish you hadn't come," she said.

I sat on the chair by the door and said, "I thought we were friends." My heart was pounding. "Lori, what's wrong? Have I done anything?"

She wouldn't look at me, but just stared at the wall, her face wet with tears.

"You're going to hate me, just like I hate myself," she said.

"Lori, I'd never hate you, no matter what," I told her.

She blurted it all out then—all the things that had been building up inside her: her affair with Edgar Rogers—who was married—and her pregnancy.

## THE THINGS I HAD TO DO FOR LOVE

Edgar was a family man with a church membership and a business on Main Street. He had promised to divorce his wife if Lori would have an abortion. She had, and now Edgar had changed his mind—for the sake of the children, he said.

I sat on the bed beside Lori and touched her arm. "Listen," I said, trying to sound cheerful, "we're going to the city this fall. We'll get jobs, an apartment, and start—"

"But I love him!" she cried.

I shut my eyes to hold back the hot tears that wanted to escape. Then I hugged her and assured her everything would work out.

I worked that night and I told Millie that Lori had the flu. Millie looked at me with that glance and said, "That isn't the way I heard it."

I just walked away.

Later on, Judy came over and nudged me. "Bruce and his folks are in the dining room—at your table," she said.

I felt shaky. "Would you wait on them, please?" I asked.

She grinned. "I already did. They just ordered drinks. They're waiting for a friend—a doctor who had an emergency at the hospital."

I thanked her and knew that I'd have to take her tables, which were across from where mine were. I still would have to pass the Calliers. Mr. Speers was very fussy about his customers being served as quickly and efficiently as possible.

Bruce saw me right away and smiled. His mother looked at me with eyes that seemed to dismiss me—like I was nothing. I got the message. She knew about us. I had that feeling. His father sort of

98

looked away. But I looked at him directly, remembering the pickup truck and my mother.

I was standing next to the Calliers' table when the doctor joined them. He sat down briskly and said there was nothing he could have done for the patient.

As his eyes skimmed the menu, I heard him say, "Her name was Lori. She used to work here. I did everything I could, of course, but that girl just didn't want to live. She took enough pills to kill two people."

His words broke my heart. Lori! Dead? I looked at Bruce and then I just left the people at my table and went into the kitchen. Bruce came rushing behind me. "I'm sorry about Lori," he said.

I started to cry.

I didn't finish work that night. Mr. Speers drove me home and after awhile the telephone rang. It was Bruce; he said he'd be right over and we'd go for a drive.

I went into his arms in the car, sobbing, blurting it out about Edgar and the baby. When I finished, I saw that Bruce's face was tense with anger. "Well, she shouldn't have gone with a married man," he said. "There's no excuse for that. I guess she sort of asked for trouble."

His words lashed through me. *What about his father?* I thought. Aloud, I said, "Bruce, I want to go home. I don't want to talk about it anymore."

He started the car, backed out of the lot by the park where we often went to talk and to make love, and he glanced at me. "I'm sorry for what happened to Lori. She could have changed her whole life around. She could have gotten away from Webster and made a new life for herself—been somebody respectable."

I stared at him. What was he trying to say? "Like me? Is that what you mean?" I asked.

He waited for a red light. His face looked different suddenly—changed.

"Is that what you mean?" I repeated. "No, don't answer. I saw it in your mother's eyes. Your father's, too. Bruce, I'm me. I'm Elaine McCall's daughter. Nothing will ever change that."

Bruce's knuckles on the steering wheel were white because he was gripping it so hard. "I know, but maybe when I get out of school, maybe we can move away."

"But there's the lumberyard waiting for you, right?"

"That's right. And Dad's putting me through school. So I owe him something. I was hoping that you could go to junior college or something. Then maybe my folks would forget about your mother and everything."

He stopped the car in front of my house. His hand touched my arm. "It will all work out, I'm sure," he said hopefully.

That was a night of deep pain. My best friend had died and my boyfriend wanted me to change. I felt so alone. . . .

Bruce went with me to Lori's funeral and kept his arm around me protectively. When it was all over, he took me home. I got out of the car and asked, "Will I see you later tonight?"

He loosened his tie. "Well, tonight my folks are having a dinner party for my dad's birthday, so I won't be around. But tomorrow is Friday, remember? Our night."

I needed him tonight, but I said okay and went into the house.

I saw Bruce all summer, every chance I got. I gladly took every free moment he would give me—it was all I had! Millie kept trying to convince me to go out with some of the guys who worked at the inn, like Steven Warren or Jeffrey Baker. But even though they asked, I refused. I had Bruce—even if it was only part-time.

One day I came home from town and Dad was there with his new wife, Gladys. He seemed nervous as he introduced us. Then he added, "Gladys, I've told you all about Beth—what a nice girl she is."

Gladys glanced at me. "Looks a little like her mother," she said. There was a sting in her words, and I got the message that we weren't going to be friends. I just said hello and Gladys shrugged. Then she said that her last husband had had three children and they had made her life miserable, so she left Phil. Her eyes met mine and she added, "I told your father before I married him that I'd never get into another bad family situation. I'd rather be alone, but you're welcome to come and visit the weekends that I work, or your father can come out here."

What had I expected? I don't know. Everyone who had been in my life was there part-time. I blinked hard to keep the tears back.

Dad and Gladys were on their way to Springfield to visit some friends of Gladys's, so they left after a little while. Dad had said Mother was home when they had arrived, but she left as soon as possible. He didn't know where she had gone.

Well, it was Friday night. Mother didn't come

home, Bruce didn't call, and I was feeling low. At nine o'clock I dialed Bruce's number, praying that he would answer, but it was his mother who picked up the phone. "Hello," Mrs. Collier said crisply.

"Is Bruce there?" I asked softly.

I heard her sigh. "Beth? Beth, if he had wanted to see you tonight I'm sure he'd have called you."

Tears sprang to my eyes. My first impulse was to give it right back to her, to tell her that her son and her husband saw something in the McCalls, but I knew that didn't say much for either my mother or myself. Instead, I just blurted out, "We love each other!"

Quickly, she replied, "Oh, I'm sure you love Bruce, but he's got a lot of growing up to do yet. Believe me, when he settles down it will be with someone—well—"

I hung up. I didn't want to hear any more. I knew that Bruce would be going back to college soon, forgetting all about me.

It was midnight when I went up to my room. I must have just drifted off to sleep when I heard the noise downstairs: someone stumbling through the house, cursing. My heart went wild with fear. It was Hank! He was coming after me!

My door crashed open, and there he was, lunging for me. I grabbed the old metal lamp by my bed—it was heavy—and I raised it. Hank laughed and came closer. I jumped out of bed and bashed the lamp against his head—hard. He fell with a dull thud and didn't move.

Shaken, I threw down the lamp. There was a pool of blood oozing from under Hank. My stomach churned sickly. I stepped around him to the telephone and called the police.

The police came right away and I heard an ambulance siren cut through the dark silence of the night. The sound filled my ears and the red flashing lights, when they got closer, flashed on the wall, off and on, like a neon sign.

A man who said he was Detective Kelly took me over to the sofa. A young police officer asked the detective, "Was he here to see her mother or her?"

Detective Kelly kept writing something in his pad and said, "Shut up."

But I knew that was what they'd all be saying—that I was like my mother.

The young policeman went out to the car, and Detective Kelly sat down on the sofa and watched them take Hank away on a stretcher. The detective looked at me compassionately. "Beth, he was after you, wasn't he?" he asked.

I swallowed hard, and my hands trembled as I rubbed them together. I felt cold and sick. I nodded. "He was looking for the—" I began.

Detective Kelly nodded and closed his pad. "Don't worry, I don't think there will be any charges against you. Do you have anyone at all that you could call—any friends?"

I looked away. "I'll be all right."

Mother didn't come home that night. I slept on the sofa because I couldn't bring myself to clean up the blood and I couldn't look at it, either. I left the lights on all over the house; there was no light to brighten the darkness inside me.

At six-thirty in the morning, I called my father. He had moved into Gladys's apartment. When he answered, I blurted it all out.

"Oh, no," he said when I'd finished. "I hope it doesn't make the papers. Gladys isn't the kind to—well, I'll send you some money, Beth. I'll help you that way, but I'm not coming out there. I want this marriage to last. Anyway, you should have kept the door locked. Anyone who doesn't in this day and age is looking for trouble."

There was some relief in daylight. I kept thinking about Hank, but once the sun had risen, I wasn't as scared. I went up to my bedroom and leaned against the door, feeling faint. I knew that it was up to me to clean up the blood, so I got a pail and mop and scrubbed it up, gagging as I did it. Then I did the dishes in the sink and opened the windows so that the cool fresh air filtered through the house.

I was wiping up the stove when I saw the police car stop out front. My heart pounded wildly and I felt sick again. I just sat down by the kitchen table and Detective Kelly came in, holding my mother's arm. She wasn't crying or anything; she just looked done in. She didn't say anything to me at all, but just went in the living room, mumbling like she did when she'd had too much to drink.

I didn't move. Detective Kelly pushed his hat off his forehead and sat down at the table across from me. "Beth," he said, "Hank will be all right. He's got a concussion but he's going to recover. But your mother—well, she was with George Callier last night, and there was an accident."

My mouth was dry. I didn't speak—I couldn't. I just waited and he went on, saying, "George Callier was killed. A trucker found them. Your mother was wandering around the side of the road and George was inside the car—dead."

## THE THINGS I HAD TO DO FOR LOVE

There was no sound from the living room. I assumed my mother had gone to her room and had gone to sleep. Detective Kelly looked toward the door and said, "You know, your mother isn't the first woman who George has dated. He was stepping out pretty regularly with some woman from Williston. Of course, I knew it because some of the men on the force would find him parking. This isn't the first time he's been out of line—only, it's the last." He stood up. "You know what I feel bad about?" he asked. "You've never hurt anyone. But maybe someday something good will come your way."

It was nice of Detective Kelly to be so kind, but I was still glad when he left. I was thankful that Hank was going to be all right; as much as I hated him I didn't want him to be dead. Then I thought about Bruce and the heartache he was going through. I knew he loved and respected his father. I had such a longing to be with Bruce—to put my arms around him, to tell him how sorry I was, to tell him how much I loved him—but of course I couldn't call him or see him.

When Mother got up late that day, I asked her if she knew that George Callier had died. She looked at me with a vacant stare and went to the sink, filled a glass with water, drank it, and shrugged. "I guess I knew it. I told him to stay on the highway, but you know how those Calliers are—you can't tell them anything."

I stared at her. *Why is she this way?* I thought.

"Hank was here last night—looking for you, of course," I said.

She turned around, eyes narrowed. "Did he try to get you again?" she asked.

# THE THINGS I HAD TO DO FOR LOVE

How I wanted to hurt her, to see her suffer, to make things even! But what purpose would that have served? I just turned away so I wouldn't have to look at her, chills going through my body from remembering. "He tried, but I got away," I said.

My mother's cold hand reached out and touched my arm. "Listen, Beth, I could get you a good job at the bar," she said. "You know, a hostess job. You don't have to serve liquor or anything. But you could make some good money, have nice things."

I turned to stare at her, and I felt the tears filling my eyes. "Mother, a man just died and all you think about is yourself and money. Why, you'd even sell me. What kind of a person are you?"

Her eyes filled with rage and she shouted, "Listen, I know you think you're some kind of a princess because you're young and you've got a good shape, but you're never going to land yourself a Callier. They wouldn't be seen in public with people like us. Why shouldn't we take from them what we can? They use us, don't they?"

My throat was dry. "Speak for yourself," I said hoarsely. "I intend to get away from here."

"I suppose you think I don't know about you and Bruce," she went on. "Well, I've known for a long time. I'm telling you right now that he's no different than his father except that his father paid well. I don't see Bruce taking you home to his house, and he's never going to, either, so you might as well face that fact right now."

Right then the telephone rang and I was standing by it so I answered. It was Millie. She'd heard about Mr. Callier and she wanted to know if I'd like to get out of the house and go for a little ride. I said I would, and she said she'd be over in a few minutes.

I told Millie about Hank and about my mother, and I said I had to get away somehow. I couldn't keep living there with the way things were. Millie offered me a room in her house if I'd help her with the housework. I guess she needed someone as much as I did. Her brother had brought their mother to live in an apartment in Webster, and since the old woman was practically an invalid the workload fell on Millie. It seemed like the answer for both of us.

I packed my things in a couple of cardboard boxes and Millie said she'd move me over on Sunday.

On Saturday the local newspaper had Mr. Callier's picture on the front page. There was a brief account of the accident, which they said occurred on his return from a convention in a nearby city. The words blurred before my eyes and I kept wishing I could see Bruce.

Millie came for me on Sunday afternoon. Mother was just getting up, and she looked into the bright sunlight with squinty eyes. "Who's that out front?" She glanced at the boxes I had brought down.

"I'm moving in with Millie," I said.

"Moving?" she asked. "You could be helping me a little."

I pulled the boxes to the porch and Millie helped me lug them to her car. Mother was in the doorway when we drove away. Surprisingly, a strange pang shot through me when I looked back to see her still watching until the car turned at the corner. I wondered then if my mother had ever loved me—even just a little.

The room at Millie's was much nicer than the

room I had had at home. There were nice drapes and plants, a carpet, and a dresser and bed that matched.

I put everything away in the closet and drawers and Millie said that I could just as well learn about everything now. She showed me how to run her washer, where the vacuum cleaner and furniture polish were kept—everything I needed to know to keep house.

That evening Millie was invited out, so she left me a list of what should be done—like making a casserole for the next day, finishing the ironing, and changing the bedding so that the wash could be started early the next morning.

There was something in her tone that cut through me. Something that made me uneasy, like a little voice inside that said I was going to be her maid, cleaning lady, and delivery girl.

I hardly slept that night. In the morning Millie was standing in the doorway saying that the wash had to be started, and when that was going I could go down to the bakery and get some fresh rolls. She was having company for ten-o'clock coffee. Hot tears burned in my eyes, but I did as she said. I showered quickly, dressed in some jeans and a clean blouse, and walked out into the coolness of the morning down to the bakery on Main.

I saw Bruce's car in front of the bakery and I walked faster, my heart pounding. We met at the doorway. He had a couple of bakery bags in his arms.

"Hi, Beth," he said tonelessly.

I touched his arm. "I'm sorry about your dad—"

His face paled. "It was a shock, that's for sure,"

he said.

"I'd go to the funeral, but I'd better not."

"No, it would be better if you didn't."

"Well, I'll see you, Bruce."

"Sure," he said, getting into his car.

Two weeks passed before I saw Bruce again. He came out to the inn on a Saturday night. Jeffrey came and got me from the kitchen. "Bruce Callier is in the bar. He said I should tell you."

Millie reminded me in a snapping voice that my order was almost ready. I just nodded and walked through the dining room to the bar where Bruce was sitting. He looked thinner, pale.

I walked up to him. "Hi," I said, remembering everything—his arms, his lips, his body. The old feelings moved through me.

He glanced at me, his eyes not meeting mine directly. He slid his drink toward him, running his hand up and down the glass in a nervous gesture. "I didn't want to leave without saying good-bye—and good luck."

"Going back to school, I suppose," I managed to say. He nodded.

I blurted out, "Will you ever call me?"

He looked away. "Sometime, maybe. But I've been thinking a lot lately—you know, about us and everything. I was thinking that you should get away from here, start over. Go to school in the city and do something with your life. Pick up the pieces and find some happiness. If anyone deserves it—deserves better—you do, Beth."

He'd come to say good-bye, to tell me to start over. But mostly he was saying it was all over. He was letting me down easy. Tears blurred Bruce's eyes in front of me. Vaguely, I was aware of Millie calling me from the kitchen, her mouth a tight, angry line. "Well, good luck, Bruce," I said quickly, "and good-bye."

I worked all night, carrying the hurt deep inside me and waiting on customers with tears in my eyes. Millie decided to stay at the bar for a few drinks after work, and Jeffrey offered to give me a ride home. Jeffrey was nice: a quiet, gentle person. I guess he was almost thirty years old, but he never dated anyone that I knew; he was just a friend to everyone at work.

When we were in front of Millie's, Jeffrey said, "I suppose Bruce came to tell you good-bye." It was a flat statement.

I shrugged and looked away. "Yes, that's what he wanted." I turned and looked at him. "I guess I knew down deep that it wouldn't last. And now with his dad getting killed and everything—" I stopped.

Jeffrey's hand touched my arm. "Well, you know what I think? You're too good for the likes of him, and too nice to have to be at Millie's beck and call."

I closed my eyes. *Not tonight! No more advice,* I thought. I opened the car door. "Thanks, Jeffrey, for the ride—and for being a friend."

"Maybe sometime we could go out," he said.

I said maybe we could. Then I went in.

While I lived at Millie's, I never heard from my mother—except once when I saw her going into the bar when I was going to the drugstore for Millie. She was hanging on some man's arm, laughing up at him, and a funny pain flashed through me.

I guess I knew I was pregnant before I went over to Williston to see Dr. Jensen. When he confirmed the fact, I thought: *Bruce's baby!* A warmth flooded through me and I had a happy feeling, knowing a part of our love was living inside of me. I'd have something of my own—someone to love!

Then Dr. Jensen said, "You're Elaine McCall's daughter, aren't you?" Then there was a silence that echoed in my ears. I just nodded. He shrugged. "Well, are you planning on carrying this baby to term?" he asked.

"Yes," I whispered.

"Do you know who the father is?"

My eyes stayed on his face. "Bruce Callier. I've never been with anyone but Bruce," I said.

He didn't even acknowledge that I'd answered. He just said, "There are several good adoption agencies that have waiting lists for children. I even know a couple who would pay all your expenses and give the child everything."

I got up, feeling faint, and walked to the door. I fought for control, and then said firmly, "I'm going to have my child, and I'm going to keep it and love it."

I had opened the door, but the doctor's next words stopped me from leaving. "You owe it more than you can give," he said. "What kind of mother would you be?"

I slammed the door behind me and ran from the clinic.

I had to sit in Millie's car for some time; I had to calm myself, to stop the tears, so I could see to drive home.

I wanted to get back before Millie returned from her club meeting, but it didn't work that way. She met me at the door, eyes fired with anger. "Where have you been with my car?" she demanded.

My heart pounded hard and fast. I set the groceries I'd picked up on the table, not answering the question. "I'll start supper," I said.

"I thought supper would have already been on," she said.

"I fixed a casserole and a blueberry pie before I left," I said. "It took a bit longer than I thought. I ran into Reverend Graves at the drugstore. He asked about you." That calmed her down, and she changed the subject.

All night I hugged my secret to my heart: Bruce's baby was inside me. I was four months along and I imagined that the little life inside me would be a boy—be like Bruce.

If only Lori was still alive. If only I had a friend to share my feelings, my fears, my hopes.

It was the second week in November when Millie got sick at work one night and went home early. Jeffrey offered to give me a ride home, and I accepted. He suggested we go for a little ride. I said I was tired, but he drove out of town anyway. He didn't say much, and I thought he looked angry.

Finally, he just looked at me and asked, "Why won't you go out with me? You don't think you're too good for me, do you?"

I was amazed at his last question. "Too good?" I asked. "Me? You must be kidding! I'm not good enough for anyone. I'm Beth McCall, remember? Elaine's daughter."

"I'm sorry I said anything," Jeffrey said. "I just like you so much, and I keep thinking about that jerk, Bruce, and what a line he handed you. You know he'll never come back for you, so why won't you give up on him and go out with me?"

# THE THINGS I HAD TO DO FOR LOVE

I started to cry. I tried so hard to hold it in, but suddenly my emotions were out of control. Jeffrey pulled the car over and tried to put his arm around me. "Beth, please, I wouldn't hurt you for the world," he said.

*Why not tell him?* I thought. Pretty soon I'd be big and there'd be no denying my condition. So I just said it—that I was pregnant with Bruce's baby.

Jeffrey swore under his breath. He stared straight ahead, silent, for a long time. Then he turned to me and said, "I'd like to kill him. If I could see him right now, I would."

He backed the car up and headed back toward Webster. We were almost home when he said, "I'll marry you, Beth. I have a nice place—old, but nicer than Millie's. But I wouldn't keep his child—never. I'd marry you, though, to make it easier for you these next months."

"Jeffrey," I said slowly, "I can't marry you that way, and I can't give up my baby—I just can't."

"Listen, Beth, I've loved you for a long time," he said. "You're so pretty and nice to everyone. I'd do anything for you—even work at the factory and make more money so you could have some nice things, like other women. I was going to go there when they had an opening, and then you started working at the inn—that's why I stayed on." He also said I didn't have to make up my mind that night, but that the offer would always be open.

When Jeffrey dropped me off at Millie's, I unlocked the door and went inside. The house was chilly and too quiet. I turned on the hall light and called her name. No answer. My heart raced and I walked slowly to the living room. Millie was lying on the sofa. I went over and stood next to her. "Are you all right?" I asked.

She woke up abruptly. "Where have you been? I called the inn and they said you left hours ago," she said.

I felt sick. My throat was dry and the words were hard to get out. "Not hours ago. Jeffrey gave me a ride home and we just drove around for a while, that's all."

She pulled the afghan close around her. "You drove around? I'll bet. I'll bet you were parking someplace. And here I was sick and you were out fooling around."

"Can I get you anything?" I asked, ignoring her remark.

"Some tea, maybe—and toast. And don't think because you're doing something for me that the subject is closed." Her words followed me to the kitchen. "You're still a McCall, and don't you forget that."

I leaned against the wall and closed my eyes around the tears. How could I forget it?

Then one day Millie came home from a meeting. It was still November, but it was already snowing. I remember that she didn't take her boots off, but came storming through the back door, trailing snow right into the dining room where I was ironing. She stared at me from across the room, stared straight at my stomach. "Do you know what I heard today?" she asked. "I heard that you're pregnant! That's the thanks I get for taking you in, giving you a roof over your head, and putting up with you."

I couldn't answer. I remember feeling dizzy, like I was going to pass out, and I remember wishing I could just die. My silence infuriated Millie and she came over in front of me. Suddenly, she slapped me—a swift, stinging blow. Then she turned quickly, went over to the sofa, and motioned for me to leave. I got my coat and put my boots on out on the porch. It had sleeted earlier and then it had turned to snow. I opened the door, walked slowly down the icy steps, and stood with the wind cutting against my face. Where would I go? The Calliers' house was closer than my mother's by about a mile, so I started in that direction. When I got there, there was a front porch light on and through the window I could see a lamp glowing warmly. I walked to the front door and rang the bell. I was terrified, but desperate.

Bruce's mother opened the door, and the warmth from inside touched my face. Her eyes were icy; her mouth a tight, tense line. "What do you want?" she asked coldly.

"To talk to you," I said. I felt frozen.

Mrs. Callier stepped back, but didn't invite me in. I went in, anyway. She closed the door behind me. "I rather expected you to show up. I heard you're pregnant," she said.

"It's Bruce's baby, your grandchild," I said.

She smiled a little. "No. No, it's not Bruce's. Who knows whose child it is? But it's not Bruce's. And don't try to contact Bruce, either, because he has a steady girlfriend and I think it's getting serious. Her mother is a lawyer and her father is a surgeon. Here—I'll show you her picture."

She moved into the living room and came back with a framed photo of Bruce with his arm around a beautiful girl. She looked at him with adoring eyes and his eyes were looking straight into mine.

I leaned against the wall and looked out the window. The wind whipped snow around like powder and I could hardly see to the end of the driveway. I turned up my collar and turned my back to Mrs. Callier. "The baby is Bruce's," I repeated. "I've never been with anyone but Bruce, and I love him."

I went outside and walked slowly to the road. I'd only gone a short way when a car pulled up alongside me. "Beth McCall?" I heard a man say. "Mrs. Callier said I should give you a ride."

I recognized him as Matt Higgins, who did lawns and shoveling and window cleaning. I guessed he worked for Mrs. Callier, too. I got in his car without a word.

"Well, where are you going?" he asked.

I looked away. "You know where my mother lives, don't you? Take me there."

Matt talked about the weather and said that he'd noticed there was a for-sale sign in front of my mother's place. Glancing at me, he said, "I hear your mother is going into the nursing home."

I stared at him. "It wasn't that long ago that I last saw her—"

"I know," he said. "I've seen her, too. The word is she's got cancer."

Matt edged his car close to the curb and stopped. I thanked him and got out, noticing the for-sale sign under the straggly old oak tree. There was a dim light on in the living room. The porch door was locked so I walked around to the back, turned the knob, and went inside. The wind made a sound that echoed through the room. It was chilly inside.

"Mother?" I called. "It's me, Beth. I've come

home for a while."

There was a strange feeling that went through me as I walked through the kitchen to the living room.

"That you, Bethie?" a weak voice asked.

I went into the living room. Mother was lying on the couch, all huddled up in a robe and quilt. Her face looked the color of putty and her eyes were circled darkly and had a faraway look in them. She kind of smiled. "So you're pregnant," she said.

I ignored the statement. I took my coat off, sat down, and struggled with my boots. "Can I stay here for a while?" I asked.

She shrugged. "I guess so. The house is for sale, you know. I'm going into the nursing home, first opening they have. That's not a cheap place to live, so I had to deed the house to them. They'll sell it and put the money in the bank. If I don't live too long, there might be something left over for you."

Mother had turned the vents off upstairs, so I went up and opened them so some heat would go into my old room. The windows were frosted over and the air had that closed-in smell. I dusted off the furniture and opened the closet door to see some empty hangers just as I left them. I looked at my reflection in the mirror: hollow eyes, pale face.

It wasn't until the next day that Mr. Speers came knocking on the back door. I opened it and he set down the cardboard box just inside the kitchen. "Millie asked me to deliver this to you—your worldly goods, I guess."

The box was cold and damp. I guessed Millie had packed it up the night before and had put it out on the back step. I shoved it over against the wall.

"She told me about you and the baby," Mr.

Speers said. "You can still work, as far as I'm concerned. I can still pick you up, or Jeffrey would, I'm sure."

I swallowed hard, feeling grateful. "I need the money," I said.

He nodded. "You want to come in tonight?"

"Sure," I said, relief filling me.

I had saved most of the money I earned at the inn—enough money to go to the thrift shop and pick up a nice crib. Each week I picked up something new for the baby—a mattress, tiny shirts, and diapers.

For Thanksgiving, I brought home a small turkey, a pumpkin to make a pie, a new robe for Mother, and a nice maternity dress for me—in case I ran into Bruce.

I put the turkey in the oven early Thursday morning. The smell of it roasting made me feel sick, but I set the table and put real napkins by the plates. Mother wore her new robe and we had our Thanksgiving meal together. She wasn't feeling well, but she picked at her food. I felt like the gap between us had closed a little.

I had to work that night; the bar was closed but the dining room was open. I sort of expected that Bruce would come in, but Millie set the newspaper on the table in the kitchen, opened to the society page. A certain column read: "Lilly Callier will be spending Thanksgiving with her son, Bruce, and his fiancée and her family."

Millie had never spoken to me after I'd left her house, but now she had a pleased look on her face. "Did you see what it says, Beth?" she said. "I guess you know where that leaves you."

# THE THINGS I HAD TO DO FOR LOVE

When I returned home that night, Mother was very sick. I called the doctor and he said that she would have to go to the nursing home—there was a vacancy now—where they could give her shots on a regular basis. He would have an ambulance come for her on Monday.

Mother was writhing in pain. I felt scared. "Can't you come now and give her a shot?" I asked the doctor.

He sighed impatiently. "Just double her pills," he told me.

I filled a glass of water and took the pill bottle in to Mother. She could barely sit up in bed. Her eyes had that faraway look, but she took the pills. I wiped her face with a warm cloth and patted her thin arm.

Someone had looked at the house that week, two different times. Mother thought it might be sold. She wanted to know what I would do then. I tried to be casual, saying there'd be plenty of places I could get a room. Everything would work out fine, I assured her. But my mind was whirling and inside I felt as though I was carrying a heavy rock.

I didn't go to work the next day, and for some reason Mother was a little better. I walked to town for a few groceries and some magazines for my mother. On Saturday morning, the realtor called and said that the house was sold. I thanked him and hung up.

Mr. Speers picked me up for work that night, and I closed my eyes around the hot, burning tears that wanted to keep coming. I just answered him briefly when he spoke to me. Inside, I was wishing I could die.

I was on a break when Jeffrey came over and sat down. "What's with you?" he asked.

## THE THINGS I HAD TO DO FOR LOVE

I just blurted it all out—about my mother, the house. "Well, you can move in with me, and after the baby—well, after it's all settled, I'll marry you."

I stared at him. "What do you mean?"

His eyes held mine. "I mean I love you and I'll marry you, but there's no way I'm going to give a name or a home to a Callier."

His words whirled around inside of me. I loved my baby, and in spite of everything I still loved Bruce—still remembered how it had been in his arms.

"Look, move in," Jeffrey said, interrupting my thoughts, "and see how it works out. I've got an extra bedroom, if that's what you want until we're married."

I said I'd think about it—I had a few weeks before I had to move.

On Monday morning, the ambulance came and took Mother to the home. I had packed up her little trinkets and sent them along in a box. I promised her I'd be up to see her later.

It wasn't so cold that day. I took the newspaper and walked to three of the places that had rooms for rent. One was really nice, but I couldn't afford it. The other two places had just been rented.

I walked over to the nursing home. Mother was lying in her bed with her eyes closed. I touched her hand and she smiled. "I knew you'd come. I'm so tired now. You don't have to stay," she whispered.

I left after a few minutes.

After another week of unsuccessfully looking for a place to live, I told Jeffrey I'd live with him. He came over and put my chest and dresser and bed in his pickup. He moved it all up the stairs to his apartment. The rooms were small, but clean and freshly

120

papered—and they were warm—and I wasn't alone.

It wasn't bad living with Jeffrey, but it was hard to let him put his arms around me and kiss me and hold me. It was hard to pretend to care when being with him brought thoughts of Bruce back to my mind more than ever.

It wasn't long before Main Street was all decorated for Christmas. The green pine boughs extended across the shopping district and the bright lights twinkled on and off as the sound of Christmas carols filled the air. One night, Jeffrey came home with a tree and all the trimmings and said that next year we'd be married, maybe even expecting our first child. The words sent a stabbing pain through me because this was my first child—the one under my heart, the one I loved.

It was the week before Christmas and I was working in the kitchen at the inn when I heard Bruce's voice. I turned around quickly, and tears burned my eyes. Bruce! He was looking at me, a stunned question in his eyes. "Beth, how are you?" he asked.

I just kept looking at him. My voice was stuck in my throat. Jeffrey came from behind me then, putting his hands on my arms. "We're getting married, Beth and I," he said. "Just like you are, right?"

Bruce paled. "I guess time changes things," he said.

"She's living with me now, at my place," Jeffrey said.

Bruce's eyes stared into mine. "Is that right, Beth?" he asked.

Jeffrey's arm went around me. "Do you really think you can pick up where you left off?" he asked Bruce. "And what about all the times you tried to call Beth? I suppose the line was busy."

Jeffrey was saying what I'd been feeling, putting it all into words. There was a brief silence that ended with Jeffrey adding, "I'm going to marry Beth. I love her and I'm going to be proud to be her husband. So buzz off, Mr. Callier. Get lost."

Bruce looked at me again, and then walked away. My eyes followed him until he opened the door and walked out, not looking back.

Jeffrey asked, "Are you mad at me?"

"No, I'm not mad," I whispered.

For Christmas, I bought a small artificial tree for my mother's room, and a rattle and a little sleeper for my baby. I hid the baby's presents in the bottom drawer of my chest along with the other baby things I'd bought. I bought Jeffrey a shirt and a necktie, and he gave me a pretty silver bracelet. I knew he wanted to make it a special Christmas for us, but all it was was a time of sorrow for me.

My mother died in February. I called Dad and he came out to help make funeral arrangements. Gladys couldn't come, he said, because of her job. It was just as well.

After the funeral, Dad asked if I knew who the father of my baby was. I just looked away.

"Of course," he said, "you won't keep the child. It wouldn't be fair. Not to the child or to you. If Jeffrey is willing to marry you, you'd better take him up on the offer. Good men don't come around every day."

Jeffrey came over to us then. I got up, walked to meet him, and said good-bye to my father.

Two weeks later I went into labor. I woke Jeffrey about three in the morning. He called a doctor and drove me to the hospital. I said he didn't have to wait, but he said he wouldn't leave me. All through my labor I prayed that the baby would be all right and that Jeffrey would look at it and tell me I could bring it home. *Please, God,* I thought, *if you never answer another prayer for me, answer this one.*

My baby was born at eleven-thirty. I heard him cry, heard the doctor say it was a perfect little boy. I looked at him, arms waving aimlessly, legs kicking. He was alive and well. *Thank you, God,* I thought.

Jeffrey came to my room later. "How are you feeling?" he asked.

"Did you see him?" I asked. "He's so perfect. I can't wait to hold him. Jeffrey, isn't he a beautiful little boy?"

Jeffrey walked over to the window. "I saw him," he said. He turned suddenly. "But when you come home with me, it's going to be alone. I told you before, no way would I raise a Callier kid."

"Not even for me? If you love me so much—"

"I hate him more than I love you," he cut in. "That was the deal, Beth."

I looked away. The tears came again. I was always crying, always reaching out and coming up empty, always losing. But not my baby! I wouldn't lose him!

A nurse came in to take my blood pressure.

"When can I hold my baby?" I asked.

She looked at me strangely. "Under the circumstances, it would be better if you didn't hold him at all. That's why you aren't in the maternity wing—so you won't hear the babies or see them." She turned on the television set. "Watch some television, and think about starting all over."

I stared at her. "I'm not starting over, and I'm not

giving him up! I want to hold him just like the other mothers."

Her eyes met mine; they were cold and disapproving. "I'll leave a note at the desk," she said.

Jeffrey didn't come around the rest of that day or that night. My doctor came in, checked me briefly, and said, "I see you want to hold the baby." He glanced at his watch and sighed. "Do you have hospitalization?"

"No, but I have some money saved—" I began.

"It's more than five hundred dollars a day to stay here, you know, and there's the delivery fee."

I closed my eyes. "I'll take care of it," I said.

"When you leave here, where are you going?" he asked.

"I'm sure that Jeffrey will let us come home with him—at least until I can make some other arrangements."

The doctor shook his head. "Jeffrey talked to me," he said. "He isn't going to let that child come into his home. You'd better give it all some serious consideration. If you leave here with that baby and have nowhere to go, the county will step in."

He closed the door when he left. I got out of bed, put on the hospital robe, and walked down the hall to the nursery. There he was against the wall—my baby—away from the other babies who had mothers and fathers smiling down at them. The poor little guy was all wrapped up in a soft blue blanket. My arms ached to hold him. I knocked on the window and pointed at him. The attendant nodded, smiled, and went to get him. She followed me to my room and handed him to me.

I sat in the rocker with him and kissed his head

lightly. I put a finger in his palm and his hand closed around it. I put my face next to his. "I love you, baby," I whispered. We knew each other already.

The next morning, I got to hold my son again. I kissed him and hugged him and took all the blankets off and looked at his perfect little body. Again, I thanked God for him.

Right after dinner the pastor came—the same man who officiated at Mother's funeral. He was direct and to the point. There was no talk about God or love, just talk about what I had to do for the baby.

I had to give him up. After all, he told me, I'd sinned, and there were a lot of good people who would bring him up properly.

I decided after that that I had to call Mrs. Callier. She answered on the second ring. "This is Beth," I said abruptly. "I had Bruce's baby—a little boy. I wish you'd call Bruce and tell him—and tell him I love him and I need him so much. If he doesn't come, they'll take our baby away—" My voice broke. There was silence, then a click. Mrs. Callier had hung up.

Finally, I had to leave the hospital. I called Jeffrey. "Can we come home with you for a couple of weeks?" I begged.

"You can come anytime—but not him."

"Please!" I cried.

He hung up, too.

The charge nurse came down to my room that night. She sat in the chair by the window. "Beth, I wish I could help you," she said, "but you can't go out on the street—not with a baby. I know that the doctor and the pastor have been abrupt with you and I'm sorry for that, but really, honey, they're right. Sometimes when we really love someone we have to give them up—we have to do what is best for them."

The room whirled around and around. I was trapped and I knew it. Like everything else in my life, this was going wrong, too. My heart breaking, I finally said I'd sign the papers.

The next thing I knew, Jeffrey was there. He told me he had come to take me home, and that there were some nice surprises at the apartment: a new television set, a new rug in the bedroom, a new set of china . . . I just listened to him, numb, exhausted, and filled with bitter resentment. Everyone moved around like nothing had happened—like my son and I didn't count at all. Jeffrey got all my things together and started to look a little impatient. "Come on, Beth, I've got the car in the emergency entrance. If an ambulance comes, I'll be in the way."

We got to the nurses' station and I stopped. I half turned to go down to the nursery. The charge nurse came over to me right away. "He isn't there now," she said softly.

Jeffrey kept nudging me on and I followed because I had nowhere else to go. But where was my baby?

The apartment was warm and spotless, but I was empty and hurting. Jeffrey put his arms around me and held me close. "I love you so much," he said. "I'll make you happy."

I shoved him away roughly. "Leave me alone!" I cried. "Just leave me alone!"

His face was angry. "I thought everything was settled," he said. He paced around the room, but I just sat and cried.

# THE THINGS I HAD TO DO FOR LOVE

Finally, he said I'd been through a lot and he would be patient because he loved me. I lay on the couch and when he thought I was sleeping, he brought in a quilt and covered me.

Life went on. I went back to work and Jeffrey kept trying to get me to set a wedding date. All the time, though, I carried the memory of my baby in my mind. Every time I saw a little one in a store, that awful hunger and lonesomeness went through me—that yearning that I feared would never leave me.

It was the last week in April when Jeffrey came home and tossed an application for a marriage license on the table. "We're getting married Saturday," he announced. "I've had enough of this." Then he left.

I sat with the paper in my hand, sobbing. Someone knocked on the door and at first I wasn't going to answer it, but then I just said, "Come in." It was Ella, the wife of the bar owner my mother used to work for.

She sat down at the kitchen table. "Jeff's been down at the bar," she said. "The way he tells it is you're getting married. Is that what you want, Beth?"

I said, "Does it matter what I want?"

She put her arms around me and held me to her. "It matters," she said. Then she suggested that I take the room above the bar and go to technical school, then move to the city and make a new life for myself. She said she was tired of seeing my life go down the drain.

Ella didn't realize it, but she was the first real hope I'd ever had. I told her I'd do it, and she helped me pack up my things. We carried them down to her car so all that was left when Jeffrey came home was me, dressed in my coat. Ella waited in the car.

He came in, put some coffee on, and said he'd gotten some rolls at the bakery. Then he asked if I wanted to order some kind of flowers for the wedding ceremony, and should we ask a couple from the inn to stand up for us.

I just stared at him. "I'm leaving, Jeffrey. There won't be a wedding," I said.

He set down the plate of rolls. "Just like that, you're leaving? Who are you going to shack up with now?" he asked angrily.

A thread of pain went through me as I walked toward the door. "No one. I'm going out on my own," I said.

"Well, you can start by paying your own hospital bill," Jeffrey snarled. "I paid it when we left the hospital, but now—"

"I'll pay you back," I said. "I'll get the money somehow."

The room at Ella's was smaller than any other I'd had, but it was clean and warm and safe. I paid Ella and Lou ten dollars a week for rent—they wouldn't take more—and I enrolled in a secretarial class at the technical school. I kept working at the inn, of course.

Jeffrey had quit work right after I left him. I heard he left town, too. Then I got a letter from him with his new address. He reminded me about the money I owed him and he told me where to send it.

After awhile, I thought I'd have to give up and quit school. I had so many things on my mind—so many unresolved hurts and disappointments and even guilt feelings. But Ella kept telling me not to give up, but to hang in there and work my way to a better life. Still, I couldn't forget Bruce or our baby, and there were many nights when I'd wake up crying.

One day I was coming down the steps of the school when I saw Bruce. I went warm, then cold with fear. He came running to meet me, and there was a hesitant smile on his face as he said, "Beth?"

All the pain surfaced. I looked away.

"I want to talk to you," he said.

Now I looked at him. "Bruce, there's nothing to talk about. I'm not interested in any more summer relationships."

He grabbed my arm and stepped in front of me. "Listen, do we have to talk out here with people going by, listening?"

I followed him to his car. "I don't have much time. I have to be at work at seven this evening," I said.

"You've got almost four hours," he said, starting the car.

We drove for a while, and as we passed the town park, I noticed a little boy romping in the grass with his father. Bruce glanced at me. "I hear we had a son," he said quietly. He pulled the car over and parked.

I stared at him. "I told your mother. She wasn't interested. And she said you were getting married."

"Listen, Beth," Bruce said, "she just told me about the baby. You could have called me yourself."

Then Bruce went on to explain that he had never been engaged to the girl in the picture—in fact, she was marrying someone else in October. His mother had made that all up to hurt me. Now she was close to having a nervous breakdown and had confessed everything to him because her psychiatrist said that if she wanted to get well she had to face the facts and deal with them. One of those facts was the baby, and the other was that she and her husband had had an unhappy marriage; Mr. Callier had always had other women and my mother hadn't been the first.

Then Bruce moved toward me and pulled me into his arms. "Another thing she has to accept is my loving you," he said. "I want to marry you, Beth. I want to find our baby and be a family—if you'll have me."

I could hardly take in all that Bruce said that afternoon. It was too unreal to be happening to me!

But the next morning Bruce called me, and I believed it was real. I cut classes and we went to Williston. We were going to get our baby! We went to the Department of Social Services and asked to see someone in charge. After awhile, a woman invited us into her office.

My heart pounded with anticipation as Bruce told her all the facts. He said he hadn't known about the baby, and that he realized that as the father he had rights and that we were going to provide a home for our son now.

The woman got up, went to the file cabinet, and pulled out a folder. She opened it, read something, and a strange look crossed her face. Finally, she said, "I don't know how to tell you this, but there was an illness. Your son is dead. Two weeks after he was placed in a foster home, he contracted pneumonia. He was taken to Webster Community Hospital, where he died a few days later. I'm so sorry."

# THE THINGS I HAD TO DO FOR LOVE

My dreams were shattered again—hope erased. I'd never see my baby again, never hold him and watch him grow—nothing.

I wanted to go home, and Bruce drove me. He wanted to come upstairs, but I didn't want him to. I needed to be alone. Whenever anything had gone wrong in my life I'd been alone, so why not now?

I was just sitting in the rocker hours later when someone came up the stairs and knocked on the door. I answered it. It was Bruce and his mother. She was crying, and her arms were outstretched to me. I stood, not moving.

"I'm so sorry, Beth, about everything," she sobbed. "I want a chance to make it all up to you—please!"

I just shrugged. "There's nothing to make up. You can't bring my baby back."

Mrs. Callier wanted Bruce and me to get married right away, but at that time, I was so full of grief and mixed-up I couldn't think about a wedding. All the bitterness from the past mingled with my sorrow, and I started crying.

Mrs. Callier came to me and held out her arms again. I went into them and she held me, smoothing my hair and comforting me. When I calmed down, the three of us talked and emptied ourselves of all our old bitter feelings. When we finished, I thought that maybe I did have a chance for some happiness at last.

The next day I told Bruce that I needed time before I could marry him. I finished my secretarial course several weeks later and got a job working in the newest office building in Webster. I saved as much money as I could, and after I paid my debt to

# THE THINGS I HAD TO DO FOR LOVE

Jeffrey, I moved out of Ella and Lou's into a nice apartment of my own. Bruce and I saw each other often,

I'd been living on my own for almost a year when Bruce and I went back to my apartment after a date. I made coffee and put out some cookies I'd picked up at the bakery.

As I poured Bruce some coffee, he looked at me and asked, "Now will you marry me?"

I looked into his eyes and saw the love in them. With a willing heart, now that I had something to offer him, now that I knew I was a person worthy of love, I replied, "Yes, Bruce. I'll marry you."

Five years have passed since our wedding. We moved out of Webster to be closer to Bruce's job. He sold his father's lumber business—and I can honestly say we've never had a bad day in our marriage. I guess because there was so much unhappiness before, I've used up my share of it.

I'm the mother of two children now—Tommy, four, and Marie, who will soon be two. I love them and Bruce in a way I never dreamed possible. But I'll never forget my first child—my firstborn son.

Mom Callier lives close by, too. She sold her house in Webster and lives just a few blocks away from us. She's a different woman from the one I knew back then—she's a woman I'm proud to call my mother-in-law.

And Bruce says I'm a woman he's proud to call his wife. I believe him, because I know it's true. Beth McCall Callier is a good and special person. THE END

# HE MADE ME A PRISONER IN MY OWN HOME!

Armed with a new library book, I climbed into my favorite "reading" tree by the creek in the park. I made myself comfortable on a branch that spread out like an easy chair, and closed my eyes to embrace the tranquility in my hideaway.

It was so wonderfully peaceful compared to the pandemonium in the rest of my life. Mom had died the year before, and Dad—in his anger and blind depression—had all but forgotten about his five kids. Our home was nothing more than an unsupervised dormitory. To save my sanity, I stayed away as much as I could.

"Aren't you afraid of falling on your nose?"

A male voice rudely awakened me from my reverie. Looking down, I spotted a young man at the base of my tree.

"I wasn't afraid until you scared the wits out of me!" I yelled down, my face flushing.

Without waiting for an invitation, he came up beside me. "I'm sorry I scared you," he said. "I was

133

so startled to see you up here—like a wood nymph or something."

"Well, I'm not a wood nymph—or a divine spirit." I giggled, eyeing my new companion. He was really cute and seemed vaguely familiar. "Do you go to Adams High School?" I asked.

"Sure do. I'm a senior." He broke off a twig. "My name is Gary Butler. How about you? Do you go to Adams?"

I told him I was a junior and that my name was Christie Muldoon. "I've seen you around," I added.

"Probably at the pep rallies," he explained. "I'm on the wrestling team. I don't remember you, though."

A new flush flooded my cheeks. "I don't do much more at school than attend classes, but I have watched the wrestling matches. I remember you now. You're a real killer on the mat."

The breeze swelled, rustling the leaves and catching Gary's hair. I closed my eyes and let the breeze soothe my face. For a moment, neither of us spoke.

"I love the creek," he said finally. "I come down here every chance I can."

I opened my eyes enough to peek at him. "I do, too. I love to hide in this tree and read. It takes me away from all my problems."

He cocked his head. "You? What problems could a sweet girl like you have?"

He was a stranger, and the question was only idle chatter, yet I felt I could trust him. "My mom died last year—"

"Hey, I'm sorry," he interrupted.

"Thanks. She had cancer—I really miss her. She
134

was sick for a long time, and our family fell apart after she died. There were so many bills, too. We had to sell our house and rent a tiny one on Putnam Street."

His eyebrows furrowed. "I know that street; those are cracker-box houses."

I laughed. "You've got that right. My sister and I share one room, two of my brothers share another, and my oldest brother sleeps on the living room couch. My dad—well, since Mom died, he's given up on life. When he's home, he just watches TV. Everyone fights all the time, and he doesn't care. Sundays are the worst, for some reasons, so I get up early and come down here."

Gary traced the twig slowly down my arm. "That's sad, babe. I don't blame you for wanting to escape."

The twig's course sent shivers racing along my spine. As I looked into his eyes, seeds of love swelled within me. "How about you?" I asked. "How come you hang out here?"

He shrugged. "Same as you, I guess. To get away from the hassle. My ma's a lush who makes life miserable. Dad drives an eighteen wheeler, and he's gone a lot. When he's home, they have some real knock-down-and-drag-out fights."

We talked for hours. Before we parted, Gary put his arm around my shoulder. "There's only a half day of school tomorrow, Christie. Why don't we meet here at noon for a picnic?"

When I looked at him questioningly, he grinned. "I'll get some soda and you bring sandwiches. We can eat in our tree."

Our tree! I thought of his words all night. I had

135

been lonely so long that the sound of "our" anything seemed heavenly.

When Mom died, everyone said, "At least you're lucky to have a big family," but nothing could have been further from the truth. There may have been a lot of us, but we never pulled together. We all retreated into our own shells after Mom died. We may have lived together, but I felt as if I were growing up alone.

I felt silly carting a sack of food to the tree the next day. *Gary won't turn up,* I told myself. *Either he was teasing or he'd forget.*

But he didn't forget, and it turned out to be the best day I'd ever had. By the time dusk turned our hideaway into satin shadows, we'd talked about everything—our goals, our fears, and our dreams. Before we parted, Gary took me in his arms and kissed me. I responded eagerly, knowing I was in love.

Gary and I were inseparable from then on. We'd both been so lonely and needy, we quickly became more than friends. We became lovers and family— our only family, we often told each other.

Gary found a construction job after he graduated. He worked the early shift, so he could meet me after school every day. We spent much of our time together, planning our future.

We eloped the night I graduated from high school—which came as a surprise to no one. Gary already had saved enough money to rent an efficiency apartment. It was small, but it seemed like a castle to us.

I found a job on the assembly line at a factory in town, and our life settled into a romantic bliss. We were so happy—we seldom went out and we ignored our family and friends.

We'd been married about two years when Gary's dad died. He left enough money for Gary's mother to retire to Georgia and for us to put down money on a house. The place we chose was in need of repairs, but it was big and was located on a large lot outside of town. There were no neighbors for blocks.

"I love it!" I shouted, rushing from room to room. "We can fix it up just the way we want, and we'll have all the privacy we need."

The house became a part of our family as we poured our energy and money into repairing and decorating it. After five years of work, it looked like a showcase. Though Gary seemed happy to keep puttering around, I grew restless. I told him it was time for us to have a child.

"Not yet, babe," he chided. "Now that the house is done, we have to start saving our money. Children are expensive to raise, you know, and we want to do it right. We don't want to end up with a family as unhappy as mine was—or yours."

I couldn't argue with him. By that time my brothers and sisters had moved away. My father had taken a job in another state, so he'd moved, too. My memories were so bad, I didn't even miss them, and I didn't want my own children to end up feeling the way I did.

Still, as another fall and winter passed, I grew more restless. When the weather warmed and the fragrance of blossoms filled the air, I tried to talk to Gary again about starting a family.

"No children yet," he told me emphatically.

"All right"—I sighed—"no kids—but we still need something more in our lives. If it's not kids, then why don't we make some friends, or join some clubs. We need to broaden our lives a little."

"Why? Don't you like my company anymore?" he snapped angrily. "Have I failed you in some way?"

"No, you haven't failed me," I responded in surprise, startled by his anger. "It's just that we're together all the time! I think it would be good for us to expand our lives to include other people, that's all."

He grabbed my arm and twisted it behind my back. "Other people?" he sneered. "Don't you mean other men? Isn't that what you want?"

"I've never been interested in other men!" I sputtered. "What on earth are you talking about? That's not what I meant at all. Gary, for—"

He stomped from the room. I didn't understand why he'd flared up the way he did, but it was clear I'd better not say anything again to upset him. I vowed to shelve any talk of making new friends, at least for the time being.

That fall, I was promoted. Joe Coleman, my manager, had the patience of Job as he taught me my new duties. When I tried to thank him for his help, he only chuckled and invited me to have coffee with him.

As we sat in the factory cafeteria, Joe studied my face. I lowered my eyes. "What's wrong?" I asked, embarrassed.

"Not a thing," he said. "I was just wondering how a woman so young and so nice could be so serious all the time. You should relax and have some fun."

I blushed, but before I could think of anything to

say, he continued. "Christie, I have an idea. The factory bowling club meets tonight. Why don't you join us?"

"No," I responded quickly, stirring my coffee with a passion. "My husband works in construction, you know. He's too tired in the evening to participate in any sports."

Joe smiled. "You could come anyway. About half the members come alone. We only bowl for two hours, so you can still get home early."

I don't know what provoked me, but I asked, "Does your wife bowl?"

"She's dead," he said, wiping the back of his hand slowly across his face. "She died of cancer eighteen months ago."

My eyes welled with tears. "I'm sorry," I whispered. "My mom died of cancer, too."

He reached over and gathered my fingers as if they were delicate wildflowers. "It sounds like you and I have something in common."

For a moment, we were silent, each lost in private thoughts. Joe finally squeezed my hand and smiled. "Back to reality. Do you want to join the team?"

His expression was so warm, I couldn't resist the invitation. "Okay." I grinned. "I'll give it a try, but I'll need to let Gary know where I'm going. He won't need to pick me up after work."

On my next break, I called the construction site. As I gave Gary's boss my message, I realized I was relieved that Gary couldn't come to the phone. He wouldn't be too happy about my new activity—I knew that. At least by not talking to him, I didn't have to feel guilty yet.

Joe drove me to the bowling alley where I recognized many of the team members. I told them I'd watch—I was embarrassed to admit I'd never bowled—but Joe coaxed me into trying. With his expert help, I actually bowled one hundred by my third game!

On the way home, my face glowed and I didn't care. I giggled with pleasure. Joe grinned. "You look like the cat that got the cream," he noted.

"It was so much fun," I bubbled. "I've never been athletic, and I never expected to be able to bowl, but I did it! I really bowled!"

Joe laughed. "And you were good, too."

"I wasn't," I protested.

He reached over and patted my shoulder. "Stick with it, and you'll master the game in no time."

When I let myself into the house, I called out happily, "Gary! Gary! I had so much fun! Where are you—I want to tell you about it!"

As my eyes adjusted to the darkness, I saw Gary by the front window. "Hi! You startled me." I gulped in surprise. "Is something wrong?"

"I always pick you up after work. How do you think I felt when I was left in the lurch?"

A chill of warning raced down my back. "Didn't you get my message?"

"I did, but I didn't get the message until after work. By then it was too late to call and find out what was going on!"

"Nothing was going on! I joined the bowling team, that's all. Some of my friends belong and I wanted to give it a try."

Grabbing my arms, he shook me like a limp doll. "What friends?"

"Janet and Yvonne," I said, remembering two

team members who worked in my department.

He shook me again. "Are you going to tell me it's an all-woman team?"

"There are men, too." I said.

Fireworks flashed across my eyes as he slapped me. My knees felt as though they'd turned to boiled spaghetti. "Do you want to mess around with other men?" he screamed, shaking me harder. "What's the matter? Aren't I good enough for you?"

He slapped me again. This time it was hard enough to knock me to the floor. He fell to his knees and thrashed my head against the carpet.

"Tell me the truth!" he shrieked. "You were there to see a man! Tell me!"

"No!" Tears streamed down my face. "No, I only wanted to try something new. I'm sorry! I didn't mean anything, I swear!"

Suddenly, he gasped and started to cry. Gathering me up in his arms, he held me tightly. "Honey, I'm sorry! I'm so sorry. I never meant to hurt you! Forgive me, please."

He held me for a long time, his tears mingling with mine. Finally, he picked me up and carried me to the bedroom. As he lowered me onto our bed, I looked into his eyes. His anguish was so obvious, my heart went out to him.

"Gary," I whispered. "I'm sorry. I was being selfish. I'm sorry."

"I never meant to hurt you." He moaned. "My dad used to smack Ma around, and I always swore I'd never be like him."

Sinking down beside me, he began trailing kisses across my face and neck. "I'm so sorry. When I thought about you out there without me, I went crazy with jealousy. It won't happen again, I promise."

I let him undress me, and I lay quietly as he made love to me. Even as his knowing caresses caused my body to respond, my tears slid silently to my pillow.

My cheek was bruised the next morning, but if anyone noticed it through the makeup I'd applied, no one said anything. I didn't say anything, either. I was so ashamed and confused, I avoided my fellow workers like the plague.

That night Gary brought home a darling calico kitten. "Another reason for you to come home nights."

When Joe asked if I was going to bowl again, I told him no.

"Why not?" His eyes were questioning. "I thought you had a good time last week."

"I did," I said, turning away and busying myself with a work order, "but I realized later I'd rather be home with my family."

"Ah, I suppose you have small children."

"No, we don't have any children, but we do have a house and a big yard and garden. There's always plenty to do. We're always busy."

Joe said nothing, but his look was one of confusion. In an attempt to change the subject, I asked, "Do you have any kids?"

His face crinkled into a smile. "I sure do. My daughter is thirteen and my son is nine and a half."

I suddenly felt foolish. I stammered, "They . . . they must keep you busy."

He nodded. "They do. Luckily, my mother lives nearby and she helps me a lot."

"I'm embarrassed. You have a heck of a lot more

responsibilities than I do."

"Don't be embarrassed," Joe admonished gently. "When my wife was alive, I rushed home every night, too."

Another employee halted our conversation, but not my thoughts about it. Joe imagined me rushing home to Gary, but—I realized with a start—that was no longer the truth. Gary's anger was taking its toll on my feelings toward him.

That night he brought me a dozen red roses, as well as a sack of toys for the kitten. After dinner, he turned the television off early and led me to our bedroom. His lovemaking was more sensitive and unselfish than I could remember.

The next day I was torn with guilt. How could I have questioned my marriage? No one else had a husband as loving and attentive as I did!

Gary went to a union meeting that Saturday. I usually stayed home while he was gone, but on this day I had a plan. I took the bus to town and had my hair fixed in a sexy chignon, with lazy wisps curling down my neck. I bought a black silk dress next—the first dress I'd bought on my own since I'd been married! Finally, I picked up a bottle of wine and two steaks and caught the next bus home. I was determined to show Gary we only needed each other to have a good time.

By the time I heard his car in the driveway, I had the dining table set and the candles lit. A salad was waiting on the counter, and the steaks were ready to be broiled. I had on my new dress and, for good measure, I'd put on my makeup with a dramatic flair.

When Gary let himself in, I made a flamboyant

entrance from the kitchen, carrying two glasses of wine.

"Welcome home, darling," I whispered. "Surprise!"

His face wore a look of total bewilderment as he stared at me. "What's going on?" he blurted.

Setting down the glasses, I reached up and clasped my hands behind his head. "I wanted to do something special for you tonight."

As I sought his lips, he slung out his arm, flinging me against the couch.

"What are you feeling guilty about?" His voice rose to the crescendo of anger I'd learned to fear.

"Nothing!" I exclaimed, struggling to my feet. "I wanted to surprise you!"

Gary roughly scraped his hand across my lips. "You look like a whore!" he bellowed. "You're all painted up—and look at your hair!"

Before I could react, he grabbed my head and tore the pins from my lovely chignon.

"Stop it!" I cried. "You're hurting me."

By now, Gary's eyes were glazed. "Where did you get the dress—from one of your hooker friends at work?"

The sound of material ripping pierced the air as he pulled the dress from my body. I stood there, hair hanging in tangles, lips bloodied and swollen. But Gary wasn't done. He dragged me to the bathroom and shoved my face into the sink.

"Wash off that paint!" he screamed.

After I obeyed, he stomped from the room. I held my face under the cool water for a long time, letting its sound muffle my sobs. With a shudder, I finally put on my robe and forced myself to walk into the kitchen.

"You look better now," Gary commented flatly as he flipped over the steaks on the grill. "Toss the salad, will you?"

Numbly, I obeyed.

As he slapped the steaks on a serving plate, Gary glanced at me. "Are you ready to tell me what you were trying to pull tonight?"

"I wasn't trying to pull anything." I groaned. "I wanted to do something different, that's all."

"Are you saying you're not happy here?"

"That's not what I meant!" I wrapped my arms around him. "Why can't you believe me?"

With a sigh, he returned my embrace. "God, Christie, when I came home and saw you all gussied up like my mom used to get when she was getting ready to go out and cheat on Dad, well, I thought the worst." I felt his tears on my neck. "I'm sorry," he mumbled. "I really goofed. I'm sorry."

The next night Gary brought home a DVD player. When I questioned whether we could afford it, he looked at me sharply. "You say we never have any fun," he snapped. "Now we can see any movie we want, and we won't have to fight the crowds at the movie theater."

We'd never gone out much before, but after that, we didn't go out at all. Our new diet of movies may have kept Gary entertained, but it drove me crazy. Our increased togetherness was getting on my nerves, too. Yet, I knew better than to complain.

A few weeks later, Joe rushed into the supply room where I was taking inventory.

"Christie, I just received a phone call from Gary's boss," he said softly. "There's been an accident. The scaffolding Gary was on collapsed and he fell.

They've taken him to the hospital."

Joe drove me to the hospital and waited with me until the surgeon came into the waiting room. Gary's leg had been badly shattered in the fall, we learned, but he'd come out of the surgery in good condition. In a matter of time, the doctor said, he'd be back on his feet again.

When I finally was led into Gary's room, I burst into tears at the sight of his battered and bandaged body. Pressing his hand to my lips, I told him I loved him. He groaned, but couldn't talk. Soon he fell into a restless sleep.

It was late in the evening when Joe drove me to the construction site to pick up Gary's car. In spite of my anguish, or maybe because of it, I laughed as I futilely tried to start the engine.

"What's so funny?" Joe asked, leaning in the car window.

"Me." I gulped, wiping my eyes. "I've never driven this car before. Matter of fact—when I think about it—I haven't driven any car since I've been married."

Joe stared at me as if I'd dropped down from outer space. With a shake of his head, he finally opened the door and motioned for me to move over. Patiently, he explained everything I needed to know.

"Tell you what," he said as he climbed out, "I'm going to follow you home."

"You don't need to do that."

"Listen to me," he chided. "You've gone through a terrible shock, and you're not used to driving. I'm going to follow to make sure you don't drive off the road and hurt yourself."

When we finally reached my house, Joe walked

me to the front door. "Are you going to be all right?" he asked.

"I am. Thanks for escorting me home. I'll have to admit, I was pretty shaky."

"Well, at least you couldn't do much damage going ten miles an hour," he teased.

"That slow, huh?" I had to smile.

"That slow." He grinned, too. "But now that you're home, why don't you go in and take a hot bath and try to get some sleep? You're going to need all your strength to help Gary recover."

As it turned out, there wasn't much I could do for Gary during the next three months—other than offer moral support. He needed a second operation, then a third, and extensive therapy after that.

For the first time in my life, I was responsible for taking care of myself and the house. After my initial shock and fear wore off, I discovered I loved it! My days seemed lighter and freer than before. I could do as I pleased.

Still, I grew lonely. Gary's therapy took all his energy, and he talked about nothing else during our daily visits. At home I had the DVD player and our cat, but they weren't enough. My family had moved away long ago, so I had no one to talk to. As my days alone turned to months, I yearned for company.

One day during lunch, I asked Joe how the bowling team was doing.

"Not bad," he said, sipping his coffee. "Janet had to quit, though."

I nodded. "She told me her arthritis was acting up."

"It leaves us one person short," he said, cocking

147

his head. "You know, Christie, we could use your help."

As I looked at him, I knew I'd been hoping he'd ask me. I told him I'd be happy to complete the team.

It may have been just another game for the others that night, but I couldn't remember when I'd had so much fun. As we walked to the parking lot afterward, Joe commented, "Christie, you're glowing. I've never seen you look so happy."

I shook my head. "I am happy!"

Joe looked at me curiously. "Did you tell Gary what you were going to do tonight?"

A ball of fear knotted in my stomach. "No, but, you see, Gary . . . Well, he has very old-fashioned ideas about what wives should do."

"He's welcome to join us when he's feeling better."

I looked away. "I don't think he'll want to. Gary doesn't enjoy doing things with other people. He feels we should be able to entertain ourselves."

Joe said nothing, but I could imagine how strange my statement must have sounded to him. My recent freedom had made me very aware of the problems within my marriage.

Gary wasn't ambulatory when he finally came home. He had to stay in a special hospital bed, which was installed in our living room. A visiting nurse stayed with him during the day, and a therapist worked with him every afternoon.

When I was home, Gary demanded all my attention. He wanted water or something to eat, or he needed his pillow fluffed, or his covers smoothed. I had to pull a chair next to his bed, so we could hold hands while we watched television. The doctor had warned me that there was going to be a period of adjustment, but I wasn't prepared for the extent of his cantankerousness. I skipped bowling for two weeks. By the third week, I was climbing the walls.

"You're going to leave me alone?" Gary shouted when I told him I was going to bowl after work that evening.

"I've arranged for the nurse to stay with you," I said, diverting my eyes from his gaze. "When you're better, you can go bowling with me. Then you'll see how innocent and fun it is."

"I bet," he said, turning away.

I really enjoyed my night out, but Gary made my life so miserable afterward I decided it wasn't worth it. The next Monday I went to Joe's office to tell him I was quitting the team. Before I could open my mouth, however, Joe burst into a big smile and announced I'd been promoted again. Now I was going to be a supervisor. Any thoughts of the team flew from my mind as I gasped in surprise.

After Joe congratulated me, he commented, "Gary's accident has had one positive effect, at least."

"What do you mean?" I asked, still grinning from ear to ear.

"You're more outgoing now. More confident."

"I'm glad. Now, if only—"

"If only what?"

In the last few months, Joe and I had become friends. I knew I could be honest with him. "If only Gary could enjoy it, too. I don't think he appreciates my new independence."

Joe took my hand. "Christie, I'm going to say

something, and I hope you won't be offended. I think you and Gary could benefit from some family counseling."

I stared at him, speechless.

"Look, Christie," he continued, rubbing my hand thoughtfully. "You've been growing while you've been on your own, and Gary might need some help understanding that."

"We don't need counseling," I blurted, too loud, envisioning Gary's temper if I ever dared mention such a thing.

"Okay!" Joe held up a hand. "But now that you're feeling more secure, you may not be as accepting of Gary's bossiness as you used to be."

"That's none of your business." Pushing past him, I stomped out the door.

Joe's words clung to me like flypaper for the rest of the day. He was right, I knew. Gary was too bossy, but I couldn't imagine him changing—not ever.

I was in for a big surprise when I got home that evening. Gary was standing at the front door.

"Look, babe! I can walk!"

"I see that." I gasped.

"I've got a walking cast!" He elevated his leg to show me. "No more attendants or therapy, and— the best news—I can move back into our bed!"

I nodded, noticing the empty spot in the living room where the hospital bed had been for so long.

He pulled me toward him so tightly it hurt my ribs. "Christie, I mean I can really sleep with you—as ~~ur~~ husband—at long last."

As I ~~sli~~pped into bed that night, I felt as nervous ~~a~~ Gary was nervous, too, and anxious. The lovemaking was forced and unsatisfactory. In the end, he pushed away from me in disgust.

"Honey, don't worry," I consoled, gently massaging his back. "You're not completely well yet, that's all." He pushed my hand away and said nothing.

In the morning, I told Gary about my promotion. He reacted with little interest. His disposition didn't improve either, and, as days went by, he still couldn't make love. After a few more attempts, he gave up trying. He even stopped making a scene about my bowling on Tuesdays.

It was well into the winter before the doctor removed the final cast. Gary had to use a crutch and was told it would be several more months before he could return to his job. Still, he was ecstatic.

"I'm going to start exercising the way I did when I wrestled," he told me the next morning. "I'll be a hundred percent again in no time!"

"I'm glad," I said, fumbling through my purse for the car keys.

"Got a problem?" he asked, watching my futile search.

"I can't find my keys," I said in disgust. "I know they're in here someplace."

Gary grinned. "No, they're not!" He waved the keys teasingly in my face. "I can drive you now."

"Gary, it would be more convenient for me if I drove," I pleaded with a sinking heart. "Now that I'm a supervisor, I often have to stay and work overtime."

"Well, babe, you'll have to tell them you can't stay late. Husband's orders."

I smiled, but I was dying inside. The thought of being totally dependent on Gary again made me miserable.

# HE MADE ME A PRISONER IN MY OWN HOME!

The next afternoon, Joe and I interviewed job applicants. It was a half hour past quitting time when we finished. As we walked outside, I heard a car horn and spotted Gary's car. Before I could react, Joe walked over to him with his hand outstretched.

"Hi, Gary," he exclaimed with a smile. "My name is Joe Coleman. I'm Christie's boss."

Gary kept both hands clenched on the steering wheel. "You've made my wife late," he snarled. "I'm warning you—don't let it happen again!"

As we drove away, I snapped, "You didn't have to talk to Joe that way!"

Gary turned to me, eyes glaring. "I have every right to talk to him any way I want! You're my wife. You'll do as I tell you! Do you hear me?"

Knowing it was useless to argue, I bit my lip and nodded.

The next day was bowling day. Common sense told me that this time, of all times, I should not go. However, more than anything, I longed for those carefree hours with Joe and my friends. I waited until late afternoon before I called Gary and told him my plans.

"I can't believe how you've changed," he screamed over the phone. "No matter what I tell you, all you can think of is fooling around!"

"I am not fooling around," I spat through gritted teeth. "Tonight is the last night of our tournament, and I want to be there. I'll come home as soon as it's over. We can talk then."

I was shaking when I hung up. I'd never defied Gary before, and it frightened me. Joe sensed something wrong that evening.

# HE MADE ME A PRISONER IN MY OWN HOME!

"You've been awfully quiet," he commented as he drove me home after the game.

"I am?" I asked, looking at his rugged face. "I guess you're right. I guess I am."

"How come?"

"It's Gary," I explained. "He's been unreasonable lately."

Even in the darkness, I saw his eyebrows arch. "Lately?"

Tears sprang to my eyes. "More unreasonable is what I meant, Joe. He was furious that I went out tonight."

Joe shook his head. "You don't have to take that. You need to assert yourself. Stand up for your rights. You do have rights, you know."

At the house, Joe came around and opened my car door. Before I knew what was happening, he drew my head up with his hand and kissed my forehead. "Call me, if you need some help," he whispered.

I fully expected a confrontation, but when I got into the house I found Gary was already in bed and asleep. As I slid in beside him, I let out a sigh of relief. Maybe he'd finally come to his senses.

I tried to talk about bowling in the morning, but Gary ignored me. He drove me to work without a word. That evening, I got the same silent treatment. When we went to bed, however, he threw himself at me with a passion I'd never seen before. For the first time since the accident, we were able to make love. Yet he was so rough, I was left shaken and unfulfilled.

The next morning, he wanted to make love again. "Gary," I protested, pushing him away, "you know we don't have time! I have to get ready for work."

He wouldn't let me go. "Call and tell them you're sick."

"But—"

"Come on," he pleaded, kissing me playfully. "You haven't had a day off in ages. You deserve it. And now that I'm well, we need to spend some time together."

He was right, I admitted as I went to the phone. We did need to spend time together. It would give us the chance to talk and get back on the right track.

As we made love this time, Gary was slower and more thoughtful. Afterward, we slept again and then spent the rest of the day watching movies and nibbling on popcorn. Gary fended off all my attempts at meaningful conversation, however. By evening, I was feeling edgy.

"Let's go out," I suggested impulsively.

He gave me a funny look. "What's wrong? Don't you like to be with me?"

"I do! But we've been inside all day. Going for a drive would be fun."

"So you can look at other guys, I suppose," he mumbled.

"What did you say?"

"Nothing. I don't want to go out."

I may have played hooky for only one day, but by nightfall it seemed like forever. I missed my job and associates and—the truth was—I missed Joe.

When we woke the next morning, Gary pulled me to him. "Gary," I protested, trying to break away. "I'm not taking another day off!"

"Yes, you are!" He shoved me roughly back on

the bed. As he twisted my arm around, I felt something cold on my wrist. I heard an unfamiliar click. Rolling my head back, I screamed in horror! Gary had handcuffed me to the headboard on our bed!

"Gary! Let me go!"

He was over me. His face was different from anything I'd ever known. "No," he said simply. "You're staying here from now on, so I can keep an eye on you."

"What are you talking about?" I demanded. "And where did you get the handcuffs? This isn't funny! I want you to take them off—now!"

Ignoring my orders, he proceeded to make love to me as if I were a robot designed for his satisfaction. Afterward, he calmly dressed and left the room. The rest of the morning, I heard him moving around the house, hammering and working on some mysterious project. I kept screaming for him to release me, but the louder I screamed the noisier he became.

It was afternoon before Gary returned to the bedroom and unlocked the handcuffs. "You can be free if you're good," he warned me.

"Gary, enough's enough," I said, rubbing my wrist. "You may think this was funny, but I was not amused."

"Then don't give me any more trouble," he said with a wink. "And, by the way, you can forget about work, too. I've already called and told them you're sick and are going to stay home the rest of the week."

Pushing back nausea, I tried to think rationally. I knew Gary had gone crazy. I had to get away from him!

Trying to keep my voice even, I said calmly, "A

whole week off? That sounds like fun, but now I want to clean up. Do you mind if I take a shower?"

When he nodded, I forced my wobbly legs to the closet and grabbed some clothes. "See you in a bit," I called as I headed down the hall to the bathroom.

As soon as I closed the bathroom door, I leaned against it, my head spinning. My eyes caught the billowing bathroom window curtains then and an idea came to me. I had to get away; that's all there was to it. I could turn on the shower full blast and make my escape through the window!

Cautiously, I reached down to lock the door.

"Wha—?" With a gasp, I whirled. The lock was gone! As I stared in disbelief, Gary pushed the door open.

"Hurry up now, Christie." He grinned slyly. "I'm going to lean against the sink and watch you."

Somehow, I managed to shower. After I dressed, Gary grabbed my arm and took me on a tour of the house, showing me what he'd been doing all day. The lock was gone from the bathroom door, but additional locks had been added to the front and back doors! Worse yet, he'd put bars on all the windows!

"I'm going to do our bedroom windows next, and then our whole house will be secure," he said. "Do you like it?"

"No! It's awful! Why have you done this?"

"Christie," he said seriously, "it's obvious you've lost interest in me."

"I have not," I protested.

His eyes were sparking anger. "All you talk about is going out or going bowling—anything but me!"

156

# HE MADE ME A PRISONER IN MY OWN HOME!

"Gary . . ." I paused, searching for the right words. "In a healthy relationship people aren't threatened by their spouse's outside activities or friends."

Gary turned on his heel and stomped to the wall. With a jerk, he tore the telephone from its socket. "Where did you hear that, little girl?" he screamed. "From your loverboy, Joe?"

"He's not my lover." I sobbed.

"Don't lie to me! I wasn't really asleep the other night when you came home. Actually, I was watching out the window and I saw Joe kiss you!"

"That was only a friendship kiss." I cried as his fist met my face.

When I came to, I was on the couch. Gary sat beside me and there was a plate of sandwiches on the coffee table. "It's time to eat," he said nonchalantly.

I moved my jaw slowly. It wasn't broken, but the last thing on my mind was food. "Gary, how long are you going to keep me a prisoner?"

"Forever."

"Seriously. I can go back to work next week, can't I?"

"No." He snarled. "On Monday I'm telling them you've had a nervous breakdown and that you have to quit your job."

"But—we need the income!"

He shook his head. "No, I've got it worked out. I get workman's compensation. Between that and our savings account, we'll be fine until I go back to work."

"And then what will I do?"

"By then you'll have come to your senses. You'll be happy staying at home. Besides, I've thrown

157

away your pills, so there's a good chance you'll be pregnant."

I was a prisoner in my own home, and I was going to be forced to become pregnant! I broke into hysterical sobs. Gary only grinned and turned up the television's volume.

He had just made fresh sandwiches for dinner that evening when the doorbell rang. Slapping his hand over my mouth, he whispered, "Keep quiet and they'll go away."

Suddenly Joe's voice boomed out, "Christie, are you in there? Are you all right?"

"We have to open the door," I mumbled through Gary's fingers. "Joe can see our car in the driveway. He knows we're in here!"

Silently, Gary picked me up and carried me to the bedroom. This time he handcuffed both my arms and used a towel to gag my mouth. After he left the room, I heard a muffled conversation. Minutes later, Gary returned with a big smile on his face.

"What did you say?" I asked when he removed the towel.

"I told him you were very sick, and that the doctor had given you sleeping pills and demanded you stay in bed. He didn't seem too happy, but there wasn't a thing he could do about it."

My eyes filled with tears. Gary had thought of everything. There was no hope. I'd be his captive forever.

Gary made love to me the next morning, then handcuffed and gagged me and left the house. He'd been gone for a half hour when the doorbell rang, and I heard Joe calling my name. I tried banging the bed against the wall, and I tried screaming, but it was no use. After a few minutes, there was silence. I knew Joe had given up.

Gary was all smiles when he returned home. He'd bought groceries and rented a bagful of movies. "See," he announced proudly, "there's enough here to keep us busy for a week."

He let me go to the bathroom, and I saw myself in the mirror. My eye was blackened, and my body was a myriad of bruises from his cruel lovemaking. Shoving my fist against my mouth, I stifled a cry. I had to find a way to escape Gary's madness or I was going to die!

Gary kept all the curtains drawn and the living room was dark as we settled down for another day of movies. I couldn't concentrate, but Gary was so engrossed he didn't notice the noise in our driveway. Not daring to breathe, I listened to footsteps and then a knock on our door.

A deep voice pierced the air. "This is the police. Let us in, please!"

Before Gary could do anything, I screamed, "Help! Help me! My husband is holding me prisoner!"

"Go away!" Gary shouted.

"We aren't leaving until we talk to you," the officer said. "Let us in."

Suddenly, Gary threw me to the floor and ran into the kitchen. I scrambled to my feet and lunged for the door. Before I could figure out the new locks, however, he was back and pushing me away. It was then I saw the pistol in his hand!

"I'm warning you," he screamed. "Go away! This is my property and my wife. Leave us alone."

"Christie, are you all right?" Joe's voice boomed

out. He must have brought the police.

"He's holding me prisoner!" I screamed as Gary grabbed me and pressed the gun to my temple.

"I have a gun!" he shouted. "If you don't all leave, I'm going to use it to protect my property. Now get out of here!"

We heard voices, and then receding footsteps along the gravel driveway.

"I told them!" Gary gloated, his voice high and strange. He pushed me back on the couch and stood over me.

We heard the policeman again, his voice magnified this time by a bullhorn. "The house is surrounded. Come outside with your hands in the air!"

Twirling, Gary fired a shot though the window. The sound of the splintering glass was followed by deadly silence. Drawing in my breath, I whispered, "Gary, please do as he says. We can work this out."

"It's worked out now," he said.

"You're right, darling," I cajoled, trying to pacify him. "I like your plan. I'll quit work and devote all my time to you. We'll have a baby. We'll be a perfect family."

For an instant, he looked like the old Gary I'd once loved so much. "Do you mean that?" he asked hopefully.

"Of course! Put down the gun, Gary. We can go outside and tell everyone to go away."

At that moment, there was a thud as a smoking canister was propelled through the bars on the window. As it hit the floor, Gary lunged for it. The moment his attention was diverted, I grabbed the closest thing I could reach—a brass lamp. Without hesitating, I bashed it over his head.

## HE MADE ME A PRISONER IN MY OWN HOME!

As Gary crumbled, I ran to the door and released the locks. Sobbing, I ran outside and fell into the safety of Joe's arms.

My nightmare was over, but Gary's had just begun. He was committed to the state hospital psychiatric section. It was discovered that he'd had mental problems for a long time, and that his condition had worsened significantly since his accident.

I had to talk to the police and doctors, and I had to have Gary committed. Thank heavens, Joe was always there for moral support. Gary asked me for a divorce, and I agreed. By the time I started divorce proceedings, Joe and I had begun dating. I'd been accepted by his wonderful children and mother. A year after my divorce was finalized, Joe and I were married, surrounded by family and our friends from work. We've been married for over a year now and—as if we already weren't blessed enough—we're eagerly looking forward to the birth of our first child together.

My love for Joe and my new family has helped erase most of my fear and anger. I don't hate Gary anymore. In fact, I hope the day will come when he'll regain his mental health and be able to enjoy a life as happy as mine is today. THE END

# THE PICTURE I HID IN MY DRESSER

The social worker, Miss Roudge, asked me again to please sign the papers. She asked as though it was easy to sign your baby away to a total stranger. How could she know what this was doing to me— how it was tearing me apart? She'd never carried a child under her heart for nine months. A heart that was now breaking.

"Angela, I know this isn't easy. But please, think of the child," Miss Roudge reasoned. I knew she was right, so with shaking hands, I signed the papers as tears slid down my cheeks. When I'd finished, she let out the breath she'd been holding in. I suppose my delay had her afraid for a moment. She quickly gathered up the papers.

"You can get on with your life now," she said. "You're still too young to be tied down to a baby. Maybe you can go back home to your parents."

I turned away from her, hiding my tears.

She touched my shoulder. "Look, honey, the adoptive parents are a wonderful, caring couple.

# THE PICTURE I HID IN MY DRESSER

They'll take very good care of him. They're just ecstatic finally to have a child. It's been four long years since they applied. You're making their dreams come true." She shifted uneasily where she stood. "Now get some rest. I'll come by and see you later."

Then she quietly walked out and left me to my misery. As I cried, I asked God and Zach—the name I'd given my son—to please forgive me.

Thinking back, I couldn't believe this was happening to me. Luke and I had been so happy just seven short months ago. It seemed as if this was all a terrible dream. Desperately, I wished I could go back and be the carefree girl I was a few years ago. Growing up in a house filled with two brothers and three sisters had been rough sometimes. It would be pure bliss, though, if I could go back to that time and forget what had happened.

I was the baby of the family for ten years. Then my mother had another child. It was a surprise for all of us, especially me. Suddenly, I wasn't the center of attention anymore. My baby brother, Brian, became the attraction. From then on, I was sort of on the outskirts and became a loner.

My sister, Maryanne, became my best friend. She was in high school at the time, while I was only ten years old. She took me everywhere she went, and she always put my hair in pigtails. But Maryanne got married and moved away after my twelfth birthday. I missed her guidance and friendship terribly.

By the time I turned fifteen, everyone had left home but Andrew, my older brother, and five-year-old Brian. Andrew was only eleven months older than I, but he was much more mature and level-headed. I was too trusting and very naive.

Mom and Dad both worked, so we were alone a lot. Even so, we were good kids and stayed out of trouble. I started experimenting with makeup and went on a few dates. Mom used to say I was pretty without makeup, but I still enjoyed using it. It made me feel grown up.

My fifteenth year holds my sweetest memories. It was the year I met Luke Tregar. Luke was the kind of boy who was always getting into trouble. He would skip school and go out drinking with his friends. I had seen him in school. He was always surrounded by his football buddies and never even noticed I was alive. Because of his troublemaking, he was on probation when I met him.

One afternoon I stayed after school to do some studying for a test I had to take the next morning. I was walking home, and, suddenly, with no warning, it started pouring. I was looking desperately for a place to duck under when Luke pulled up to the curb. He motioned for me to get in his car. I gladly jumped in.

"What's a pretty girl like you doing out in a storm like this?" he asked with a grin.

I blushed and couldn't say a word. I explained that I'd been studying and gave him directions to my house.

But Luke cruised the main drag first and turned up his stereo. I caught him giving me sideways glances, and I felt uneasy, wishing he would hurry and get me home. When he finally pulled into my driveway, I thanked Luke and started to get out. He grabbed my arm.

"Wait a minute. Is that all I get for rescuing you?"

he asked with a smile. "Your knight in shining armor would like to know what you're doing tonight."

I felt my cheeks getting hot. "Well, nothing really," I said. "How about I pick you up at seven?" he asked.

"I'll have to ask my mom, but I'm sure she won't mind," I said.

Luke looked me up and down once with his gorgeous eyes. "Good," he said. "See you at seven."

I went into the house as he squealed out of the driveway. I was really excited as I went to my room to change my wet clothes. Andrew stopped me.

"Who was that?" he asked.

"Luke Tregar. He saved me from the rain. He also asked me out tonight," I told him.

"I hope you said no," Andrew warned.

"I said yes. What's wrong with you?" I exclaimed.

"He isn't your type, Angela. He's always in trouble, and he only wants one thing from girls."

I walked into my room, saying, "That doesn't mean he's going to get it."

I asked Mom after supper if I could go out for a few hours with a friend. Andrew looked up. I shot him a warning glance. She said it was okay, so I ran off to my room to get ready.

I was outside on the porch swing when Luke pulled up. I got in his car, and we drove off.

"You look nice, but I can't see you very well over there," he said. "Why not sit here?" He patted the spot next to him.

I blushed with pleasure as I scooted closer. He put his arm around my shoulder.

Luke was a couple of years older than I me—seventeen and a senior at the time. And he was really good looking, the kind of guy all the girls had crushes on. He was tall, athletic, and had a great build. In fact, Luke was handsome enough to get any girl, even with his bad reputation.

We pulled up to a drive-in and I went to use the rest room. When I came out, I saw the waitress leaning over the tray, laughing and talking to Luke. *She's flirting with him,* I said to myself. When I got in the car, she winked at him and left.

Luke looked over at me, still smiling. "Why are you sitting over there?"

I didn't answer.

"Oh, I get it. You're mad because of that waitress. She's just a friend. Don't take it personally." He grinned. "You're cute when you're mad," he said and reached around my waist and pulled me close. Before I knew it, he kissed me on the cheek and handed me a soda.

I took a big sip and almost choked. "What did you do to this?" I asked.

"I just added a little zest. Don't tell me you've never had any whiskey," he said, laughing.

I didn't want to sound too straight, so I said, "Of course, but this is pretty strong. And I really shouldn't drink. My dad would ground me for a year if he found out."

"I have some gum in the glove compartment and one drink won't hurt. It'll just make you feel good. Loosen up," he urged as he gently squeezed my shoulder.

It felt so good to be close to Luke, with our legs pressed together and his arm protectively around me. I felt safe and warm. We drove to the park and got out, then sat on the ground, leaning against a big tree.

The more I drank, the more I talked. I was basically a quiet person, but the whiskey and Luke made me open up like a book. I told him about my family and my problem making friends.

"It's just because you're shy," he said. "And I like you that way. Don't change—just stay the way you are, Angela." He lifted my face and looked into my eyes. "You're easy to talk to, and I'm really beginning to like you. Will you go out with me again?" he asked suddenly.

I was startled, but I replied, "Sure, Luke. You know, I really like you, too."

Then he kissed me. It was like no other kiss I'd ever experienced. But when he opened my mouth with his own, I jerked away from him.

"I'm sorry," I said, totally embarrassed. "I–I've never been kissed like that before." Luke laughed softly, pulling me close. He kissed me again as he gently lowered me to the ground. Suddenly, I became frightened. I wasn't so dumb that I didn't know what he had in mind.

I pulled his hands away. "Please, Luke, no!" I said. He groaned and rolled away from me. Then, sighing, he helped me up and led me to the car.

"I better get you home before I do something I'll regret," he said. "I'll pick you up at eight and drive us to school, okay?" I just nodded my head.

When we pulled into my driveway, Luke gave me a peck on the cheek. "See you in the morning, Angela," he called, and I was on cloud nine as I walked into the house.

I had wonderful dreams that night. Dreams I wouldn't dare tell anyone except my best friend,

# THE PICTURE I HID IN MY DRESSER

Linda. Linda and I were as close as you can get. She was a loner like me. I called her to tell her about my dream, and that Luke was picking me up before school. She was excited for me. "He better not steal my only friend," she joked.

Luke picked me up right on time. When I started to get into his car, he patted the spot next to him. I gladly scooted up close. This time, instead of putting his arm around me, he put his hand on my knee. His hand felt warm through my jeans.

"I have a surprise for you this afternoon," he teased. "I'll give it to you after school."

"That's not very nice, making me wait and wonder all day," I said, smiling.

"I'll be here to pick you up after school," he told me as he walked me to my locker. "I'll see you later, Angela." Then he gave me a kiss on the cheek and was gone.

Linda caught up with me as I walked to my class. "I saw him give you a kiss," she said. "You weren't kidding about how much he likes you. But isn't he moving kind of fast, though?"

"Not any faster than I'd like him to. Isn't he great?"

"He's gorgeous and you know it, Angela," Linda said. Just then the first bell rang, and we rushed to get to our class.

I daydreamed about Luke all day and couldn't wait to see him after school. I really wanted to know what he had for me. He was the first boy I'd ever really liked. I caught glimpses of him all day in the halls until after lunch, so he must have skipped out that afternoon. But he was waiting in his car when school let out.

# THE PICTURE I HID IN MY DRESSER

"Will your mom be mad if you're late getting home?" he asked when I got in.

"Not if I'm there before she gets home from work," I answered.

He motioned to the spot next to him. "Come here. This is your place, and I better not have to tell you again," he joked.

"So what's the big surprise?" I asked as I scooted up next to him.

"You can wait till we get where we're going," he said, and drove out to the lake.

We got out and sat on the high rocks overlooking the water. It was beautiful there. The wind was blowing, tousling Luke's hair. It made him look like a little boy. Then he pulled a little blue box from his coat pocket and handed it to me. I opened it and couldn't believe what I saw.

"I want you to be all mine, Angela. So I'm giving you my class ring. It's too big, but I got a silver chain for it. Will you wear it?" he asked, sounding unsure of himself for the first time since we'd met.

I didn't answer because I was so surprised.

"I know it's kind of soon to ask," he went on, "but I really like you. You're the first girl I've dated that's—well, not so experienced. You don't make yourself up like a streetwalker or come on to me like one. And your blush is real, like now."

"I've never gone steady before, Luke," I admitted, "but I can't think of anyone I'd rather try it with."

He put the necklace around my neck, and we sealed it with a kiss.

After that, we drove to and from school every day together. I kept my necklace under my blouse, except when I was alone with Luke. I didn't want my parents to know yet. I was waiting for the right time.

We went out a few times a week to movies or school activities. Luke played on the football team and wrestled. It took up at least four nights a week for practice and games, so I would go to the field some nights just to watch him practice. Luke had quit skipping school because they threatened to throw him off the team. And when my parents met him, they seemed to approve.

Luke never pressured me to have sex. He would kiss and touch me, but he was usually the one who pulled away first.

"I want to save that for marriage," he said once.

We'd been dating that whole school year, and it was nearly June when suddenly everything blew up in my face. Luke had taken me to school that morning, but must have skipped out after first period. When school was over, he wasn't around. When I got home, I called his mom.

"He really did it this time, Angela," she told me. "He's been picked up again for drunk driving. Since he was on probation, I'm not sure what will happen. But you can bet it won't be good."

My parents came home shortly after that. They had already heard about it. One of the police officers who'd arrested Luke was a good friend of my dad. He must have called Dad and told him about Luke, because as soon as he walked in the house, he started yelling.

"I don't want you around that Tregar boy again! To think I let you ride in his car every day. How often was he drinking when you were together?" he demanded.

"Never, and why are you all over his case just

because of a D.W.I.?" I asked, nearly in tears.

"This isn't the first time, young lady. It's the second offense. And you will not see him again!" Dad told me.

I ran to my room, threw myself on the bed, and cried angry tears.

Mom came to my room a while later to talk. "I'm sorry your dad was so hard on you, Angela," she said. "But we both agree that it would be best for you to stop seeing Luke for a while. Maybe if he straightens out you can date again."

I didn't agree, but didn't want to argue. I cried myself to sleep that night while I held Luke's ring to me.

Luke called me the next day after school. "Angela, I need to talk to you right away," he said. "Can I come over?"

Mom was home, so I said, "I'll meet you at Mario's Pizza in five minutes." Then I hung up, grabbed my jacket, and called, "I'm going over to meet Linda at Mario's Pizza, Mom. I'll be home for supper."

I rushed out the door before she could question me. I ran to the pizza place and there was Luke, sitting in his car waiting. I got in and we hugged and kissed a long time.

"Mom and Dad won't let me see you again," I cried. "What are we going to do?"

Luke looked worried. "Listen, I'm leaving tonight. Please come with me? If I stay, they'll send me to reform school until I'm eighteen. That's nine months away. I couldn't take not seeing you for that long." He held me close. "Please, Angela. I'll take care of you. I have some money. And I promise not to drink unless we're at home and together." What could I say? I knew then that I truly loved Luke and couldn't bear to stay behind.

"Okay," I agreed. "But how? When?"

"I'll pick you up at midnight behind your house. Take just the clothes you need, and all the money you can get your hands on. We have to go tonight because they'll come for me tomorrow. Now go home, get ready, and at midnight we will unofficially be Mr. and Mrs. Tregar," Luke said.

He kissed me passionately, then he kissed my face and neck, murmuring, "I love you so much, Angela. I can't wait to have you."

We got caught up in the heat of the moment. His hands were all over me, and it felt so good and right that I didn't want him to stop. But a bunch of noisy kids walked out of the pizza place and broke the spell. So we kissed good-bye, and I walked home. I was dizzy with everything that was happening. I had no time to think things through. I was going totally by my feelings. I called Linda when I got home. Mom and Dad were out buying groceries, so I used their bedroom extension. I told her what I was about to do. She immediately tried to talk me out of it but finally gave up.

We said our teary good-byes and hung up. I quickly went to Mom's jewelry box and took some money I knew was hidden in the secret compartment. She put away money there for special occasions. I wrote a note and put it where the money had been. I told Mom I would be okay and not to blame herself or Dad. Only she and I knew about the secret place. I'd caught her slipping money in there one day, and I knew she would check to see if I took it.

I locked my bedroom door and packed some

clothes in a small suitcase. Then I opened my window and snuck the suitcase out and hid it between the garage and a thick hedge. I used my window so the boys wouldn't see me. They were watching television as usual. I came back in through the window and unlocked my door. Then I packed all my personal things from the bathroom into my purse, and I was ready for Luke to pick me up. At dinner, I pushed my food around and was deep in thought. My stomach was full of butterflies, and I was a nervous wreck. Mom noticed I wasn't eating.

"Angela, honey, try to cheer up," she said. She gave my hand a gentle squeeze. "I'm sure Luke learned his lesson. If he stays out of trouble, you can start dating again, all right?" I looked into my mother's loving eyes and almost burst into tears. We had always been close and it was hard to hurt her this way. I couldn't think about that, though, or I'd never go through with it.

The rest of the evening I stayed in my room and read until it was time to go to bed. I set my alarm for a quarter to twelve and put it under my pillow, so only I would hear it go off. I fell asleep quickly. The day's events had worn me out. When the alarm went off, I woke up immediately. I lay there quietly to see if anyone else was awake. My parents' room was on the other side of the bathroom and Andrew and Brian had rooms upstairs, so I wasn't afraid of waking anyone. I climbed out my window and went out to the hedge to pick up my suitcase.

I saw Luke's car parked beside the back gate. His car was running, but the lights were off. The car was so quiet that I didn't hear it until I got to the gate. I threw my suitcase in the back through the window.

# THE PICTURE I HID IN MY DRESSER

"Crawl in the window. My doors are too noisy," he whispered.

So I got in, and we crept down the street and took back roads through town so the police wouldn't see us.

When we were out of town, I asked, "Where are we going?"

"My parents take care of my aunt and uncle's cabin. It's about two hours from here. Mom knows I'm leaving. She gave me the key. I had to tell her and she understands, so don't worry," Luke explained. "We can only stay one day. Then we can take the back roads to Tennessee and the interstate to Delaware. The cops will be looking for my car on the highway in this state."

I kissed his cheek. "I love you," I said as I lay down on the seat with my head in Luke's lap. The day had just been too much for me.

I woke with a start as Luke grabbed me when he slammed on the brakes. I jumped up.

"What is it?" I asked.

"Just a deer. But we're almost there. Might as well stay awake."

Soon we pulled into the driveway of a well-kept log cabin and parked the car in the back where it couldn't be seen. The cabin was sheltered by tall hedges and big oak and fir trees. *It's the perfect place for a honeymoon,* I thought to myself with a shiver. This was going to be a scary and exciting night for me. I had this uncontrollable urge to jump in Luke's car and say, "Take me home. I'm not ready for this." But I didn't.

We walked to the back door. Luke put down our bags and unlocked the padlock. He put the bags inside the door, then picked me up and carried me over the threshold.

"Now we are unofficially married," he said softly as he put me down. We hugged and he gave me a long kiss.

Luke showed me around, and then I put fresh sheets and blankets on the bed while he started a fire in the fireplace. The cabin was basically one big room. There was a blanket hanging in one corner for enough privacy to change your clothes.

Luke rummaged through his duffel bag. Then he pulled out a short, white silk nightie. "I bought this especially for tonight," he said as he held it up to me. "Can't wait to see you in it."

I shivered and turned away from him. "Luke, I'm scared. You know I've never—"

"Hey, Angela," Luke interrupted, putting his arms around me, "I understand. Guess I'm coming on a little too strong. All the other girls I've dated fall into bed with anyone. But I would never hurt you. If you don't want to make love, I won't force you. When you're ready, I'll know."

He held me until I stopped trembling. Then I quickly changed behind the blanket. I put on the nightie and put my bathrobe over it.

When I came out, Luke got some whiskey out of his duffel bag. He mixed up drinks with soda he'd bought back at home. We played cards and drank. I was too tired to stay awake, but I was more afraid of going to bed with Luke.

After I won a game, he playfully tackled me and we wrestled on the floor. Then our wrestling turned into kissing and caressing. Luke picked me up and put me on the bed. He slowly untied my robe and pulled it away. He was so gentle and it felt so right that no thoughts of stopping him ever entered my mind. . . .

The next morning we washed up and ate candy bars for breakfast. That was all we had. But it didn't matter, because pretty soon we ended up back in bed.

"I never thought it would be like this. I'm glad you were my first," I whispered.

"You're like a dream come true for me, Angela," Luke said, pulling me closer. "I really love you. Let's always stay together."

Later we stopped at a little town near the cabin and bought some food and gas. I called home to let them know I was okay. My brother answered.

"Angela, are you crazy?" Andrew yelled. "What do you think you're doing? Dad swears he's disowned you, and Mom's so worried, she's sick!"

"I just wanted Mom to know I'm okay. Please don't holler," I said, feeling guilty.

"Is Luke there? Let me talk to that creep! If I ever get my hands on him, I'll kill him!" Andrew shouted.

I started to cry. "You'll never understand, will you?" I sobbed. "Just tell Mom I'm fine, and I love her."

I hung up and got in the car. Then I cried on Luke's shoulder. "It's okay, Angela," he assured me. "They're just upset. Things will cool down. It's important that you keep in touch."

We drove back to the cabin, and when we got inside Luke said, "Let's get packed and load up the car. I want to be gone early in the morning."

I looked sadly from him to the bed. "I'll miss this bed," I told him. "It's the first one we've shared."

# THE PICTURE I HID IN MY DRESSER

Luke put his arms around me. "If we stay here, they may come looking for us." He took my hands and we sat on the couch facing each other. "Look, Angela, we're going to Delaware. We can see the ocean, and I'll find a job. Please believe in me. I promise I'll take care of you."

"I do," I said. "It's just that this is all so new to me, and I feel safe here."

He held me close. "We'll visit your sister in Delaware. What was her name?"

"Maryanne," I said, smiling.

"She won't put the cops on us, will she?" Luke asked.

"I don't think so, but I'll call first to see how she's taking all this," I said.

In the morning, we left and drove most of the way there before Luke got tired. So we pulled into a rest area and slept together on the backseat. We slept until the sun came up. Then we used the rest rooms and hit the road in search of food and coffee. How I longed for a shower and clean clothes. "There's a truck stop up here shortly. We'll get breakfast," Luke said. He knew the area, since his family used to take trips to the surrounding beaches.

At the truck stop, I went to the bathroom to wash up. Luke did the same. He was in the restaurant when I came back, and he looked so handsome with his hair combed and shining. I felt a surge of love and joy and pride. I couldn't believe he really loved me.

He'd ordered me a big breakfast and coffee. I liked the taste of coffee, but only with lots of cream and sugar. Luke talked about the beach. He had been there several times with his folks. We finished our coffee and I was feeling excited about seeing it for the first time.

Luke drove straight to the beach, only stopping for gas. We parked and the two of us ran barefoot together to the edge of the water. I stopped and stared. The noise of the waves was incredible, and the gulls flew by squealing as if to welcome us to their home. I took in the beauty of it all, the deep-green water and the waves rumbling along the shore.

We decided to spend the night in an old rundown motel close to the beach. The place was perfect, since the beach was almost deserted there. Luke signed us in as Mr. and Mrs. Tregar, and asked for their honeymoon suite. It was probably the same as all the other rooms, but it included a bottle of chilled champagne and a "Do Not Disturb" sign for the door.

We bought some hot dogs, buns, and marshmallows from a convenience store and went down to a secluded spot on the beach. We roasted our hot dogs and marshmallows and drank our champagne. Luke chased me down the beach and we made love there in the sand as twilight fell. It seemed as though we were the only two people in the world. It was frightening and romantic and carefree. We reluctantly went back to our room and took a shower, washing the sand from each other.

I really slept well that night, pressed close to Luke. I was becoming more at ease with my new life with him.

I woke with the sun streaming in through the blinds. I was always an early riser. I felt refreshed and excited, since we were going to see my sister that day. I called Maryanne before waking Luke. She asked us to come see her and promised she wouldn't notify the police. I told her we were going to look for jobs at the beach, and that we'd be there that evening.

We drove to several beach towns looking, but neither of us found jobs that day. So we headed for my sister's. We had trouble finding her house since it was getting dark. But when we drove up, she was waiting at the door. We hugged and I introduced Maryanne and her husband, Michael, to Luke. We peeked in on her one-year-old son, Randy. He was sleeping at the time. Luke and Michael went outside to see Luke's car. It was his baby, his pride and joy. While they were outside, Maryanne and I sat and talked.

"Angela, why did you run away?" she asked. "Mom called the day after you left. She thought that you might show up here."

"They wouldn't let me see Luke anymore because he was picked up for drunk driving. The cops were going to put him in reform school until he turned eighteen. We really love each other, Maryanne," I explained. "We couldn't stand to be apart that long. I know what I did hurt Mom, but they gave me no choice."

"Well, you're welcome to stay here for a while, but jobs are scarce this time of the year. If you don't find a job, you'll have to go back. Deal?" she asked.

"Deal," I said confidently.

But neither of us could find decent work. Luke got on part-time at a garage. After two weeks, I finally found a part-time job bussing tables. But it wasn't enough to keep us going, so we pooled our money, and went back to Kentucky. We stayed in Luke's uncle's cabin for a few weeks. We had no idea what we were going to do. Luke decided one evening to go back to our hometown, to ask his mom for money. He never came back.

Luke's mother came to the cabin late that night and picked me up. I spent the rest of the night at her house. Luke had been seen and chased by the police. He was in jail. They were taking him to reform school the next morning. I wasn't even allowed to see Luke before they took him away. I wouldn't be able to see him again until he was eighteen. Seven months away.

I'd called my mom from Luke's, and when she came to pick me up, she looked older than when I'd left. It had only been two months. She hugged me but didn't start the car. We just sat there.

"Angela," she finally began, "I have some bad news. Your father doesn't want you to come home. He said when you left that you were never setting foot in the house again. I've tried my best to change his mind, baby, I really have," she said shakily, her eyes filled with tears. "I've talked till I'm blue in the face. I've even cried, but he won't budge. I don't know what else I can do. He said that you made your bed, and now you have to lie in it!" Mom reached in her purse, fumbled around, and handed me some money. "I've talked to Linda's parents. They said you can stay a few days there."

I started crying then. "Mom, I never meant to hurt you," I said. "I've lost Luke and now I've lost you."

I didn't tell her that I'd missed my period last month, and this month. I was pregnant and Luke didn't even know. Now what was I going to do?

# THE PICTURE I HID IN MY DRESSER

Mom held me until I stopped crying. Then she dropped me off at Linda's. Linda came running out to meet me.

"I'm so glad you're back. I've really missed you!" she said. Then she rushed me up to her room. "Come and tell me everything, and don't look so sad. Luke will be out in seven months, and then you can get back together."

"But what do I do in the meantime?" I asked. "I think I'm two months pregnant. Luke doesn't know yet. I wanted to make sure before I said anything. The police have already taken him away."

"Your mom said she's going to send you to Arkansas to stay with your sister Suzanne," Linda said. "You could go to school there, and if you're pregnant you could have the baby there, and then come back when Luke's out."

Five days later I stepped off the bus in a little hick town in Arkansas. My sister and I hadn't seen each other for a few years. She looked the same, though. She hadn't aged much. Suzanne had two children of her own, and two from her husband's previous marriage. So we were pretty crowded in her three-bedroom house.

I told her I was sure I was pregnant. She took me to see a doctor a few days after I arrived. He confirmed what I already knew. I really wanted this baby, but I was afraid without Luke. Suzanne talked about abortion, but I told her no. Then she asked me about adoption.

"I want to keep this baby," I told her. "Luke would never forgive me, and I'd never forgive myself if I gave it up."

But Suzanne worked on me every day about it. I

knew she was only doing what she thought was best, and I loved her for it. Still, it got to where I knew everything she was going to say before she said it.

I wrote Luke every day at first. I told him about the baby and how I was studying to take my G.E.D. exam. He never answered my letters. I couldn't understand why he wouldn't write me. So I talked to Suzanne about it.

"It seems to me that he's scared off by the baby. You'll probably never see him again!" Suzanne told me. "He wasn't as serious as you thought, Angela. And if he doesn't care enough to write, then why are you bothering to keep his child? You'll only end up raising it yourself."

"That's not true!" I cried. "Luke loves me. A baby would make him happy. Something is wrong, because he would never run out on me. I just know something is wrong."

I ran off to the bedroom and cried my heart out. *So this is love,* I thought. *Loneliness and feeling hopeless.* It was a love that had been destroyed nearly before it began. But even then I knew it was a love that would remain with me for the rest of my life. And I would never believe that Luke didn't love me anymore. Never.

I wrote Luke one more letter and told him it was my last. I wrote: *You promised to take care of me. You said you wanted to be with me forever. If you don't write back, I'll know you don't want me—or our child.*

A few weeks went by. Then a month. Nearly five months had passed, and each day I became more numb. I decided maybe Suzanne was right. I finally let her take me to see a lawyer about adoption. Suzanne knew a couple who were in their late thirties. They couldn't have children themselves. The husband drank a lot, but she thought a child might settle him down. I liked the woman but not him. But I was so numb that nothing mattered. I just wanted it all over and done with.

By my seventh month, I was still skinny. Suzanne called me a pregnant toothpick. I couldn't eat or sleep. I was a walking zombie. At least I'd passed my G.E.D. test and had gotten my high school diploma. Then one day as I was getting ready to take a walk, my other sister, Loretta, called from Louisiana. I told her everything that was going on.

"Things don't sound right," she said worriedly. "Let me talk to Arnie. We'll call back tonight."

Loretta and her husband, Arnie, had two children who I'd never seen. Arnie called back that evening. "Angela, I'm paying for your plane ticket here," he told me. "I want you to come tomorrow if possible. I've talked to a lawyer and made some phone calls down there. It doesn't sound good. Suzanne doesn't know it, but that lawyer you're going through is involved with the black market. His organization sells babies illegally for money. Call me just before you get on the plane."

I hung up and I told Suzanne what he'd said. She was upset but let me go. So, a few days later I was on my way to Louisiana.

With my sister and Arnie's help, we set it up to place my baby legally. Loretta was very sympathetic and felt it was a good idea. I gained some weight and looked more like I should have. I took her kids to the park every day. They were such little sweethearts.

# THE PICTURE I HID IN MY DRESSER

The day I had Zach was more horrible than I'd imagined. I was terrified to begin with. But when my labor started, it was more pain than I'd ever felt—physically or mentally. I had asked the social worker to take a few pictures for me. One for me and one for Luke, if he ever showed up. That's all I figured I owed him.

I was brought back to reality by a nurse bustling into my room with a dinner tray. "Time to get some nourishment," she said.

I did try to eat, but everything tasted like cardboard. I pushed the tray away, lay down, and went to sleep. I must have been really tired, because I slept through to the next morning.

The nurse woke me up for breakfast. I drank some juice, and then went into the bathroom. I was still a little shaky, but I managed to take a shower. I was sore all over and could barely walk. Still, it felt so good to be clean again. Later, Miss Roudge brought my pictures in, and we said good-bye. I couldn't look at the pictures then.

My sister picked me up at noon. All I wanted to do was go to bed when I got home. But Loretta wouldn't let me. "Come on, you're young and full of energy. Let's get you packed and ready to leave tomorrow."

So I was on the bus bright and early the next morning, waving good-bye to my sister. Loretta had done so much for me. She knew how much I wanted to get Luke out of my life for good. I hated him for all he'd let me go through alone. Yet deep down, I knew I still loved him. But I tried to hide it—even from myself.

While I was in Louisiana with Loretta, my sister

# THE PICTURE I HID IN MY DRESSER

Maryanne had gotten divorced from Michael. She was now living back at home with her son, Randy, so I moved in with her. I went to visit my family—even my dad. Linda's family had moved away while I was gone, and that was really sad for me.

"I've seen Luke a few times. He asked about you," Maryanne confided, watching me to see my reaction. "When I told him you were in Louisiana, he said he was going to go find you. So I said you had a new boyfriend."

"Why?" I asked.

"I didn't want him messing up your life again, Angela. He's already messed it up so bad. He's no good for you," she warned. "Let him go. Forget him."

"I can't leave it at that," I said. "I have to find out for sure why he did this to me. And I want to give him a picture." I took out the picture of our son from my purse and showed it to Maryanne. The one I'd saved for Luke was in my dresser drawer.

"Oh, my gosh. Even this young, he looks just like Luke!" she exclaimed.

I rested up for a week before looking for Luke. Then I called his mother's house.

"Is Luke home?" I asked.

"He isn't living here," his mother said. "He moved into town. He should be at the New Day Health Club where he works now. He usually gets off at five o'clock. May I ask who's calling?"

"Thank you," I said quickly and hung up.

Then I changed my clothes and brushed my hair. I looked at my image in the full-length mirror. You couldn't even tell I'd just had a baby. I was a little more filled out, but I was still slender. My hair was

# THE PICTURE I HID IN MY DRESSER

longer, too. I was pleased with what I saw. *Will Luke be?* I wondered. *Will I be able to forgive him?*

I made sure my pictures were in my purse and left at four-thirty. I could walk to the club from Maryanne's. I saw Luke's car and decided to wait in it for him. It was starting to get dark, and I didn't want to face him in the light. Maybe I was afraid of what I'd see in his face. I also wanted to see him alone.

I sat on the passenger side as it got dark. I was so nervous I chewed a few fingernails off. It seemed like I'd waited an hour, but I'm sure it was only ten or fifteen minutes.

Then I saw him. Luke looked so handsome under the front door lights as he came out. He must have showered. His hair was wet and shiny. He was still lean and well muscled. He didn't even see me until he was in the car.

"Angela!" he yelled, turning on the inside light. "Honey, where have you been?" he cried in surprise, grabbing and hugging me so hard I could barely breathe. His mouth found mine, and he kissed me passionately. "I've missed you so much. I love you, Angela," he whispered.

I stiffened, pulling away from him. "I know how you love me. You proved that months ago," I said.

"What do you mean?" he asked, confused by my anger.

"You never answered my letters. You forced me to give up our baby. How can you sit there and say, 'I love you, I miss you?' Maryanne was right. You'll say anything to get a girl into bed!" Then I lost all control and let loose all the anger and pain I'd held in for so long, screaming, "I hate you!" over and over as I hit his chest with my fists.

# THE PICTURE I HID IN MY DRESSER

Finally, Luke grabbed my wrists. "Angela," he pleaded, "I didn't know you had a baby. I didn't know anything. I just got out a month ago. I never got any letters from you, I swear it. If you wrote, then they threw them away. They screen the mail. If it's unsuitable, they toss it. They must have known I'd run off if I knew you were pregnant," Luke explained. "Angela, please, I didn't know. When I got back, I couldn't get anyone to tell me exactly where you were. They told me you were in Louisiana with a new boyfriend."

"That isn't true. They just thought you didn't really care about me," I protested. "I would have kept the baby if I had the smallest hint that you loved me, but we were cut off completely from each other. I couldn't raise him alone, Luke. I don't have a job, no job skills, no way to support a child. I couldn't be selfish and deprive him of a good home and family. I loved him too much for that."

I reached in my purse for the pictures. "This is Zach," I said. "He looks like you."

Luke's eyes filled with tears as he looked at his son's picture. He looked over at me. "Angela, I'm so sorry. I didn't know. I swear it."

He broke down then, and we both held each other while we cried.

"I'm taking you to my apartment," he said.

We went to his place and he started pacing. "This is too much to take in all at once," he said. "We're seeing a lawyer tomorrow. Don't get your hopes up, but I'm going to fight to get our son back."

I looked up at him. "But I signed all the papers. He's legally their child now."

Luke was still pacing the floor. "Well, maybe so.

But I have to give it my best shot. I've got some money saved from my last paycheck that I was going to use to go look for you. If we need to, I'll borrow from the trust fund my grandfather left me. I'm sure Mom will loan me money to help find her grandson. We'll hire the best lawyer we can find," he insisted.

We sat and talked for a long time, filling each other in on what we'd been through. We hugged and laughed and cried, and it was as though we had never been apart.

"I can't let you leave ever again," he said. "Stay with me tonight, Angela."

So I called Maryanne to let her know that I wasn't coming home. She wasn't there, but I left a message with her baby-sitter.

Then Luke turned on the radio and pulled me to my feet. "Let's dance," he whispered, and held me in a tight embrace as we danced to a slow song.

It felt so good to be against his warm body. It had been so long since he'd held me. I put my arms around his neck and pulled his face to mine. He kissed my mouth softly at first, then with more eagerness. His hands felt like fire as they slid under my blouse. Then he led me to his room. I put my arms out to him, and we made the sweetest, most tender love ever, holding each other all through the night. . . .

In the morning, we were up bright and early. We went to Luke's mother's and explained what had happened. She agreed to lend us any money we would need but insisted we not touch the trust fund until Luke went to college.

So our next move was to see a lawyer. We called

several before we found one who would take our case. When we were seated in Mr. Ahern's office, we told him what we wanted to do. He listened carefully, and then finally spoke up.

"Do you realize what you'll be doing to the adoptive parents if you win this case?" he asked. "I'm sure they've gone through plenty of pain not being able to have their own child. Then when they are able to adopt, the natural parents come along and take the baby away. Are you willing to sit across from these people and hurt them like that?"

Neither of us could speak. We hadn't thought of what it would do to those people, only what it was doing to us.

"They have taken care of a child you couldn't care for," Mr. Ahern went on. "And I'm sure they've grown to love him very much. More than you do right now."

"Mr. Ahern," Luke broke in, "we don't want to hurt those people, but we're hurting right now."

"Let me ask you something else," Mr. Ahern said. "Can you have more children?" His question was directed to me.

"Yes, I guess so. But it's not the same," I insisted.

"Look, kids, go home and talk this over. If you still feel the same, come back and see me tomorrow," he advised.

"Tell me one thing. Do we have a chance of winning?" Luke asked.

"Yes, you do," Mr. Ahern admitted. "Because you are the natural father, and you didn't sign anything. You would have an even better case if you were to marry, but under the circumstances you still have a very good chance. Please think about what you'd be doing to the adoptive parents."

We left his office. Luke had to go to work, so I went back to Maryanne's house. I told her everything. Lucky for me, she was hesitant at first, but then supportive about Luke and me being back together.

I packed my things and moved into Luke's apartment. I got some groceries and had supper made when he came home. By then I had a splitting headache.

We ate in silence, neither of us wanting to bring up the adoption case. Finally, I couldn't take it any longer. "Luke, I can't stand the thought of hurting those people," I blurted out. "At least we've never held him. I'm sure if I'd taken care of Zach and I was in the adoptive parents' shoes, it would kill me to lose him."

"I know," Luke agreed with pain in his eyes. "I've been thinking the same exact thing. I guess we should just try to start over."

We both cried at the thought of giving up our baby. But I called Mr. Ahern the next morning and told him about our decision.

"I don't care to lose a client ordinarily," he said. "But this time I'm happy. I think you're doing the right thing."

Luke started night school while he worked during the day. I didn't see much of him except on Sundays when the health club was closed. Then we would go to his mom's or sometimes to my mom's for dinner. Things were pretty strained between me and my father. There was a lot of tension. But I figured it would get better with time.

I was so bored while Luke was working or at

school. I wanted a job. I decided to talk to him about it. We were just finished with dinner one night, and I'd started the dishes when I brought it up. "I want to find a job, Luke. I'm bored to death around here," I said.

"No way. I want you at home, Angela. Besides, I make enough. There's no reason for you to work."

"But, Luke, I don't have anything to do all day. You're always gone. It takes me an hour to make supper and an hour to clean the house. Then all I have to do is sit and watch soap operas. I hate soap operas," I argued.

He took my face in his hands. "I don't want to talk about it. I said no, Angela," he repeated calmly as he kissed me. "My mother's never worked, and my wife isn't going to, either."

I was getting angry then. "But I'm not your wife yet, and we don't have enough money. If I had a part-time job—"

"No," Luke interrupted loudly.

"Don't you talk to me like that! I'm not your daughter, and I don't like being treated like a child," I said coldly.

"Angela, the way I grew up, the man always made the decisions, paid the bills, and worked a job. The woman's place was in her home—keeping house, making meals, and raising kids," he said, trying to make me understand his reasoning.

"Well, I didn't grow up that way. My parents both work, and they share housework and making decisions!" I retorted angrily. He put his arms around me, trying to soften me up with kisses. He wouldn't let me say another word, just kept kissing me. I melted as usual.

# THE PICTURE I HID IN MY DRESSER

"I want you all to myself. I won't share you with a job," Luke murmured in my ear. Then he took my hand and led me to the bedroom. That's where the discussion ended.

It was totally unfair and selfish of Luke to deprive me of any kind of social life of my own. He worked and went to school. He had no time to sit and think of his son, but that's all I did. So without telling him, I went out to look for work.

It took me a week, but I finally found the perfect job. It was perfect because my boss worked it so I could have the same day off as Luke and be home before he was. It was a waitressing job, and I had to train a few days before I knew what to do. I worked from ten to four and had an hour to change, shower, and fix supper for Luke.

Every night I tried to tell Luke. He didn't suspect anything because I left an hour after him and was home before he was. I was so afraid of what he might do if he knew. I felt like a little girl hiding something from her parents. I finally decided I'd wait until I had a few checks in the bank, then he couldn't object as much.

I opened a checking account in my name and deposited my first paycheck. I had been putting my tips in a large wine bottle. It was already half full of dollars and change. It was hidden in our closet behind some boxes.

After my first month, my boss gave me a raise, and I was assigned to more tables, which increased my tips. My job was in a diner on the edge of town where mostly truckers and people from out of town stopped to eat and drink coffee.

I decided to push my luck for two more weeks. By

then I could save enough to convince Luke I should work. He could argue with me but not about money. His trust fund barely covered all his school expenses. His paycheck covered our bills, but there wasn't anything left over for going out or buying extra things we needed. So I knew the money I earned would be hard to argue with.

My mother knew about my job and didn't approve of my keeping it a secret. She helped me roll and count my tips once my jar was full. Then I took it all to the bank and deposited it. I couldn't believe the amount I now had. I smiled, totally satisfied with the money I'd worked for and saved by myself. I just knew Luke would be pleased. I had almost reached my goal of one thousand dollars. Just one more check would make it that much.

A few days later, I received my check and planned on taking Luke out to dinner to tell him. It was a quiet afternoon, with the diner completely empty for a change. I was about to take a break after cleaning up from the lunch rush. Then, just before my break, a couple came in with a baby. They sat in my section, so I took menus and water to their table. I knew they were from out of town, since I'd never seen them before.

The woman put the baby on the table in his infant seat. I didn't look closely at babies anymore; it made me miss mine too much. But for some strange reason, my eyes were drawn directly to this little one's face. And all at once I felt myself sway and my mouth dropped open. I caught myself before anyone noticed and quickly went back to the waitress station to sit down and try to make sense of it all. That little baby looked just like Luke! I sneaked a look their way again and noticed neither parent had the child's coloring or looks in any way.

I took the couple's order and then served it to them, trying to figure out how to ask them questions without arousing their suspicions. After they ate, I took them the bill, still staring at the baby. I knew he was my Zach even before I asked, "Are you folks passing through?"

"Yes," the young woman said. "We're on our way to New Jersey to visit my parents. They haven't seen little Timmy yet." She put her hand gently on my son's leg.

I felt a lump forming in my throat, but I managed to say, "With those eyes and that hair, he must take after his grandparents."

"No, as a matter of fact, he's adopted," she said. "We waited four years for this child. But it was sure worth it."

I couldn't help but ask, "Aren't you afraid his natural mother might come and want him back?"

She looked at me, obviously startled by my question. "Well, actually, the adoption agency told us to be prepared if something like that did happen. But I'm not afraid," she said. "I figure the mother wouldn't have given him up if she really loved him."

I just couldn't let her go on thinking that way about me. "Well, I can tell you from experience that girls don't give up babies because they don't love them. It's exactly the opposite," I blurted out. "She loved him enough to be unselfish and give him up to a family that can provide him with more than she can. If we were all selfish, where would that leave you? Maybe you should be more compassionate to the mother of that baby. After all, you would still be childless if it weren't for her."

They both stared at me, speechless, as I walked off. I still couldn't believe I'd said that. The words just wouldn't stop once they started. But I knew that if I wanted to hold my baby just this once, I would have to apologize to them. I walked slowly back to their table, waiting for a bad reaction.

"Look, I'm sorry I blew up." I talked fast before they could interrupt. "It's just that—well, I'm pretty sure Timmy is the baby I gave up. He looks just like my boyfriend," I said.

"I don't know who you are or what you're trying to pull," the man said angrily as he roughly grabbed my arm. "Where do you get off talking to us like that? Come on, Tina, let's get out of here." He let go of me.

"Wait a minute, Ron. Let's at least hear what she has to say," his wife said. "There's no harm in that."

I jumped at the chance. "I had him in Louisiana, on the third of March at Bayou Hospital. My social worker was Miss Roudge, and I have a photo of him. It's in my wallet, if you'd like to see it," I offered.

The two of them looked pale and shaken, and I knew they realized their baby was mine.

"No," Tina said, "I believe you. Why would you lie about it? So what do you want?" she asked.

"I just want to hold him and give you my address in case he'd like to meet me someday. I don't have to know your last name or anything," I pleaded.

"I don't know," her husband said nervously.

"Of course, we can do that," she agreed. "I'll get my address book out of my purse." She got it out, and I gave her my name and Mom's address and phone number in case Luke and I moved. She wrote it all down.

"I can't thank you enough," I told her.

She motioned for me to pick Zach up while her husband paid the bill. I lifted Zach up and smiled. He looked at me, happy for some attention. I held him carefully and rubbed my cheek against his. "Oh, Zach," I whispered, "I'm your mother. Please don't forget that I love you with all my heart."

Tears sprang to my eyes as I held him close. He was so soft and small. I don't know how long I held him while wild thoughts of running out the door with him whirled through my mind.

"We have to go. I'm sorry," Tina finally said as she took him from me. "I promise to keep in touch, and when Timmy is older I'll tell him who his natural mother is. I'll never hide the truth. He will always know he was adopted," she promised.

"Thank you," I said with a weak smile.

"No, thank you for giving us this child. We love him so."

I touched his cheek one last time, and then they were gone.

When I went back to the waitress station, Margo, the other waitress, asked, "What in the world was that all about? Hey, Angela, are you okay?"

"I don't feel so well," I mumbled.

"You look like you just lost your best friend and you're a white as a sheet," she said with concern.

"Look, Margo, I'd like to go home, if you can handle it from here," I told her.

"Sure I can. Go on home," she assured me.

I grabbed my purse and rushed out the back way. I gulped the cool air, trying to keep from crying.

When I got home, I showered and changed

clothes, going through the motions as if in a trance. *I have to tell Luke,* I thought. By the time I left, it was four. I walked toward the health club, stopping at the bank first to deposit my check. Luke was instructing a class in weight lifting. I sat on a bench inside the front entrance after leaving a message with the man at the front desk. I had to wait a long time, so I tried to prepare a speech. I didn't know how to tell him about the job and seeing Zach. I couldn't believe it. The chances of that couple stopping there at all—and during my shift—were one in a million. Yet it had happened.

Luke came down the stairs from his class, flushed and sweaty. "Hi, honey, what's up?" he asked.

"Can we go out to dinner tonight? Maybe to Harger's?" I suggested. "I know it's expensive, but it's quiet and dark." I talked fast so he could hear me out before he said no. "I've saved some money from the grocery budget. Also, I have something important to tell you."

"If you're sure we can afford it, I suppose so. Let me get showered and changed," he said.

When we got to the restaurant, we asked for a secluded table. The hostess lit the candles on our table. She brought drinks and a waitress took our order before Luke asked, "So what's so important that you had to tell me here? I have an idea it's bad or you would have told me at home where we can argue." He smiled. "Am I right?"

I didn't answer.

"Come on, Angela. I know something's bothering you. Go ahead. I can take it," he assured me.

"Let's wait until we've eaten, then we won't be interrupted," I hedged.

# THE PICTURE I HID IN MY DRESSER

Luke was famished, but I just picked at my food. I could never eat when I was upset. It seemed my life would never be normal. It was always in some kind of turmoil. I couldn't see ruining Luke's dinner, though. When he'd finished, we ordered another drink. The waitress cleared our table and brought our drinks and the check. "Now will you tell me?" he asked.

In answer, I took my checkbook from my wallet and showed it to him. He glanced at it.

"What's this? You been holding out on me?" he joked. Then he looked at the deposits. "Wait a minute. You've been depositing a lot of money. How can that be? Where did you get this money?" he demanded in an angry tone.

"I-I've been working the last month and a half," I stammered, terrified by the look on his face. This wasn't the reaction I'd expected.

"Where?" he asked, his lips drawn tight and his jaw set.

"I've been waiting tables at the Valley Diner," I told him.

"Oh, this is great," he said, totally disgusted. "Not only do you take it upon yourself to get a job, but you decide to be a waitress, letting truckers pay you to run back and forth like a slave while they watch your cute little behind traipsing in front of them. I bet they tip you real good," he said as he glared at me.

I couldn't believe what he said. "Well, who waits on you at home?" I asked, angry and hurt.

"You do. In our own home, where you belong," he said.

"I get it," I snapped. "I'm your own personal wait-ress at home, huh? I keep your bed warm, serve your meals, and clean up after you. You, in turn, pay my bills. All without the benefit of marriage!"

That shut him up long enough to think a minute. "Okay," he said as he sighed. "Maybe you're right."

"I have something else more important to tell you, anyway," I said. "I saw our son today."

"You what?" he exclaimed. "Where?"

"At the diner, while I was working." As I explained the details, Luke's face registered disbelief and his eyes grew bigger. As I finished, pain washed over the disbelief.

"Why didn't you call me, Angela?" he asked. "I would like to have seen him, too."

"I didn't have time, Luke," I apologized. "They were only there long enough for me to hold him a second. It was all so strange. And it was horrible, saying good-bye again," I said, my eyes filled with tears.

Luke put his hand over mine. "I bet it was. Now I hope you've told me everything. I swear, you sure keep our life hopping. There's never a dull moment." He smiled trying to get me into a better mood.

The next morning we argued over my job again. "You will find a different profession—or else!" Luke declared.

"Or else what?" I challenged.

"Or else I'll turn you over my knee!"

Luke chased me around the house, but I wasn't in a playful mood. When he caught me, I slapped his hands away. "Stop it, I'm not feeling well."

Then he became angry. "Angela, let it slide. If you keep thinking about our son, it will only get you down. There isn't anything you can do about it.

# THE PICTURE I HID IN MY DRESSER

You've been depressed since you saw him."

I just looked at him with a hurt expression.

My depression didn't stop there, though. It got to where all I thought about was when I held my Zach. I dreamed about someone chasing me down the hospital corridors. When I turned around, it was Luke. I was holding Zach, and Luke would grab him from me, laughing cruelly. Then the faces of Zach's adoptive parents would appear. They would all laugh, even Zach. Then they all disappeared and I was left alone in the dark. I never seemed to get any sleep because I was afraid I'd have that awful dream.

One afternoon as I was working, my mother stopped by the restaurant. It was about two months after I'd seen Zach. "I thought you might want this letter," she explained. "It came to the house this morning. I was coming to town anyway, so I thought I'd drop it by."

I looked at the return address. "I don't know any Mrs. Perrino," I said. "Or anyone from Red Bank, New Jersey."

I dropped the letter in my purse, since I was too busy to read it. I finished out my shift and forgot the letter. I didn't remember it until I was home, lying on the bed with my feet propped up. It had been an awfully busy day and I was exhausted. I got the letter out of my purse and lay back down, puzzled by who it could be from. The woman wrote:

Dear Angela,
I'm sorry for the tragic news I must tell you. I went through Tina's address book and feel it's my duty to tell all her friends. I'm a friend of her parents. I'm ter-

ribly sorry to tell you this, but there was an accident over two weeks ago. While Tina, Ron, and little Timmy were on their way home from shopping one night, a drunken driver hit their car head on. The car spun off an overpass and they were all killed instantly. The other driver wasn't hurt. He is going to be tried for manslaughter.

Any money you could contribute would be deeply appreciated, since Tina's parents aren't well off. They are both retired and living on a small pension. Please accept my deepest sympathy.

Mrs. Emily Perrino, friend of Tina's parents

She'd included an outdated funeral announcement and her address.

I lay there stunned. "No, no, no!" I cried. "My baby's gone!" I cried and cried hysterically. I was still holding the letter in my hand when Luke came home, but I didn't hear him. When I didn't answer him, he took the letter from my hand and read it.

"Oh, no!" He groaned, looking at me as tears filled his eyes.

I got up to hold him. We cried together for a long time. Then we called our bosses to say we were taking a few days off because of a family crisis. The next morning we left for New Jersey.

By sunset, we drove into Red Bank. We called Mrs. Perrino, and she gave us directions to her house. Minutes later we knocked at the door and a little white-haired woman answered.

"Come in," she said. "I've made some coffee."

# THE PICTURE I HID IN MY DRESSER

She was very old, but seemed like a girl in her twenties, full of life and energy. "Tina's parents are dear friends of mine," she told us. "We've been next door neighbors for over twenty years now."

She had such a kind face that I knew it would be easy to talk to her. "We never knew Tina or Ron," I admitted. "I met them only once when they passed through our town. In fact, it was only by chance that we met. You knew Timmy was adopted, didn't you?" I asked.

She nodded, looking puzzled.

'Well, we're his natural parents. I'm very thankful you wrote, or we would never have known." I broke down then, and she ran over and patted my shoulder.

It was cold and drizzling the next day. The weather matched my mood. Mrs. Perrino went with us to show us where Tina and Ron and our baby were buried. They had buried Zach between his adoptive parents.

"Oh, my little Zach, you never even had a chance to live!" I cried, and then I said a silent prayer: *Dear Lord, I know You'll keep my baby happy until I come to meet him. And I thank you with all my heart for giving me the chance to hold him before You took him away.* Then Luke gently pulled me up from my knees and we drove back to Mrs. Perrino's house. We said good-bye and promised to keep in touch.

Luke and I went on home, and life took up where it had left off. Our grief didn't last as long as it could have. Since we really had no memories of our son's short life, there was nothing to keep reminding us of him. Also, I had suspected I was pregnant. But with all that had happened, I'd let it slip my mind. Then I woke up one morning, sick to my stomach, and I remembered.

"Luke, I'm pregnant!" I announced.

We were both so happy. We went right down and got blood tests taken. We were married four days later in his family church. Just our families were present. We had a honeymoon for four days at his aunt and uncle's cabin. It was filled with memories of our first special night together. Luke and I just relaxed and enjoyed each other's company. And we had some very romantic nights in front of the fireplace.

When we got back from our honeymoon, there was a letter from Mrs. Perrino for us at my mom's. We took it home to read it. She'd sent a short note and a picture of our son's headstone. In her note she thanked me again for the contribution, saying that there might not have been any markers if I hadn't given that much.

After I read the note, I looked at the picture. The headstone had his legal name and dates in the middle, but along the top was engraved: Zach—Cherished in his parents' hearts.

No one would ever understand that but Mrs. Perrino, Luke, and me. But it meant the world to Luke and me. Zach would be cherished in our hearts forever. Even if we had ten other children, there would always be a special place in our hearts for Zach—our firstborn son. THE END

# DON'T TELL DADDY WHERE WE ARE!

My son, Jason, yelled at me, "Hey, Mom, you just passed the exit to Grandma Clarke's house." He leaned forward to get my attention from the backseat. "Didn't you see that exit sign?"

"We're passing Virginia, period," his older sister, Katie, said, her voice suspicious. "Where are you going, Mom?"

"Well, remember when I picked you all up, I said I had a big surprise for you?" I stammered, trying to sound casual. "Well, this is it. We're going to Florida!"

"Florida?" Katie repeated. "You told Daddy you were taking us to visit Grandma Clarke."

"Okay, so we'll visit her on our way back," I answered, smiling at them in the rearview mirror. "Don't you two want to go to Florida and swim in the ocean?"

"No, I want to go to Grandma Clarke's house and play with her dog," Jason said. "This road looks too long. I'm tired of riding so much."

"Oh, big seven-year-old boys don't get tired of riding this fast," I replied, slowing down so a big truck could get in front of us. "Just wait until we get there. You'll have lots of fun."

"Yeah, but it's kind of telling a lie," Katie insisted, with all her ten-year-old honesty. "What if Daddy calls Grandma Clarke and we're not there? He'll be worried."

"Daddy gets mad when he doesn't know where we are," Jason explained, jiggling the seat. "Let's go back to Grandma Clarke's and call him."

"Oh, we can call him when we get to Florida," I assured them, wondering how I would get out of it. "You can collect some pretty shells on the beach to take home and surprise him with, too."

"That's a good idea, Mom. Let's get enough to give Gramps and Grandma Porter some, too," Katie suggested. She had always been real close with them. "We'll take big shells to Gramps, so he can put them in his cactus garden."

"We have to get Grandma Clarke some, too," Jason answered, determined to keep her in the conversation. "She'd like some little ones for her flowerpots, wouldn't she, Mom?"

"She sure would," I agreed, relieved that they were finally accepting the trip without more arguing. "You can gather shells, and swim, too. We'll have a great time."

They settled back, happily discussing shells and all the things they'd do, forgetting the serious conversation we'd just had. But it opened up a whole new bag of worries for me.

I'd been so busy planning how to get my kids, that I'd never given a thought to their feelings. I just took it for granted that they'd be excited about traveling and love to be with me.

Maybe they'd still be happy with me, I decided as we left Virginia behind. It was only natural for them to miss their father. I would just have to change their minds a little at a time.

When the court gave my ex-husband, Kenny, custody of our two children, I didn't object. Maybe that's where I made my big mistake. But I honestly thought they would have a more normal home life with him than with me.

I'm a country music entertainer, and my first record was just released a few weeks earlier. It was getting lots of air play, which meant I had to stay on the road. I spent most of my time traveling all over the country, putting on shows. But I wasn't making nearly enough money yet to hire somebody to travel with me to look after the kids. Like so many others are doing today, I was mostly making enough to get by and try to keep pushing my record.

"Mary Jo, we won't upset the kids' regular schedule as much if they live here with me," Kenny had pointed out when we discussed things before the court decision. "I'm always here with them at night, anyhow. They're getting used to you being gone on tours. Besides, you know you can always see them, or take them to keep, whenever you're in town."

"All right, whatever is best for them," I'd finally agreed, choking back my tears. Kenny taught junior high school and spent lots of time with kids. I figured he knew more about what was best for ours. "Divorce is hard enough on the poor little things."

"Now, don't worry about them, Mary Jo. Kids adapt fast," Kenny had assured me, going over to look out the window at them playing in the yard. "Katie is ten years old and Jason is seven. They understand what we tell them. Remember, Mom and Dad are right next door to help with them, too, if they're needed."

"I'm going to stay in town and keep them as much as I can," I answered, not daring to make any comment about my in-laws helping.

Kenny's parents living right next door was the main reason we'd broken up. They always made our decisions for us, and Kenny would go right along with them, regardless of how much I disagreed. We even had to spend all our vacations together, and they'd decide where!

The Porters had three children, but Kenny was the baby and their only son. His sisters were several years older than Kenny. Both of them lived in other states and seldom came home. So Kenny felt obligated to stick close and make sure his parents weren't lonely.

The only time he ever took my side against them, was when I got this chance to get into music. But he did that more for himself than for me. He had always wanted to buy a big farm and raise horses. This looked like his chance to do it, since other working-class people were sometimes getting big breaks in country music.

A close friend of Kenny's, who taught at the same school with him, had gotten a lucky break and gone into music a couple of years before. He made a whole string of hit records and was practically a millionaire. So when he came back and heard me singing at a school carnival, he'd offered to help me get an audition with his record company.

# DON'T TELL DADDY WHERE WE ARE!

Kenny was overjoyed at the suggestion. He insisted we get right with it the very next day.

"This is our big chance, honey," my husband told me as we got ready for bed later that night. "With Sam backing you we can start looking at farms by this time next year."

"Oh, I don't think I'll ever get that popular," I answered, laughing at his big dreams. "Sam is a single, good-looking, sexy man. That, alone, is enough to make him a big star. And he's very talented along with it. But I'm just average. An average-looking, average singer."

"No, you're not, Mary Jo," Kenny interrupted, more serious than I'd ever seen him. "You've always had an unusual voice. Sam says it's just different enough to put you over. You've just got to try it, Mary Jo."

"But what if I can't?" I picked up my hairbrush, but he put it back on the dresser.

"All those other famous women have made it, so you can do it, if they can." He put his hands on my shoulders, looking deep into my eyes. "I'm counting on you, Mary Jo. You're my ticket out of teaching school. I love kids. But staying cooped up in a classroom just kills me. I want to be out on that big farm. At least try for me."

"I'll have to be away from you and the kids a lot," I objected, eager to please him and try for myself, yet afraid. "You know musicians have to work the road a lot to even get started."

"Just until we get enough money to buy that farm and stock it," he'd promised, taking me in his arms. "After that, you can retire. You can just be a full-time mother and my wife forever, honey."

# DON'T TELL DADDY WHERE WE ARE!

I wasn't so enthused about buying a horse farm, but I would have moved anywhere to get away from his parents.

"You've got yourself a deal, Mr. Porter," I answered, slipping my arms around his neck. "If Sam's company offers me a contract, I promise, I'll sign."

Oddly enough, Kenny never breathed a word about our plans to his parents, until I had passed the audition and signed a contract. I guess he was afraid they would talk us out of it. They had talked him out of being anything except a schoolteacher. For some unknown reason, they'd been obsessed about that.

They certainly were upset when they learned we had done some business without consulting them. We pretended not to notice, as we thought they'd be proud once my record came out. But the better I did, the more they resented it. When I started touring, they became furious.

Both of them started working on Kenny while I was away. Mrs. Porter kept pointing out how I was neglecting him and our kids, leaving him with all the responsibilities, while I had fun.

Dad Porter made sure Kenny heard all those gossip tales about the wild things musicians do when they're on the road.

It didn't take long for my husband to start believing them and feeling sorry for himself. He completely forgot that he was the one who had insisted I do it in the first place, and began to doubt me.

Life became a hassle. I'd rush in off a long tour, eager to spend time alone with my husband and kids, and find our house overflowing with relatives his mom had invited for the weekend, expecting us

# DON'T TELL DADDY WHERE WE ARE!

to put most of them up at our house.

Or my father-in-law would "surprise" us with tickets to a ball game or movie they had wanted to see.

If I brought home gifts, I was spoiling my kids; if I didn't, they would make it seem like I hadn't thought of the kids. Both Mom and Dad Porter encouraged Katie and Jason to break any rule I made for them.

I knew my in-laws were trying to cause us trouble, but Kenny refused to believe me. They had never liked me much because of my background.

Mr. and Mrs. Porter had had their hearts set on Kenny marrying a girl with money, or at least a college degree. I had neither. Growing up, Mom had to raise me and pay a stack of bills. She and I both had to work and scrimp just to put me through high school.

This was another reason I was so eager to succeed now. I wanted to show them I was good enough for their son.

The worst times were the ones when Kenny accused me of cheating on him. We both knew some musicians did, but not nearly as many as it seems. I certainly didn't. My lead guitarist's wife, Peggy, was our manager. She always traveled with us. What bit of spare time we had, I usually spent with her, but Kenny wouldn't believe me. He wouldn't even believe Sam, when we did shows with him.

I finally offered to quit and stay home, if Kenny would sell our house and move away from his parents, but he wouldn't. Things got so bad we argued all the time, so we decided to just call it quits. The only thing we could agree on was who should keep the kids.

Those next few months were torture. I kept trying

to spend time with the children, but seldom succeeded. Kenny's mother would convince him they were too sick to be out, or have other plans already made to take them elsewhere. They'd say the kids were in the shower, in bed, at a friend's house, or any one of a dozen more excuses to keep from calling them to the phone when I called.

When I tried dropping by the house to see them, it was worse. Kenny and his parents were coolly polite, but they all stuck so close, I couldn't have a minute alone with my kids. Finally, I just gave up and booked more shows out of town. If I couldn't be with my kids, at least I could make some money to maybe one day be with them.

But working one-night stands is mighty exhausting. Especially if you are already under strain like I was. My voice just couldn't take it. I started getting so hoarse I could hardly speak, much less sing. Several of our shows had to be cancelled.

The doctors all assured me that the best cure was taking time off to give my throat a rest. If that didn't work, they'd have to consider an operation, which I sure didn't want.

I really hit bottom that day. I'd have to tell my band I was quitting. They had stuck by me in the rough times, and now we were just starting to make money. Our name was beginning to get known.

My heart felt heavy as rocks when I called the band together and explained I couldn't keep them on the payroll any longer.

"Don't you worry about us," they all told me. "We'll find work. Everybody needs musicians this time of year. You just try to get well, so we can get back together real soon."

"Yeah, just relax and have fun with your kids this summer," Peggy said, forcing a smile through her tears. "Nothing's going to get us down. Why, you'll be back in a couple of months better than ever. We'll take up right where we're leaving off now."

I didn't make any promises, for if I could find a way to earn a living and stay with my kids, I was going to. Kenny had promised I could keep them if I stayed in town, so I was going to try.

The flimsy excuses they had been making to keep the children from me wouldn't work now that I was off the road, either. Kenny must have realized it, because when I told him I was taking the summer off and wanted to keep Katie and Jason, he became flustered enough to blurt out the real reason he'd refused to let them visit me.

"My folks think you shouldn't take them to your place anymore." He ran nervous fingers through his thinning hair. "Jason told Mom you had men in there drinking beer when they visited you last, Mary Jo."

"What?" I had gone to the house, and we were standing in the yard beside my car. "I don't believe this. The only man at my place was my lead guitar player and his wife, Peggy. You know them. They live in the apartment right across from mine. He was drinking a beer and watching TV when Peggy left him and came over to bring us a fresh batch of chocolate chip cookies she'd just baked."

"Then where did Jason get the men drinking?" Kenny asked, sneering.

"I'm coming to that," I told him, moving over near the rosebush. "We all got to talking, and Peggy stayed, so her husband came when his TV program ended. He hadn't finished his can of beer, so he just carried it along with him. I never thought a thing about it. You often drink a beer in front of the children, you know."

"I don't get drunk," Kenny snapped, looking over my shoulder toward his folks' house next door. "Jason said he was drunk."

"Why, he'd only had one beer." I defended him, surprised. "I can't imagine why Jason would tell such a story."

"Children tell what they see," Kenny's mother spoke up, so close behind me that it made me jump. "Kids Jason's age speak truth."

"Yes, but grown-ups don't always repeat it as the kid tells it," I shot back, angry at her sneaking up and eavesdropping on us. "What does Katie say about it?"

"We thought it best not to call her attention to it," Kenny said, glancing at his mother. "Sorry, Mary Jo, but you will just have to see them here, if you see them at all."

I knew it was useless to argue, so I left. But I wasn't giving up. There must be a way to see my babies without those vultures always hovering over us!

The answer hit me that night as I talked to my mother on the phone. She lived in Virginia. It would seem perfectly natural for me to take the kids to visit her.

The few times Mom had visited us, she had hit it off fine with Kenny and his parents, because she's real easygoing. They even stopped by to visit her overnight once, when we were on vacation.

"Yes, I guess you can take them to your mother's for a week," Kenny agreed, when I mentioned it to him. "But only for a week."

# DON'T TELL DADDY WHERE WE ARE!

I guess that's when I actually decided to kidnap them and go on to Florida. If I could just get to spend the rest of the summer with them, my kids would have the chance to get to know me again. Of course I'd have to take them home when school started, for I had no idea where or how to get false papers to enroll them elsewhere. But I would enjoy them while I could. I honestly didn't think of it as a criminal offense. I just wanted to hold them in my arms again, and share their lives like I used to. Oh, I had no doubts that Kenny would be furious, as well as his parents, but I figured they'd just refuse to let me see the kids, and they were already doing that.

Kenny and his parents could stand to worry until they figured out what happened. I didn't care, though. It would serve them right if they never saw the children again. After all, they'd kept them from me and still tried to turn them against me.

Mom could have been a big help, but I didn't dare let her in on my plans. She loved me and my kids dearly, but Mom wouldn't lie for anybody. If she was questioned and knew where we were, she'd believe she'd have to tell. I'd call her later, but not yet.

Katie broke into my thoughts. "Mommy, I've got to use the bathroom."

"I've gotta use it, too," Jason declared, perking up as we came in sight of his favorite fast-food restaurant just off the interstate. "I'm hungry, too."

"So am I," I agreed, flipping on the turn signal as we neared the exit. "How about a hamburger with fries?"

"Daddy's got a girlfriend," Jason announced while we were eating. "She's rich. But she's not as pretty as you, Mom."

# DON'T TELL DADDY WHERE WE ARE!

"She's not Daddy's girlfriend," Katie snapped, glaring at her little brother. "Grandma Porter invites Miss Donna to dinner all the time. She wants Daddy to like her, because she thinks she's rich, but I hate her."

"Hey, you shouldn't hate her if it's because you think she is Daddy's girlfriend," I explained, adding more catsup to my fries. "He needs a grown-up companion to talk with, like you all need your own friends. How come you think she's rich?"

"Aw, her folks own a big ranch and some oil wells in Texas," Katie muttered, her eyes on her plate. "She bought that house for sale near ours, and she's going to teach school."

"I hope Daddy doesn't marry her," Jason blurted, wadding his napkin. "She'd be a teacher at home all the time. If he does, I'll just run away."

"Yeah, if Daddy marries that nerd, I'll run away, too," Katie agreed, still keeping her head down. "She already tries to boss us."

"Well, I wouldn't worry about them marrying now," I consoled them, making my voice cheerful. "Lots of people are friends and don't marry, you know."

That first week was great. We checked in at a hotel and spent two nights and three days right there at Disney World, living it up. Katie and Jason were so excited they forgot all about calling home.

"Let's just stay here, Mommy," Jason pleaded when we started to leave that third day. "I love it here."

"We don't have enough money to stay longer, honey," I explained, letting them take a last look as we left. "Besides, we have a lot more places to see and things to do."

"Yes, we've got to call Daddy." Katie put both hands to her face in alarm. "Oh, Jason, I bet he's looking everywhere for us. We forgot to even call him."

"I bet he's awfully mad because we forgot," Jason said, looking scared. "Will he spank us, Katie?"

"Oh, I called him," I lied, unable to stand seeing them so upset. "Daddy is real glad you two are having so much fun."

"When did you call him?" Katie stared up at me suspiciously. "You wouldn't even let us call Grandma Clarke."

"Oh—uh—I called while you were asleep," I stammered, hurrying them on. "Sorry, I forgot to tell you all. Let's get the car and roll."

"Let's call Daddy now, Jason," Katie suggested, just after we'd checked into a motel in another town several hours away. "We can tell him what we did and all the souvenirs we bought to bring home."

"I'm going to tell him about everything," Jason said, heading for the phone. "Can I dial all by myself?"

"No, you can't call tonight." I blocked his way. "Daddy isn't home."

"Where is he?" Katie gave me that look again.

"He's helping Miss Donna redecorate her house," I blabbed, grabbing the first excuse that popped in my mind. "He said they'd be working real late every night until it's finished."

"Then we'll just call Gramps and Grandma Porter," Katie decided, pushing past her brother. "They can tell Daddy."

"No, they aren't home, either." I forced a smile. "Daddy said they were all going to help Miss Donna."

"I'll just call and see," Katie said, trying to reach for the phone."

"Wait. I've got a better idea." I grabbed my purse and car keys beside the phone. "Let's run back to that little shopping mall we passed and get them some pretty postcards. You can find some with pictures to show them where you two have been."

"That would be better," Katie agreed, always eager to shop.

"Let's go." Jason tugged at my arm. "Can we get a sundae, too, while we're there?"

"Sure thing," I promised, feeling sort of dirty. Lying to my kids wasn't part of my plans, but now it was becoming very necessary. "Let's hurry before they close."

I made sure we stayed out until they were too sleepy to think of calling home anymore that night. But the next morning, I had my first taste of what was to come. We'd been on the beach a couple of hours, and had come out of the water to dry off a bit. I lay back on my towel, closing my eyes, while they built a sand castle beside me. It kept caving in and they blamed each other.

"Let's go some place else where there are other kids to play with," Jason said, flopping down on his own towel beside me. "I'm tired of this beach."

"Yeah, I'm tired of this place, too, Mom," Katie agreed, grabbing her things. "Let's go. I want some kids my size, too."

"I wish I was home now," Jason whined. "I'd be playing with Kyle and his new puppy. We're teaching it all kinds of tricks, Mom."

Kyle was our neighbor's little boy, who had lived across the street from us ever since the kids were small. He and Jason had been friends all their lives, and were almost inseparable.

"You'll get to see your friends again when school starts," I told them, sighing as I gathered our stuff to go. I felt kind of let down, too. "We'll just have fun until then."

"This beach doesn't have any pretty shells," Jason complained, slipping his sandals on. "I want some boys to play with. I wish Kyle was here."

I didn't answer, because I knew how he felt. I loved my kids dearly, but I was getting hungry for some adult companionship, too. I'd spent most of the last few months with people my own age, and now we all needed some space from one another.

"Mom, school doesn't start until fall," Katie cut into my thoughts, laughing. "We'll be seeing our friends next week. Daddy said you could only keep us at Grandma Clarke's this week."

"Yeah, when are we going to see her?" Jason squinted as he faced the sun to look at me. "Let's go right now, Mom."

"We'll have to go soon, won't we, Mom?" Katie spoke up, digging her toe in the sand.

"We'll be going home Sunday, you'll see," I mumbled, wondering how I could tell them they were going to stay in Florida and spend the rest of the summer with me.

Finding a way to tell them wasn't easy. I thought it best to tell them when we were having lots of fun. But that wasn't easy, either. Both kids were getting as bored as I was, shopping in the mall and staying at the beach. They were bored with each other, too, and had started fighting over every little thing. I was ready to scream.

Real trouble hit the next day. We'd bought a new game at the mall the night before, and they were eager to try it out. I thought I'd use the time to take a nice bath, knowing they wouldn't be fighting. But I had figured all wrong.

When I came out of the bathroom, Katie was hanging up the phone. Jason jumped in his chair, looking guilty, but she didn't.

"You lied to us, Mommy!" she shouted, her dark eyes blazing with anger. "You never called Daddy at all."

"Katie, what have you done?" I felt myself shrinking.

"I called Daddy," she retorted, lifting her stubborn chin. "Grandma Clarke had called to see why we didn't come. Daddy says they've all been worried to death. They were scared somebody had kidnapped us and killed us all. You should be ashamed of yourself! And you always told Jason and me never to lie!"

"Katie, I'm sorry I had to lie to you and Jason," I apologized, wanting to shake her. "But it was the only way I could get to be with you. You know they won't let you visit me anymore. Did you tell Daddy where we are?"

"Yes, he wanted to know." She inched over by her brother, looking uncertain now. "Daddy said to tell you if you don't call him right back, he's having the police pick us up."

"Will they spank us and put us in jail?" Jason asked, his eyes filling with tears.

"No, honey." I knelt in front of them, my anger gone. "They will put me in jail and take you all home to Daddy. Rather, I guess they will keep you someplace until Daddy can come here and get you. But they will not let us stay together."

"We don't want you to go to jail, Mom." Katie wasn't angry anymore, either, just scared, like Jason and me.

"Then you all be good and do exactly what I tell you," I replied, hugging them both. "We'll have to hide for a while. See, the law believes I'm a criminal because I brought you here. And Daddy is mad at me over it, so he'll tell them to put me in jail. The only thing we can do is to hide until Daddy cools off, and I can take you home then. Maybe he'll be so glad to see you that he won't make me go to jail then."

They agreed, but it wasn't easy to hide two children, even in Florida. I'd splurged and spent most of my money, thinking we'd live simply the rest of the summer. But now I'd have to change all our appearances, which meant buying all new clothes for both kids. Then we'd need to find a larger city, where lots of tourists crowded the beaches, so we wouldn't be noticed.

But everything went wrong from the start. I tried to dye Katie's hair, but it turned out a carroty red. This made her angry at me again, and at Jason for laughing at her.

Jason got carsick all over the backseat as we headed for a bigger city.

I had planned to get as far from the area Kenny thought we were in as possible. But the old station wagon I'd traded my nearly-new car for to hide our trail, conked out on us after we'd gone about seventy miles. It happened at the edge of a small town.

Everything there was old, including the run-down motel room we had to rent until the one garage could repair our car.

# DON'T TELL DADDY WHERE WE ARE!

"I hate this stinky place," Katie said, wrinkling her nose at the fishy smell coming from the fleet of fishing boats close by. "Let's call Daddy and tell him we'll come home if he won't let them put you in jail, Mom."

"Daddy wouldn't listen," I answered, pretending not to see the big bug crawling across the floor of our motel room. "All those boats will be gone out to sea when we get up in the morning, so it won't be bad then."

But it was. We stayed on the beach until the heat drove us back inside, but it wasn't interesting, either. There was nothing to do except swim or lie on the sand. We'd already done that, so both kids were bored stiff. The only good thing about the whole place was that the beach was right across the two-lane highway from our motel, so we could run back and forth.

"I want to go home," Jason declared, when I finally had to scold him for quarreling. "Why doesn't Daddy come get us like he said he was going to?"

"Daddy doesn't know where we are, stupid," Katie growled. "I bet he's looking for us."

"Don't kid yourselves," I snapped, irritated at my own silly plans that had gotten us into this mess. "Daddy looks out for Daddy. He doesn't give a darn for anybody else."

"That's not true." Katie jerked around to face me. "Daddy takes good care of us. He'd never make us stay in a crummy old place like this. We want to go home. We don't like living with you."

"Yeah, you're mean, Mommy," Jason accused, taking sides with his sister. "You won't even take us to see Grandma Clarke."

# DON'T TELL DADDY WHERE WE ARE!

"I'm doing the best I can, kids," I answered, close to tears. "I took you to Disney World, didn't I?"

"Yes, but now you're making us stay in this awful place," Katie said. "If you really love us, why don't you take us to Grandma Clarke's house? Daddy could find us there."

"Let's go, Mommy," Jason pleaded, shivering as he glanced around the room. "It's too spooky here. I had scary dreams last night."

"Oh, stop whining and let me have some peace," I scolded, wanting to complain myself. "We can't go anywhere until our car is fixed. You two are driving me nuts."

"Well, it's not our fault your old car broke down." Katie glared at me with pure hatred. "You promised we'd have fun in Florida, but you won't do anything we want to."

"You just want to lie on the beach." Jason's voice quivered. "Daddy played with us, and took us places."

"But I've explained why I can't play ball and stuff." I shook my head. "I have to rest a lot. Let's walk down to the garage and see if they've done anything on our car yet."

"No, Jason and I will go look for some shells for Daddy on the beach," Katie replied with a sly look. "I'll look after him, and we won't go in the water."

"Well, all right, if you promise," I agreed, thinking it would just take a minute to run to the corner garage. "But I'll see you across the highway first."

I watched until they were safely on the beach, where several families were scattered around, then started on my way, wishing I was back on the road with my band and the kids were at home. I'd forgotten how restless kids their age became, if there's not lots of action. Much as I loved my kids, I just couldn't take the place of their friends. Yes, and their daddy and grandparents, I had to admit. They had had to adjust to life without me for too long. Well, we couldn't hide out much longer. My money was almost gone.

A nice surprise awaited me at the garage. They had just finished fixing the car and it was ready to go. But the cost encouraged me to stick to the decision I'd almost made walking there. We had to start home. I paid them and drove back to tell the kids, happier than I'd been since we left. This was the right thing.

But the kids weren't there to tell, or to take home. I'd parked beside the motel and rushed across to get them, but they weren't on the beach. The family at the beach said they'd returned to the motel as soon as I left them. *Probably Jason had to use the bathroom,* I thought, thanking them and hurrying back.

I called their names as I opened the door, but silence answered. They hadn't come back—or had they? Suddenly, I realized both of their overnight bags were gone. Then I saw the crumbled sheet of paper propped on my pillow. It was a note saying they were going home.

All I could think to do was call the police and confess everything. A policeman picked me up. He used the radio to start an Amber alert for them. He described both kids and what they were wearing, while we drove. We checked several side streets, but there were no signs of them. I just knew somebody had already picked them up.

About halfway to the interstate entrance we saw

them and beeped the horn as we approached. Katie heard us and turned, sticking out her hand like she'd seen them do on TV. Then she realized it was a police car and recognized me inside. They started to run away as fast as they could. I think that was the worst moment of my life.

"Please don't make us go back with Mommy," they begged the officer when we got them in the car and headed back to town. "We want to go home to Daddy."

"You're not going back with her," the policeman promised with a disgusted look at me. "Your daddy is being notified. We'll keep you safe until he can get here."

Kenny asked them to hold us all. He was flying right down. They offered to let me make one phone call, advising me to get a lawyer. But I called Mom instead. I needed to hear her voice.

It was the smartest thing I'd done, although I didn't know it at the time. I just felt she was all I had left in the world, now that my kids had turned against me.

I still don't know what she said to Kenny or his parents, but it must have been as strong as what she blasted me with. They all arrived together, a few hours later, and Kenny refused to press charges against me!

"You and Kenny don't own these kids like property," Mom said, looking us both right in the eye. "They're not pawns to use for revenge. These poor little children are being caught in the middle, and I won't allow it! They are real people, with hearts and feelings of their own. God just loans kids to parents to make their world a little brighter. I trust you two to figure it out from here."

I knew Mom was right, and I think the rest of them did, too, for they convinced the police there to let me face charges back home. Kenny never pressed them, but I did have to appear before the judge, because I'd kidnapped my kids and had taken them across state lines. But the judge put me on probation, with visitation rights to see my kids only with a counselor present.

This all happened almost a year ago. But the kids still refuse to see me. I'm not pushing them, because I know I have only myself to blame. I should have gone back and talked to the judge in the first place, instead of taking the law into my own hands. I have also discovered another reason for the stupid thing I did. Much as I love my kids, I realize now, I partly did it to get back at my ex-husband, like Mom said.

I'm back with my band now, playing music, but the thrill is gone. There are no more rosy dreams of getting rich or famous. It's just a way to make an average living. More to keep me on the move, I guess, for we stay on the road a lot.

But my kids are still on my mind. Maybe someday when they're older, they will understand and forgive me. Their daddy already has.

"You did wrong, Mary Jo, but so did I," Kenny told me the last time I tried to see our kids. "I realized that when they were with you and I couldn't see them. Just give them time. They'll want to see you again. Remember, kids do adapt."

I hope and pray he is right, but I can't expect too much. After all, I did give my kids bitter memories.                    THE END

# *LOVING A MARRIED MAN*

When Lloyd asked if I'd go to a party with him, I said sure, although I didn't really expect to enjoy it much. I figured it would be more tiresome than fun. Little did I dream that it would mark a turning point in my life, and that nothing would ever be the same again.

It was to be a fancy, catered affair that Lloyd's boss, a successful building contractor, was hosting in his lavish home for a number of his business associates and key employees. Lloyd was one of the firm's accountants.

I'd been dating Lloyd for nearly a year. One of the girls at the office where I worked had introduced us shortly after I moved to the city, and we'd been seeing each other once or twice a week ever since. What we had going was just a friendly relationship—or, rather, a one-sided romance. Lloyd had asked me to marry him, but I'd turned him down, explaining as kindly as I could that while I enjoyed his company immensely and thought the world of him as a friend, what I felt for him was fondness, not love.

Lloyd was attractive in a boyish way, and his eyes were steady and sincere. He was dependable and a gentleman, the type my mother would have called "the salt of the earth." For some girl, he would make an ideal husband. But not for me. When he kissed me, his kisses were pleasant enough, but pleasant wasn't what I wanted. What I longed for was a wild, flaming love that would set my blood on fire, thrill me to my toes, and send me rocketing off to the stars. With Lloyd, the magic just wasn't there.

That was a wonderful time in my life. I was twenty-two and reveling in my independence and the freedom to come and go as I chose. I had my own cozy little apartment, a job I liked, and a used car that wheezed a bit with age, but generally got me where I wanted to go. I was caught up in a busy social life and loving every minute of it. Having been raised in a small town where my parents still lived, I was dazzled by the city—the bright lights and bustle and the many diversions it offered.

There was only one thing lacking—that special man. So far, he hadn't appeared on the scene, and I was beginning to wonder if he ever would. But I kept telling myself he had to be somewhere out there and that, if I just bided my time, sooner or later he would come along.

And, sure enough, one night he did—at a moment when I was least prepared for it. The last place I expected to find him was at that cocktail party, which I assumed would be composed mostly of stuffy older men.

Lloyd and I were a little late in arriving, and the

room was already filled when we walked in. Lloyd's boss, after welcoming us, supplied us with drinks, and we spent the next few minutes talking with him and his wife. Then Lloyd, who knew most of the guests, began introducing me around, and we wandered from group to group, joining in the chatter and laughter.

We'd been there for an hour or so and were standing with several other couples, exchanging jokes and banter, when I heard our host say, "Hi, Rick, glad to see you finally made it," and I heard a deep voice answer, "Sorry for the delay, but better late than never." Looking around, I saw a new arrival come in the door. The man's head was turned partly away from me, and I scarcely paid attention to him. Lloyd, at my side, was in the midst of telling an amusing story, and I tuned into the conversation again.

Lloyd, having finished his story, went off to freshen his drink. I drifted over to the window and stood for a moment looking out at the gathering dusk of the soft summer evening. All at once, a funny little feeling ran through me, and sensing that I was being watched, I turned to glance about and spotted the man who'd arrived late. He was standing across the room, one elbow propped on the bar, his gaze fixed intently on me. As our eyes met and held, my breath caught, and I felt my pulse quicken. He was extremely handsome, but more than his looks, what rocked me was the jolt of instant attraction that passed between us as we stared at each other.

*There he is,* I thought with a flutter of my heart. *He's the one.* It was crazy. I knew nothing about the man beyond the fact that his name was Rick, yet I'd never felt more sure of anything in my life.

Slowly, he started toward me. As he drew near, I stood transfixed, barely breathing. In that rapt, suspended moment, everything else faded away. I was conscious of the man approaching. I knew, with a simple certainty, that this was the beginning.

Lloyd intercepted him midway, breaking the spell. "Hello there, Rick, good to see you," I heard him say as he clapped a hand on Rick's shoulder. Briefly, they fell to talking, and then Lloyd introduced us.

"I don't believe you two have met," he said. "Rick Tarone, Kim Sloane."

Again, Rick's gaze held mine, and for a swift, breathless moment, I saw something potent and burning flicker in his eyes. In the next instant it vanished as he glanced from me to Lloyd and back to me. He frowned slightly, and I could see he'd drawn a conclusion.

"Nice meeting you," he murmured, his voice neutral, and we nodded politely at each other.

For a while, the three of us stood there making small talk. Then two other couples joined us, and Rick strayed off to another part of the room. I watched his retreating back, and then turned to Lloyd.

"What kind of work does Rick do?" I asked.

"He's an architect," Lloyd told me. "He's been drawing up the plans for some of our company projects. That's how I came to know him."

"I see," I said, catching sight of Rick through the crowd as he moved from one group of people to another. I was dying to ask a million more questions about him, but didn't know how to put them without appearing too obvious, and since Lloyd offered nothing further, I had no choice but to let the subject drop.

Lloyd became absorbed in a discussion with another man, and I turned away and began circulating on my own. By then, the party was in full swing, and with so many people milling around, I caught only occasional glimpses of Rick. Although our paths never seemed to cross, I was keenly aware of his presence, and I couldn't keep my eyes from roaming about, seeking him out. Once or twice, I glanced up to find him looking in my direction, and I began to wonder if that magical moment we'd shared had been real, or if I'd only imagined it. Maybe it had all been wishful thinking, my own private little fantasy, and nothing was going to come of it.

I grew more and more discouraged as the evening wore on and Rick continued to keep his distance. Then, suddenly, when I was standing at the edge of the crowd, momentarily alone, he appeared at my side.

"This thing between you and Lloyd—is it serious?" he asked abruptly.

His unexpected approach took me so by surprise that a few seconds passed before I could reply. Then I said, "We're friends—nothing more."

"Can we go someplace and talk?" he asked. "There's a garden out back. It will be quiet there."

I nodded, my heart soaring, and we went out the door.

As we rounded the side of the house to the back, the din of babbling voices and loud laughter receded, and the night took on a soft enchantment, heightened by the moonlit garden and the fragrance of roses scenting the air. We walked along, neither of us speaking. I think we both knew something important was happening. At the far end of the path, we came upon a wooden bench that was sheltered by beautiful trailing wisteria. There we sat, only inches apart, our shoulders almost touching. I was vividly conscious of his nearness and of being all alone with him. I looked at him out of the corner of my eye, marking the contours of his features. In the silence, the very air seemed alive with something vibrant.

Rick leaned toward me a little, his hand moving as if to take mine, then hesitated. "Kim," he began softly.

"Kim?" came a louder voice from around the side of the house. "Kim, are you out there?"

My heart plunged. *Oh, no,* I thought, *not Lloyd—not now, of all times.* I sat up straighter, peering into the darkness as the faint sound of footsteps reached my ears.

"Kim?" Lloyd called again, and I could see his form at the opposite end of the garden.

"Yes, I'm coming," I called back. I cast a helpless look at Rick and stood up.

He caught my wrist. "I'll see you again?" he asked, his voice low and urgent. "Are you listed in the phone book?"

"Yes," I whispered. "It's under—"

"I know, under Sloane," he said. "Kim Sloane. I remember."

He released my wrist, and I turned away and walked to where Lloyd stood waiting.

"What were you doing out here?" he wanted to know as we headed back inside.

"Just getting a breath of fresh air," I told him. "It was so warm in there."

"Well, I've been looking all over for you," he complained, a bit crossly. "The party's breaking up. Are you ready to go?"

"I'm ready," I said, glad we were leaving. I really wasn't in the mood for any more partying. All I wanted to do was go home and be alone to think about Rick.

The next day was Sunday, and I woke up in a euphoric glow, filled with a delicious sense of anticipation. Dreamily, I lay there replaying the events of the previous evening, remembering Rick's face and his voice and the feel of his warm, firm hand on my wrist. Then I got up, put on some clothes, and went into the kitchen to get breakfast out of the way. I was sure I'd hear from Rick shortly, and I wanted to be prepared for whatever he might suggest.

All afternoon, as I fiddled around the apartment, I was in a good mood, expecting the phone to ring at any moment. But the hours passed with no word from Rick, and by evening my spirits were dragging. I'd been so sure he would call that his failure to do so was a real letdown, and I could scarcely contain my disappointment. But I comforted myself with the thought that he'd probably already made plans for the evening and would get in touch with me as soon as he had some free time.

For the next five days, I hurried home from work each night and spent the evening hovering near the phone, willing it to ring. Several times it did, but the right voice was never on the other end of the line. Mostly, it was Lloyd, asking me to go out with him. I kept turning him down, wanting to keep myself available for Rick in case he called—refusing to give up hope.

But the days went by with still no sign of Rick, and by the time Sunday rolled around again, my hopes were all but gone. Apparently what had passed between us hadn't made a lasting impression on him, but had been no more than a brief attraction, a fleeting thing that had faded with the dawn. A dismal feeling that I would never see him again descended on me, and I spent a dreary day, too gloomy to accomplish much of anything.

The phone rang late in the afternoon, and listlessly I went to answer.

"Kim?"

At the sound of that deep, rich voice, my heart turned over. It was his voice.

"Oh, hello," I breathed, my whole body suddenly weak with relief and joy. Then, realizing I was coming on like a lovesick teenager, I began again in a more mature tone. "Yes, this is Kim."

There was a pause, and then he gave a low chuckle. "I liked it better the way you said it the first time."

I laughed, too, a little nervously, and again there was a pause. Then Rick asked, "I know this is pretty short notice, but can I take you out to dinner tonight? Dinner and dancing?"

"I'd love it!" I said, a warm ribbon of happiness flowing through me.

"Wonderful! I'll be by to pick you up in a couple of hours. Say, around six. Or is that too early?"

"That will be fine," I told him. *It can't be too early for me,* I added silently, so excited at the prospect of seeing him again that I could hardly wait.

## LOVING A MARRIED MAN

For all my glowing excitement, though, when Rick rang my doorbell that evening, I knew a moment of panic. *What if he wasn't as pleased with me on this second meeting as he'd been on the first? What if I fell short of his expectations and the whole thing ended up just fizzling out?* My stomach gave a nervous flutter as I opened the door.

But as soon as he stepped inside, I knew it would be all right. "You look lovely, as lovely as I remember," he murmured, his gaze lingering on my features like a soft caress, and again I felt something strong and compelling flow between us. Never had I been so drawn to anyone as I was to him.

Rick drove us several miles out of the city to a nightclub that had a hushed, intimate atmosphere, excellent food, and a dance floor that overlooked a marina. Dancing with him was sheer heaven, and as we glided over the floor, swaying in time to the dreamy music, I gloried in the feel of his arms about me and of his warm, solid body so close to mine. We did a considerable amount of dancing, but not much talking. It was enough for me that we were together, and it seemed to be enough for him, too.

Once, we wandered out onto the pier and stood watching the moonlight shimmering across the water and the boats bobbing gently up and down. As the faint strains of a sad love song drifted out, Rick's arms encircled my waist and we began a slow dance, our feet barely moving. In the dusky stillness, his cheek pressed to mine, he whispered: "Where did you come from, Kim? Are you real or only a fantasy out of my dreams?"

For me, too, it was all like a fantasy, a dream

come true. Right out of a storybook.

When we arrived back at my apartment, Rick took the key from my hand and unlocked the door for me. Bending down, he lightly touched his lips to mine. "I'll call you," he said. Then he was gone.

It wasn't the impassioned kiss I'd been expecting, but that was probably just as well. As keyed up as I already was, I probably couldn't have handled any more excitement that night, and Rick must have felt the same, because his kiss was so brief that it really held more promise than substance.

A whole week went by before I heard from Rick again, but this time I wasn't worried. He'd said he would call, and after the enchanted evening we'd shared, I knew he would. And he did, the following Sunday.

Again, we drove out of the city and had dinner in a cozy little restaurant that featured hanging plants and flickering candles. This time, unlike the previous Sunday, we did a lot of talking. Rick told me about his job as an architect, speaking of it with such enthusiasm that I could see how committed he was to his work. He said he put in long hours, hoping to build up enough capital to strike out on his own and maybe make a name for himself someday. He asked me about my job, and I told him I worked in the office of a sporting-goods outlet as a secretary. We talked on and on, scarcely noticing the passage of time.

That night, when Rick took me home, his kiss was far more than a promise. It was a deep, throbbing, fiery kiss that left me breathless and almost too weak to stand. I floated off to bed in a daze, tingling all over. I knew that for the one and only time in my life, I was in love.

I hoped I wouldn't have to wait another week to see Rick again and was afraid I would, what with all the overtime he'd said he was putting in on his job. But he surprised me by calling on Tuesday night around eight.

"I just got through working, and I'm in the mood for pizza and wine," he said. "How about if I bring some over? Have you eaten yet?"

"Yes, I have," I told him, and then added hastily, "but don't let that stop you."

"It won't," he said, laughing. "See you in a little while." He arrived a short time later with a huge flat box and a chilled bottle of wine. We sat at the kitchen table while Rick feasted on pizza and I nibbled at a slice and discreetly feasted my eyes on his face as we talked. Then we carried our wine into the living room and settled down on the sofa. I was in a rosy glow from the wine and from his intoxicating nearness, and when he pulled me into his arms and closed his lips on mine, I went weak. At first, his kiss was light and tentative, and then it deepened and grew more probing.

"Kim?" he whispered thickly, his breath warm against my cheek.

"Yes," I whispered back, swept away by a storm of need and desire.

He picked me up and carried me into the bedroom, and the lovemaking we shared was so beautiful it made me want to cry.

Afterward, wrapped in his arms, I lay listening to the sound of his breathing and waiting for him to say those three words I longed to hear. When he didn't, unable to help myself, I burst out, "Oh, Rick, I love you!"

He shifted slightly, cupped my cheek in his hand, and then, with a little groan, pulled me even closer. "I love you, too," he said, his voice husky with feeling, and I knew he meant it.

I hoped he would stay all night, but when I suggested it, he declined, saying he had a busy day ahead and that if he woke up beside me, he might not make it in to work at all. He rolled off the bed, got dressed, and gave me one last, lingering kiss good night. "Till next time," he murmured against my lips and went out the door.

In the days that followed, thoughts of Rick filled my every waking moment. Never before had I felt so totally alive. Everything in my world took on a richer hue. It was as if Rick had found a part of me that I hadn't even known was there.

If I could have had my way, I would have spent every night of the week with him, but his heavy workload not only left him little time for leisure, it prevented him from making plans in advance. So I did the next best thing. I curtailed my social life to almost nothing and stayed home evenings to make sure I wouldn't miss a chance to see him. When Lloyd called, asking for a date, I said I was busy. Then, since there didn't seem to be any way to let him down easy, I had to just say it straight out—that somebody new had come into my life and I wouldn't be seeing him anymore.

"I'm sorry, Lloyd," I told him, meaning it. I knew I was hurting him and hated to do it, but I couldn't bear the thought of going out with another man when I wanted only to be with Rick. Lloyd was silent for a long moment. Then he mumbled a stiff goodbye and hung up.

The rest of the week passed with no word from Rick, and time just dragged. He finally phoned on Sunday evening.

"I'd like to drop by in a little while, if that's all right with you," he said.

"It's more than all right," I told him, filled with joy, as always, at the sound of his voice.

But my joy didn't last long. The moment I opened the door to his knock, I sensed that something was wrong. He stepped inside with a somber look on his face and kissed me almost absently, then walked to the window and stood gazing out, his head lowered as if weighed down by some big problem. Feeling a twinge of apprehension, I was about to ask what was troubling him when he turned and came over to put his hands on my shoulders.

"Kim," he said quietly, "there's something I have to tell you. I'm married."

At those words I stood absolutely still, saying nothing. The room suddenly seemed to grow too warm, then icy cold.

"I'm sorry, Kim. I should have told you before," he said. "I started to, that night in the garden. . . .I was going to tell you how it was with me. But then Lloyd interrupted, and after that I lost my courage. I was afraid that if you knew, you wouldn't let me see you again."

Feeling sick inside, I made a move to pull away, but he tightened his grasp on my shoulders, holding me fast. "Kim, listen to me," he pleaded. "I know what you're thinking, but you're wrong. I'm not just out for a fling. I told you that I love you, and I do—so much it almost scares me. The moment I first laid eyes on you, something hit me. I've never felt this way about anyone before."

"But you're married," I said dully.

He sighed. "A piece of paper says I am, but the meaning went out of our marriage a long time ago. We've been going our separate ways for years."

"Then why do you stay married?" I asked.

"Because of the kids. We've got two boys. Michael's almost eleven, and Bud just turned eight. We're sticking it out until they're older and a divorce won't be such a traumatic thing for them. But there will be a divorce," he said positively. "And when that time comes"—he paused, his eyes searching mine—"well, I just hope you'll be there waiting, Kim."

His face wore such an anxious, hopeful look that I felt my resistance crumbling, and a rush of the desperate, aching love I felt for him flooded my heart.

"Oh, Rick!" I moaned, and he knew it was surrender. He gathered me into his arms, and I trembled and buried my face in his neck, holding him tight, wanting never to let him go.

I had to let him go, though, time and again. Whenever he came to see me, which was as often as he could—but never often enough for me—I savored each precious moment we shared. But, always, there was that painful parting at the end of the evening, followed by another long, lonely interval of waiting, waiting until we could be together again.

As the weeks and months went by, my love for him grew deeper and more consuming. Rick was so sweet to me in so many ways. Often, when I reached my office in the morning, he would call me just to say hello.

"I wanted to start my day off right by hearing your voice," he'd tell me. And he almost never came to see me without bringing some thoughtful little gift. Once, knowing I adored anchovies, he showed up with a dozen tins of the kind I liked best, with capers. And when he found that I was driving around on tires that were nearly bald, he bought a whole new set for my car and refused to let me pay for them.

"I'm really doing it for myself," he told me, planting a kiss on the top of my nose. "I want to keep my girl safe from harm." I felt infinitely cherished, and I could hardly wait for the day to come when I would join my life with his and be truly a part of him, instead of having to make do with seeing him only a few times a week, in hurried hours together.

How I hoped and prayed that day wouldn't be too slow in coming! I just wished Rick would give me something definite to go on, but he didn't, and I hesitated to ask, afraid he'd think I was hassling him. But the uncertainty was getting to me, and I knew that sooner or later I would have to pin him down, find out how much of a wait we were in for.

Then one night Rick supplied the information on his own.

I was lying on my bed after we'd made love, and Rick was getting dressed, preparing to leave. As I watched him fasten his belt, I felt the familiar pang of parting, and a small sigh escaped me. Reading my thoughts, he came to sit beside me on the edge of the bed and gave my hand a reassuring squeeze.

"It won't always be like this, sweetheart," he said gently. "One of these days, our time will come. As soon as the boys are through high school, I'll go ahead with the divorce. Then it'll be you and me all the way."

I sat bolt upright. "Through high school!" I echoed, staring at him, aghast. "Rick! You told me Bud is only eight. That means ten more years!"

Rick's eyes clouded. "I know it seems like a long time, but . . ."

"It's an eternity!" I cried in dismay. "Oh, Rick, surely the boys will be mature enough to handle the divorce sooner than that. Surely in another year or two . . ."

"No!" It came out with such force that I jumped. Rick got to his feet and began pacing the floor. "I won't do that to my boys," he said fiercely, and I could see how agitated he was. "I won't do to them what was done to me. My parents split up when I was nine, and my whole world caved in. It was like having the ground drop right out from under me. I lost my sense of security—I couldn't see anything left to trust. It took me years to get over it." He stopped pacing and frowned at the floor. Then he looked at me with a slow shake of his head. "I can't let that happen to my boys," he said miserably. "I just can't."

My mind reeling, I said nothing. I could understand the concern he felt for his boys, knowing how fond he was of them and what a dedicated father he was. But ten years!

He came to sit beside me again. "Don't think I don't know what I'm asking of you, Kim," he said, taking my hand in both of his. "It's an awful lot, I know that. And I wouldn't ask it if I didn't think we had something special together, something worth waiting for." He lifted my hand and put it against his cheek. Then a shadow seemed to pass across his face, and he frowned. "I guess it's horribly selfish and unfair of me to want to keep holding on to you when there's so little I have to offer you for now," he said unhappily. "But I can't help it. I never knew it was possible to love a woman as much as I love you."

His eyes made an appeal that made my heart turn over. With a small, strangled cry, I went into his arms, knowing that, no matter what, I was committed to him, body and soul. I simply wasn't capable of saying good-bye, of facing the desolate place my world would be without him. Loving him as totally and passionately as I did, I was left with no choice but to wait for him for however long it might be—until the end of my days, if necessary.

He cradled me close. "Honey, it won't be so bad, I promise," he murmured, stroking my hair. "I'll find ways to be with you more often, and we can go off on a weekend trip every now and then. The time will pass more quickly than you think, you'll see."

I had little hope of that. I knew those ten years were going to seem more like fifty and that there would be endless hours of waiting in between his visits. But, mercifully, there weren't as many of them as before. Rick, true to his word, arranged things so that we could have more time together. He came to see me each Tuesday and Thursday evening, and sometimes on Sunday. Sunday was his family day, and he always devoted the afternoon to his boys, playing with them or taking them places. Then later, if he could manage to duck out of the house, he would come to spend the evening with me.

And every so often we would slip away for a weekend together. Mostly, we would just drive, with no particular destination in mind, stopping whenever and wherever we chose, spending the night in a motel. How I treasured those golden hours—having him all to myself for two full days, drifting off to sleep in his arms, waking up beside him in the mornings—it was pure bliss. And how I hated it when the weekend was over. Yet I believed that some sweet day, we would come to the end of our partings and be together forever.

I centered my whole life around Rick, going all out to make things pleasant and comfortable for him when he was with me. I knew his life at home couldn't be too great, caught as he was in a loveless marriage, and I tried to make up for it by creating a cozy, inviting place for him.

Rick never failed to appreciate the efforts I put forth to please him.

"I love coming here," he would say, sighing contently as we snuggled on the sofa. "This is my real home. You're the one I really feel married to."

I felt married to him, too—but only when we were together and I could see him and touch him and feel secure in his love. In his absence, my comforting sense of unity with him ebbed away, and there were dark moments when the silence of my apartment was so oppressive I thought I would drown in it. I kept telling myself I was no worse off than wives whose husbands were salesmen. They often had to do without their husbands for a week or more at a stretch. But that was poor comfort when the solitude of my nights apart from Rick came crowding in on me, reminding me that although we were married in spirit, we weren't in fact, and wouldn't be for a long, long time to come.

Still, for the most part, I was fairly happy and content, knowing I could count on seeing him at least two evenings a week. Fall faded into winter, bringing chill rains, and then snow, and after contending with the raw weather and slushy streets, I was glad to get home at night and didn't mind quite so much spending most of my evenings alone. And when Rick and I were together, it was cozier than ever in my apartment, with the wind and sleet battering the windows and the two of us warm and snug inside.

It was during the holiday season—Thanksgiving and Christmas—that I missed him the most. He had to spend the time with his family, of course, so I went to be with my parents on both occasions. It wasn't the same as being with Rick, but at least it took the edge off my loneliness.

The winter months crawled by, dark and dreary. Then, seemingly overnight, it was spring, and then June and the end of school. Both Michael and Bud brought home excellent report cards and would be advancing to the next grade in the fall. Rick told me this with pride, and I was relieved to hear it. It meant that Rick and I had hurdled the first obstacle—one year of waiting was over. I didn't let myself dwell on the long wait that still lay ahead—that would have been too depressing. So I looked backward instead of forward, fixing my sights on the year that had passed, not on the nine that were yet to come.

That summer, Rick began talking about our taking a week's vacation together. He said he'd figured out a way he could swing it. His wife had wanted to visit her parents, who lived a few hundred miles away. He would drive her and the boys there, then leave, with the excuse of having to attend an out-of-state seminar. He would then come back for me, and we would take off to wherever we pleased, not returning until it was time for him to take his family back home.

I was ecstatic at the prospect of spending an entire, uninterrupted week with Rick—it would be nothing short of paradise. Excitedly, I went on a clothes-buying spree and spent hours looking at travel brochures, all the while keeping my fingers crossed that nothing would happen to ruin our plans. It all seemed just too good to be true.

And that's the way it turned out—too good to be true. In July, Bud broke his leg falling out of a tree, and Rick didn't have the heart to go off and leave him stuck at home, hobbling around on crutches and a cast. So he devoted his vacation to keeping the boy entertained, and there went our trip. I was crushed, but Rick promised that we would go the following summer for sure, and that took a little of the sting out of my disappointment. At least it gave me something to look forward to.

But the next year our plans again fell through. Rick's wife came up with the idea of taking the boys to Europe, and Rick, unable to think of a plausible reason for refusing, had to go along with it. So it wasn't until another year had passed that we were finally able to get away.

We went to a beach resort and spent six glorious days just playing and being lazy, splashing in the surf like a couple of kids, sunbathing on the beach, having late, leisurely dinners on the terrace, taking strolls along the water's edge. One night in our room, when I was brushing my hair, Rick came up behind me and bent down to wrap his arms around my shoulders.

"We could be shipwrecked on a desert island for the rest of our lives, and I'd never grow tired of being with you," he murmured, resting his chin on top of my head. As I viewed our two images in the mirror, Rick's face above mine, his gaze tender in the lamp's mellow glow, I thought how good—how right—we looked together. I leaned back against him.

"That's because we were meant for each other," I said softly, and he nodded gravely.

All too soon our trip was over and it was time to return to the city. Once home again, I found I was no longer quite so content to go on as before, seeing Rick just now and then when I yearned to be with him each and every day. I was getting tired of counting the months and years that still had to pass before he would be truly mine, living only half a life while I waited and waited. Having tasted that delicious little slice of unbroken togetherness made me hungrier than ever to have him all to myself, and the thought of waiting for seven more years was almost more than I could stand. I began falling into spells of restlessness and depression that grew more and more pronounced as time went by.

And there was another disturbing thought that kept nagging at me. Rick and his wife were the same age, I knew—they'd gone to high school together and had married right after graduation. She, like Rick, was thirty-two. In another seven years, she would be thirty-nine, crowding forty. At that age, she might be unwilling to disrupt a lifestyle she'd grown accustomed to and refuse to grant him a divorce. The thought sent a chill to my heart, but when I voiced my fears to Rick, he assured me there was no cause for concern.

"I don't anticipate any problems on that score," he said. "She doesn't want me any more than I want her, so don't worry about it, honey."

I did worry, though, because, despite all his confident words, he couldn't absolutely guarantee that his wife would go through with the divorce. Even though she no longer wanted him, she might want to keep him around to avoid the inconvenience of maintaining a household without a husband. It wouldn't be the first time a woman had held onto a husband she'd stopped loving for the sake of preserving her marital status. I was dreadfully afraid that Rick's wife would make that choice. What bitter irony it would be if, after waiting so long, I ended up having no more of him than the little I already did.

That anxiety kept eating at me, and the thought that I would have to go on living with it for another seven years made me more depressed than ever. Finally, I knew I would have to find some means of getting out of the despondent state I was in. Part of the problem, I realized, was that I stayed home too much at night. In the three years I'd been seeing Rick, I'd become a recluse, hardly ever going anywhere except to work each day, and I knew that, to keep from going crazy, I'd have to create a life for myself apart from him. I joined a bowling team and began having dinner occasionally with the women friends I still had.

The increased activity helped a little. At least it

got me out of the apartment more and gave me something to do. But nothing was much fun without Rick, and my heart wasn't really in any of it. It was just a way of killing time until I could be with him again. So, although I managed to keep myself fairly busy, my only moments of true happiness were the ones I spent with my lover.

A year went by in that fashion, and then another, and Rick and I reached the midway point—five years down and five to go. By then, I was twenty-seven and very conscious of the fact that I was nearing thirty with nothing much to show for my life. To make me even more conscious of it, one day as I was walking along a downtown street, I ran into Lloyd. I hadn't seen him in ages, not since I'd broken off our relationship, and at first I felt awkward, wondering if he still had bad feelings about me. But he greeted me in a friendly manner, with no trace of ill will, and we stopped to chat for a moment. Lloyd asked what was new with me, and I just shrugged. Then I asked what was new with him.

"Well, for one thing," he said, smiling broadly, "I'm getting married in a couple of months."

"Oh, are you? Lloyd, that's wonderful!" I cried, genuinely happy for him. But when he turned to leave, walking off with a breezy wave of his hand, I felt filled with envy and frustration. His news had brought a jarring reminder that the years were slipping by, that the rest of the world was moving onward while I stood still.

Rick had once said, "The time will pass more quickly than you think, you'll see." How wrong he had been. For me, the time had dragged, and would go on dragging for another five years.

## LOVING A MARRIED MAN

That thought was weighing on my mind the afternoon Rick and I took a stroll through the park. We
were spending Sunday together, which we'd been
doing more and more often lately, now that his boys
were in their teens and engrossed in their own pur-
suits. It was a lovely fall day, and as we wove our
way through the woods, I looked about apprecia-
tively at the leaves ablaze with brilliant crimsons and
golds. But my enjoyment was tinged with melan-
choly as I reflected that winter would soon be
here—another long, gray winter to be endured, with
four more to follow. I sighed, and Rick gave me a
questioning look.

"You're awfully quiet today, honey," he said. "Is
something bothering you?"

I gave him a faint smile. "Tell me again how quickly the time is passing," I said wryly. "I keep forgetting."

His face clouded over. He rested his foot on a fall-
en tree and was silent for a moment. Then he said,
"I feel so guilty. You miss out on so many things
because of me. This isn't much of a life for you, is it
honey?"

I couldn't deny the truth of his words, so I said
simply, "I love you, Rick."

He took my hand. "I know," he said softly. "And I
know how rough it is on you, having to wait so long
for us to be married. But I promise I'll make it all up
to you when our time comes."

I looked away. "If and when," I mumbled.

Rick sat down on a log and pulled me down
beside him. "You're still worried about the divorce,
aren't you?" he asked. "Kim, there's nothing for you
to worry about, believe me. You have all of my

heart, now and forever, and there's no way I'll go on living the rest of my life without you. There will be a divorce, and that you can count on."

He spoke with a solemn conviction that got rid of doubts, and from then on, I was able to rest assured that we really would have a future together. But that shimmering future was still a long way off, and I was so tired of waiting that sometimes I thought I would die. Just to add a little variety to my life, I quit my job at the sporting-goods outlet and went to work at an engineering firm. There was no real advantage in it—the pay was about the same—but at least it gave me a change of scene. Other than that, the year passed uneventfully, as did the next.

During the following year, Rick struck out on his own and became an independent architect. Since he was known throughout the construction trade and had established a good reputation, he was busy right off. It was an exciting time for him, and for me, too, because I got to see more of him. Often, when he visited an out-of-town project site, he would stay over the weekend, and I would join him there for two days.

Those extra days together helped to speed the passage of time, and before I knew it, two more years had melted away. When the next summer came, Rick's son, Bud, finished his junior year in high school. Michael, Rick's oldest, was already attending the state university, and in another year, Bud would be going off to college. So finally, miraculously, incredibly—Rick and I were on the homestretch, with just twelve months left to go. At long last, the end of all the dreary waiting was almost over, and I could let myself look ahead to the start of our new life together and believe in the reality of it. I was elated, and so was Rick.

"Tell me what kind of house you'd like and I'll design it for you," he declared one night, dancing me around my living room. "I'll build you a mansion, a palace, whatever you want."

"A cottage will do just fine," I told him happily. "As long as I'm sharing it with you."

We began planning where we would build our home and where we would go on our honeymoon, and I went about in a fever of joy and anticipation. Now that the long-awaited day was drawing near, time seemed to crawl, and summer passed into fall, then into winter with maddening slowness. The holidays came, and again we had to spend them apart—Rick with his family and me with my parents—but for once I didn't mind so much, since it would be for the last time.

The new year got off to a bad start. During the first week of January, I saw Rick only once. He dropped by the apartment one evening looking tired and tense, and when I commented on it, he said he was under a lot of pressure at work. I served him a glass of wine to help him relax, but it didn't seem to have much of a soothing effect, and after a short time he left.

Then two weeks went by without my seeing him at all. He called once or twice, but just to say hello and to tell me he was still swamped with work and didn't know when his next free evening would be. When he finally showed up again, he stayed for just a few minutes, and then hurried off, saying he had to get back to work.

February went pretty much the way of January,

with Rick putting in long hours on his job and seeing me only occasionally. He looked increasingly tired and strained as time went by, and on the few evenings he managed to spend with me, he was moody and preoccupied, with scarcely anything to say. I was getting really worried about him, afraid he was wearing himself out by taking on too many projects at once. But when I protested one night that he was driving himself too hard, he gave an impatient shake of his head and said, "No, work isn't the problem," and changed the subject. When I tried to bring it up again, asking what was the problem, he mumbled an inaudible reply. Before I could say anything more, he looked at his watch, said he had to be on his way, and went out the door.

That was the first hint I'd had that something other than business was weighing on his mind. Yet, in thinking it over, I could see that the signs had been there all along, signs I should have recognized weeks ago. Knowing that Rick loved what he was doing and thrived on hard work, I should have guessed that his job wasn't the source of his low spirits. And I'd seen so little of him lately—that, too, should have told me that something was wrong. Never before, even at his busiest, had he made himself so scarce. It all added up to some kind of trouble brewing, and whatever it was, I knew it had to be serious; otherwise Rick, usually so open, wouldn't be keeping it hidden from me.

At that realization, I had a sense of impending doom, and it was then that an old fear came back to haunt me—the fear that Rick's wife had no intention of ever setting him free. That would account for his behavior. And now, burdened with the bitter knowledge that our long wait had been in vain, that the shining future he'd been promising me for years was nothing more than a mirage, he was finding it hard to face me. It was the only reason I could come up with to explain why he'd been avoiding me, and my heart grew faint at the thought. Then I reminded myself that I was just guessing, that I could very well be wrong, that whatever was troubling Rick might have nothing at all to do with us. But a fearful little voice inside of me kept insisting I was right, and a chill went through my body.

I lived with that anxiety for a week. Rick didn't come by, or even call, and I was growing more apprehensive each day. I tried to calm my jumpy nerves by remembering that Rick had once said, "There's no way I'll go on living the rest of my life without you." I hugged those words to me, telling myself repeatedly that I should have more faith in him, trust him to find a means of persuading his wife to grant him a divorce. But his prolonged silence seemed like a bad omen to me, and I couldn't still my doubts and fears.

It was on a raw, blustery evening in March that Rick finally appeared at my doorstep. By then, I was worried sick, and his manner as he came inside was anything but reassuring. Wearing a solemn look, he greeted me with only a slight nod, and then crossed to the window to lean against its frame and stare out into the dark. As I watched him from the center of the room, my mind flew back to the night, so many years ago, when he'd stood in that same spot, in that same way, just before breaking the news that he was married. I knew with chilling certainty that what he was about to tell me would be equally bad—that there would be no divorce, that we would have to go on as before, snatching our stolen moments here and there, with no real life together, ever. I waited with half a breath as the silence stretched out unbearably.

Finally, he turned to look at me, his eyes bleak. "Kim, I don't know how to tell you this . . ." he began, then stopped and swallowed visibly. "I don't—I can't . . ." he tried once more, and again his voice trailed off. Then, all in a rush, he said, "There's somebody else."

That was so unexpected that at first it hardly registered. "Somebody else?" I repeated blankly. Then his words sank in, and shock waves rocked through me. "What are you saying?" I gasped. "Are you telling me you no longer want me, that you don't love me anymore?"

Rick took a step toward me. "I still care for you, Kim," he said gently. "I guess a part of me always will." He made a helpless gesture with his hands. "But—"

"But not enough to marry me," I finished for him, my voice thin and hollow.

He let silence be his answer.

A trembling started inside me. "You can't mean what you're saying!" I cried. "You can't mean we're through, after all we've been to each other, all we've shared, Rick! I've waited ten years for you. Ten whole years!"

"I know," he broke in. "Don't you think I know that? Kim, I feel so rotten, like the worst kind of heel." Pausing, he cast an anguished look at me, and then said in a lowered tone, "I never thought a thing like this would happen. I don't know why it did.

Maybe it just went on too long with us. I guess it just wore itself out." He passed a hand across his brow. "I'm so sorry, Kim. I know that doesn't help much, but I can't tell you how sorry I am."

As I stood there listening to him apologize for shattering my life, a dull roaring began in my head. "Rick, you'd better get out of here," I said through stiff lips, suddenly feeling a desperate need to be alone. "Just leave. Now."

He opened his mouth as if to speak, but apparently realizing there was nothing more to say, he sighed instead and walked to the door. "I'm sorry," he murmured once again. I stood perfectly still, my back toward him, not answering. He left then, closing the door quietly behind him.

I can't remember what I did the rest of that evening, or if I did anything at all. I can't even recall feeling much of anything, other than a stunned disbelief that Rick was no longer a part of my life. It all seemed unreal, like a nightmare, and I felt only an emptiness, as if my every emotion had drained away, leaving nothing but a big hollow inside. Eventually, I went to bed, and to sleep. I think I just blacked out, welcoming a blessed, dark oblivion.

I was still in that strange, unfeeling state when I awoke the next morning. I got up and, except for skipping breakfast, followed my usual routine—showered, dressed, and drove off to work. The day seemed to pass in slow motion, and I moved through it in a kind of haze, functioning mechanically, scarcely aware of my surroundings.

It was when I walked into my apartment that evening that the shock wore off and the enormity of what had happened hit me. At the thought that Rick would never again come knocking on my door, that I would never again feel his arms about me or his lips on mine, a suffocating weight lodged in my chest, and my whole body began to shake. It was the most dreadful night of my life. I paced endlessly from room to room, swamped in a sea of pain that gave me no rest. I could hardly stand the way I felt, could hardly endure drawing breath, being alive. There was no point in going to bed—sleep was out of the question—and I just kept pacing the interminable hours away, too upset to settle in any one spot.

Toward dawn, my legs finally gave out on me, and I sank down onto the sofa in an exhausted heap. As I sat staring out the window, watching the pale gray morning light soften the sky, my dulled mind cleared enough to remember something Rick had said the night before: "I still care for you, Kim. I guess a part of me always will." With a small hope sprouting in me that was born of desperation, I seized on those words, telling myself that surely all was not lost. Surely the bond of love and closeness we'd formed through the years was too strong to be broken. Surely that "somebody else" who'd come into his life was just a passing fancy that he would soon get out of his system. And once he did, he'd realize that I was his one true love, that nobody could take my place in his heart, and he'd come back to me.

I pushed myself up from the sofa, my stomach sick from lack of food and a sleepless night, my legs stiff and sore from all the pacing I'd done. The sun was just peeping over the horizon, heralding the start of a new day, and I wondered bleakly how I would ever survive it, and the many others I would have to face without Rick. "But it won't be like this forever," I told myself firmly, saying the words aloud. "Just until Rick comes to his senses and sees what a terrible mistake he's made. Then he'll come back to me."

That thought was what sustained me in the stark and empty place my world had become with no love there to give it meaning. As day followed dreary day, it was all that kept me going. It was my hope, my prayer, and my strength, and I kept clinging to it sadly.

I went on like that for six months, until, sitting at the kitchen table one Saturday morning, I opened the paper to the society page and came upon Rick's picture. A woman stood beside him, and in the caption beneath, my eye caught the word "newly-weds."

I read no further. The paper slipped from my fingers and fell to the floor at my feet. Later, much later, when I could summon the will to move, I kicked it into a corner, and there it lay all day, like some poisonous thing that I couldn't bring myself to touch, or even go near.

Finally, that evening, driven by a gnawing curiosity, a kind of morbid fascination, I gathered it up and studied the picture intently.

The woman standing beside Rick wasn't especially young—about my age—nor even very pretty. But as she stood close to her new husband, leaning her shoulder against the man I'd once called mine, her smile was radiant with happiness. Rick was smiling, too, gazing down at her in that tender, loving way I knew so well, and he, too, looked blissfully happy.

My fingers shaking, I twisted the paper into a wad and dropped it into the garbage. Then, retrieving it, I carried it outside and shoved it into the trash, away from sight and out of my life.

So now, after all the years of waiting, I am alone, and soon I will be thirty-three. That's not very old, to be sure, but the youthful bloom is gone, and so are my dreams and illusions.

As for Rick, he had it both ways. He had me for as long as he wanted me, and then, when somebody new came along, he replaced me with her. Yet, lost and forsaken as I feel, I can't really condemn him too much, for I know he truly did love me and had every intention of marrying me. In my less bitter moments, I can see that I have to accept my share of blame for not having acted more wisely. I should have known from the start that time was against me, that a ten-year wait was too risky, that with a married man there are no guarantees. I should have called it quits with us right after I learned he already had a wife and before he became such a central part of me that I couldn't do without him. Instead, I plunged in recklessly.

I'm slowly getting my life back together. I'm putting more into my job these days and working toward advancement in case it turns out that I have to settle for a career instead of marriage. I've also started dating a little. I hope that, in time, I will find someone to fill the empty place Rick left in my heart, but I'm no longer looking for a grand passion—a quiet, steady love will do. And he doesn't have to be gorgeous. Just an ordinary kind of guy who's decent and caring and there when I need him will be all right with me. But whatever else he might or might not be, I know one thing for sure—he will be single.                    THE END

# MY X-RATED FILM SHOCKED MY HUSBAND

I came awake slowly as Lenny turned toward me in his sleep, flinging an arm across me. Then I felt his warmth, and his hairy chest against my arm, and smelled his nice, masculine smell. Then I felt a warm stirring in the pit of my stomach. I nibbled at his ear, and then put my lips on his. Still half-asleep, his arms tightened around me as his lips responded to mine. Our bodies pressed together, and he began to touch me. Suddenly, he pushed me away and sat up abruptly.

"Hey, it's Saturday morning!" he exclaimed. "We gotta get moving. It's the kids' weekend with us."

I felt like a deflated balloon! "Darling, it's still early. You aren't due to pick them up until noon. There's plenty of time for love," I said, forcing lightness to my voice that I didn't feel. I tried to pull him down beside me again.

But he unwound my arms, threw his legs over the side of the bed, and stood up. "Donna, honey, we've got a million things to do—straighten the house, shop for snacks, and buy soda for Tiffany and Sam." He gave me a swat on the backside as he headed for the bathroom. "Come on, baby, up and at 'em."

He disappeared into the bathroom as I groaned and burrowed deeper into the bed. *Damn—damn—damn,* I thought. *Now our lovemaking was taking second place to his kids.* If only I'd known what I was getting into when I married a divorced man with two kids! *I'd probably have married him anyway,* I thought with a sigh, *because I love the guy so darned much.*

But this business about Tiffany and Sam spending every other weekend with us was beginning to put a strain on our not yet one-year-old marriage. It didn't have to be that way if Lenny weren't so paranoid about his kids. His guilt about the divorce and leaving the kids was like an albatross around his neck, even though his first wife, Carla, wanted it as much as, if not more than, he did.

Lenny emerged from the shower, nude, and I felt that tremor in the pit of my stomach again at the sight of him. He started pulling on shorts, saying, "What do you want to do, hon? Make breakfast while I dust and vacuum, or vice versa?" One thing about Lenny, he did believe in giving a working woman a hand with the chores.

I bit back the nasty words that were on the tip of my tongue—like what good would it do to clean the house because by the time the kids left Sunday night, the house would be a pigpen.

"You know I can't stand drinking your coffee," I said, reluctantly dragging my body off the bed. "I'll make breakfast."

# MY X-RATED FILM SHOCKED MY HUSBAND

"Good girl!" Pulling a knit shirt over his head, he gave me a quick kiss on the tip of my nose and headed for the vacuum.

*Be content for little favors,* I told myself, slipping into a robe. A kiss on the nose didn't compare with lovemaking, but on the weekends the kids came over I was lucky to get that.

Fifteen minutes later, Lenny slid into a chair opposite me at the kitchen table and started gulping his bacon and eggs as if he were competing in time trials.

"What's on the agenda for the weekend?" I asked, knowing as I did it would be so crammed full of "fun" for the children. We'd all be exhausted by Sunday night.

"I promised Tiffany I'd take her shopping for some clothes this afternoon. I talked to her on the phone yesterday, and the poor kid says she doesn't have a thing to wear."

"My God, Lenny," I said, my thin veneer of tolerance cracking. "You give Carla enough child support money so that a twelve-year-old girl shouldn't have to say that she has nothing to wear."

"Aw, come on, Donna, don't give me a hard time," he said with a sheepish look. "You know how rough it's been on the kids since Carla and I split. So, okay, I spoil them a little to make up for it. You can't begrudge them that."

*Oh, yes I can,* I wanted to cry, but I didn't. Lenny couldn't believe that the children weren't traumatized by the divorce. Sure, I know it's hard on kids when their parents separated, but Tiffany and Sam had learned in the almost two years since the divorce that they really had it made as far as their father was concerned. Tiffany, at twelve, could wrap him around her little finger, like the most experienced courtesan. And ten-year-old Sam had learned a few tricks, too, on how to get whatever he wanted from Lenny.

"Eat your eggs," I mumbled unable to stand the pleading look in Lenny's eyes.

"You'll come shopping with us, won't you? I don't know much about girls' clothing. You can give Tiffany advice on what to buy."

*And Tiffany won't give a hoot in hell about my advice and will pick just what she wants anyway,* I thought. I tried to wiggle out of the chore. "Wouldn't you, I mean, don't you think maybe you ought to go alone? The kids might have things to talk over with you, and they'll feel freer if I'm not around."

"Baby, you're family. Okay, so the kids aren't yours, but I want you in on everything, understand?"

I knew he was trying to be sweet, but that kind of sweetness I didn't need. Now this morning in bed— if he had made love to me that would have been sweet.

I remembered the lovemaking a few nights before. When Lenny touched me, I came alive with burning, hot sensations. Our passion always drove us wild with feverish excitement.

My thoughts reverted to the present. "Okay, if you're sure," I murmured.

We scurried around like mad, cleaning, running to the grocery store, and, finally, Lenny took off to pick up the children. I dropped into a chair, and slid way down. My feet stretched in front of me, and I tried to gather strength for the coming onslaught.

The sad part about the whole thing was that I

could probably love Lenny's kids if it weren't for him. They were good-looking, bright kids, with a lot of appeal, but Lenny indulged them so badly when he had them, he was turning them into a couple of spoiled little monsters.

I should have trusted my first instincts when my friends Jim and Mary Hartley invited me over for dinner one night "to meet this really great guy, who's sort of at loose ends since his divorce."

"Mary," I said, "I don't think I want to get involved with a divorced man. There are bound to be headaches."

"I said meet him, not get involved with him, for goodness sake!" Mary cried. "It's been five years since Jerry died. You gotta start thinking about getting married someday. You're twenty-seven."

Jerry! His memory had dimmed almost completely in five years. We'd been engaged, on the verge of marriage, when he'd been killed in a car accident. But it wasn't the memory of Jerry that kept me from getting married. I just hadn't met the right guy yet or something.

"These days it isn't a crime to be unmarried at twenty-seven," I snapped to Mary. "And if I do marry, I think I'd rather it be someone who hasn't been married before."

"Donna," Mary said patiently, "I repeat. I said I'd like you to meet Lenny, not marry him. I think you two would get along great and could have some fun together."

Mary didn't know she was an excellent Cupid. I agreed to meet Lenny, we fell madly in love, and there I was married to him and his kids.

My thoughts were interrupted by the pounding of

feet, and Lenny's voice yelling, "You ready, Donna? Tiffany wants to get going before the shops get too crowded."

The kids trailed Lenny into the house. Tiffany was a lovely looking little girl, with her mother's golden hair and blue eyes. *She'll probably never go through the awkward, homely stage,* I thought, with envy, remembering my own awkwardness at her age. Sam looked just like Lenny, which was beautiful to my eyes.

"Hi, kids," I said.

"Hi," they answered, not with or without enthusiasm.

I believed in being straight with the kids. They weren't yet ready to love me, and I wasn't quite ready to love them, so our relationship was strictly on a sort of endurance basis. They—I guess they tolerated me. And I guess my reaction to them was about the same. I'd have liked it to be more, but it was darned hard to love a couple of spoiled brats.

"I hear we're going shopping for some clothes for you today, Tiffany," I said.

Sam's lips puffed in a pout. "Yeah, Tiffany's getting new clothes. What am I getting?"

Lenny ruffled his hair. "Don't worry, buddy, you'll get something, too."

*Sure you will,* I thought. *If the kids wanted the moon, and Lenny could buy it for them, he would.* Thank goodness he made a good salary as a steel salesman, and I worked as an executive secretary. We'd never have managed otherwise.

We spent a wearying couple of hours in and out of shops at a nearby shopping plaza. It seemed as if Tiffany tried on a couple of hundred outfits before she finally made a selection. Meanwhile Sam ended up with a new baseball mitt—which he needed like a hole in the head—and a jacket.

We'd stopped for hamburgers somewhere along the way, and when we got back to the house, I plopped into a chair while Lenny went out in the yard to play ball with the kids, so Sam could try out his baseball mitt. Exhausted, I was on the verge of dozing in my chair when I heard a clatter at the back door.

Lenny came dashing in with Sam as if the world were coming to an end. "Where's the iodine, Donna, and the bandages? Sam fell and he's got a big gash in his knee."

The big gash turned out to be barely a scratch about an inch long. I took him to the bathroom and poured antiseptic over it, while Lenny hovered anxiously. "Maybe we ought to take him to the hospital emergency ward. Maybe he should get a tetanus shot or something. Gangrene could set in." Sam's eyes grew big and round with apprehension as Lenny went on and on, citing all the catastrophes that could happen.

"Lenny, it's a mere scratch," I said, then turned soothingly to Sam. "It's okay, Sam. I washed it out, we'll put a bandage on it, and you'll be okay."

"You sure?" Sam asked. Lenny's over anxiety had communicated itself to him.

"I'm sure," I said firmly.

"Well—" It was Lenny again. "Guess we can wait and see if it gets infected or not."

I wanted to scream that all little boys and girls get scratches and bumps and bruises. They wouldn't be little boys and girls if they didn't. Lenny magni-

fied the smallest mishap into frightening propor-
tions. It had become a little sickening. But I swallowed the words and said in a steady voice, "I'll
start dinner. Why don't you go watch TV or something, give Sam's leg a rest."

I fumed through dinner preparation. When the
kids were around, Lenny forgot that I worked at an
eight-hour, five-day a week job, as he did. Women's
Liberation flew out the window.

We went to a movie after dinner, and then it was
more TV until it was time for the kids to go to bed. I
surveyed the disorderly living room that we'd so
laboriously cleaned early that morning. Apple cores,
empty soda bottles, and potato chip bowls lay
strewn around. "How about everybody pitching in
and straightening up the living room before we go to
bed," I said. "Tiffany, you collect the bottles. Sam,
you—"

I got a reprimanding look from Lenny. "It's been a
long, hard day for the kids, honey. They're tired." He
turned to them. "Go to bed, kids. I'll help Donna."

I saw the sly look cross Tiffany's face, relief flooded Sam's. Daddy didn't believe in working his darlings. Forget that he and I had had as rough a day as
they had.

They gave Lenny a big, loving good night kiss. I
got a perfunctory one on the cheek.

As Lenny and I picked up the mess, I muttered
softly, "It isn't going to hurt your kids to learn to
clean up the messes they help make, you know."

"Donna, I want their time with us to be, you know,
fun, not full of work and—"

"Picking up a few bottles is hardly what I'd call
work," I snapped.

# MY X-RATED FILM SHOCKED MY HUSBAND

"Gee, baby, I don't know why you can't be more understanding," he said with a scowl, banging down bottles on the kitchen counter. "More patient. The kids have gone through a lot of pain the last two years. It seems to me—"

"It seems to me, you've got a guilt complex so bad you wouldn't say no to them if they suggested going out and murdering a few people just so you can do everything they want."

His voice was flat, cold. "I do think you're exaggerating things a bit. And I'd rather not talk about it. That's all we do lately is argue about the way I handle the kids, and I'm tired of it. After all, they are my kids." With that he stomped off to the bedroom.

I wanted to yell after him that he was doing a rotten job of bringing up his kids, and that I was tired of living with the results of his handling. But I didn't. I followed him ten minutes later, when I'd made some order out of the disorder in the kitchen.

Lenny was already in bed. He had turned away from me, pretending to sleep. *So be it,* I thought. I bounced onto the bed so hard, if he really were asleep, I'd have jolted him awake.

I slept little that night; I really tried to be honest and objective with myself. Was I simply jealous and resentful of the kids, and thus imagining a lot of abuses that didn't exist, or was I right in believing Lenny was indulging the kids far beyond what was good for them? And by so doing he was lowering my respect for him, and he was hardly endearing his children to my heart.

By the time I finally fell asleep, I was convinced that I was right and Lenny was wrong. If I could only make him see how his indulgence was hurting them, and my relationship with them without preaching or getting into an argument about it. But we couldn't seem to talk about them without fighting.

In spite of little sleep, I was the first one up the next morning. I started breakfast, aware a few minutes later of the patter of feet and giggles. With coffee started and batter for waffles made, I went toward the sound of the commotion, which was coming from our bedroom. There were the kids in bed with Lenny, giggling over the Sunday comics, Tiffany cuddled close to her father.

*What's wrong with that,* I asked myself as resentment gnawed at me. Nothing! But the answer didn't satisfy me. It wasn't simply that they were in bed with Lenny, it was the way Tiffany was cuddled up to him, all beguiling smiles and fluttery lashes.

Tiffany was always snuggling up to Lenny. I wasn't afraid of competing with Carla, Lenny's ex, who was a bitch on wheels, but I wasn't sure about Tiffany. Too often I got the feeling that I wasn't dealing with a girl-child, but with a rival. *You're losing your perspective, Donna, my girl,* I told myself angrily—jealous of a twelve-year-old girl! I said as brightly as I could, "Breakfast will be ready in a few minutes. Waffles suit everybody?"

I shouldn't have asked. Tiffany wrinkled her nose. "They're too fattening."

"At twelve I don't think you have to worry about a weight problem," I said dryly.

"Well, they're sweet, with the syrup and all, and they make my face break out."

"They're no sweeter than soda and all the glop you had yesterday," I said testily, then threw her a look over my shoulder as I returned to the kitchen.

# MY X-RATED FILM SHOCKED MY HUSBAND

"Anyone who wants waffles better be in the kitchen in ten minutes."

For someone who was afraid of pimples and putting on weight, Tiffany had her share of waffles. *She'd better eat 'em,* I thought, *'cause I'm sure as hell not going to make a separate breakfast for her.*

That afternoon we went to a baseball game. Sam wanted a sample of everything from every vendor— popcorn, soft drinks, hot dogs, candy, ice cream— and vomited in the car going home. As we tried to clean up the mess, Lenny asked anxiously, "Do you think Sam should see a doctor? Maybe he's sick, throwing up and all."

I groaned. "Dear Lord! Lenny, Sam ate so much junk today, he was bound to throw up. Did you ever think of saying no to the kids once in a while when they want something?"

He glared at me. "Not if I can help it. Anyway, a baseball game wouldn't be a baseball game without hot dogs and stuff."

"I give up," I said, throwing up my hands.

Thank God we only had them every other week. On alternate weeks, Lenny saw them Saturday afternoons, usually taking them to lunch or a movie or something. But even the every-other-week visit was getting to be too much the way things were going. It took me a week to recover, and the next week to gather the strength for the upcoming visit.

For the second night in a row, we fell asleep back-to-back. I tossed and turned, trying to find a solution to the problem of being a weekend step-mother. In the almost year we'd been married, the situation had worsened instead of getting better. I wanted to love Lenny's kids as much as he did. I wanted to enjoy our weekends with them. And I probably would have if it weren't for Lenny and his obsessive belief that the only way to repair the damage to the kids because of the divorce was to indulge their every wish. Maybe marrying me had filled him with more guilt, as if he were trying to replace their mother. Whatever it was, he was blind to what he was doing to them—and to us.

I found myself sniffling into my pillow. My anger was gone, and feeling sorry for myself took its place. But the situation was serious, and if our differences about the kids continued, it could be bad enough to break up our marriage. I snuggled close to Lenny's unresponsive back. I did love him so. And when the kids weren't around, he was a strong, intelligent, sensible man. But their appearance reduced him to a jellyfish—a puppet on a string, which they made dance to their tune.

The next morning, both tired, we had little to say to each other in our usual frantic rush to get off to work in the morning. But by that night, both of us had had more than enough of our cold war. Lenny got home before me and started dinner, and when I entered the house I could smell delicious smells coming from the kitchen.

He came dashing out when he heard me, took me in his arms, and kissed me long and lovingly. "Baby, what the hell's happening between us? I miss you."

I wanted to tell him what was happening, but I hated to destroy the nice warm feeling between us. It was so good to feel his arms around me again, to taste his sweet, soft lips on mine. "And I miss you, too, darling."

"This sleeping, back-to-back—it's got to go,

you know."

"How about trying something else right now," I whispered softly.

"Yeah," he breathed against my lips. "I got a roast in the oven. It'll be a while before it's ready."

Our lovemaking was sweet and wild, tender and abandoned, all at the same time. And when it was over, we finished making dinner together, and I did the dishes. Then we went to bed and made love again.

The loveliness between us made me forget our problem for a while, but long after Lenny was asleep, I found myself wrestling again with the problem of Tiffany and Sam. Maybe you think being an every-other-weekend stepmother shouldn't have been that much of a problem. But aside from the differences of opinion between Lenny and me about how the kids should be raised, I hated to see Tiffany and Sam, who could be sweet and lovable if it weren't for Lenny's overindulgence, turn into little monsters. I didn't want them growing up thinking they could have anything they wanted and that they'd never to assume any responsibilities.

I fell asleep at last, but the next week my mind whirled with thoughts, trying to find a solution. If Lenny could only see himself when he was with the kids—see what a weak, spineless creature he was around them, and how they selfishly twisted and manipulated him. The seed of an idea was planted that week. It began to grow, and by the following week, I was prepared for a last-ditch try. If it didn't work, then I'd just have to pray real hard that our marriage didn't go down the drain because of it.

When Lenny went to pick up the kids Saturday

morning, I scurried around carrying out step one of my plan. I'd begged, borrowed, and almost stolen every tape recorder I could. I placed one in the kitchen, the mike concealed behind the bread box. I put another in the parlor, a bowl of artificial flowers making a nice disguise for it, and I put a third in our bedroom.

We had planned a visit to an amusement park Saturday afternoon, and as we got ready to leave I said, "I think I'll take the video camera. I can get movies of you and the kids."

"Yeah, sounds great," Lenny said. "We haven't had any videos of us together for ages."

Sam made a face. "Yuk, who wants videos of us?"

But Tiffany preened a bit, running her hand through her long silky hair, like a movie star preparing for a close-up.

Well, I'd bought enough tape to shoot a twelve-hour blockbuster if needed, and there wasn't a shot I missed. I caught Lenny scurrying around like a robot trying to obey the kids' every wish—buying tickets for every ride, doling out money like it was peanuts at shooting galleries and stands and arcades, purchasing every gadget and toy that everybody was selling. It made quite a picture—if Lenny would only see it.

Then Tiffany sneezed a couple of times, and Lenny leaned toward her anxiously. "You okay, honey? Are you catching a cold? Maybe you should have worn a sweater today." It was in the eighties!

I hovered over Tiffany as solicitously as Lenny, but my eyes were on his, faintly mocking as I said with all seriousness, "Maybe we'd better get her home and to bed, Lenny. After all, if she's catching a cold, that's nothing to fool around with. It could turn into pneumonia, or a strep throat. We don't want her ending up in the hospital because we didn't pay attention to a couple of sneezes."

For a moment his eyes met mine, widening in perplexity. Then he got the message, my mockery of his always making a big thing out of nothing. The red crept up his neck and flooded his face, and he mumbled, "Maybe it was just some dust that got in her nose."

I thought—score one for me—I hope! Later that evening as we sat around watching TV—with the usual assortment of popcorn, potato chips, and soda—I sneakily switched on the tape recorder.

I really got some gems, such as when Tiffany cuddled up to her Dad, her eyes glued to the TV, and asked, "Will you get me another soda, Daddy?"

"Sure, honey, sure," Lenny said, jumping to his feet and dashing into the kitchen.

And when Sam said, "That baseball mitt you got me last week is no good, Dad. It's a fielder's mitt, and I decided I want to be a catcher. Will you buy me another one?"

"Well, baseball mitts are pretty expensive, Sam."

Sam's face scrunched up and he whined, "Gee, Dad, I'm not much good as a fielder. And all the kids want to be fielders. If I had a catcher's mitt—"

"Okay, okay, son. We'll get you one next week."

Those were just a random sampling of the demands and selfishness and whining my trusty old tape recorders picked up that night. The one in the bedroom recorded a few more the next morning when the kids climbed into bed with Lenny to read the comics, and a few more at breakfast that morning.

After the kids were gone, and we climbed into bed Sunday night, Lenny said, "You think you're pretty smart, don't you?"

My heart gave a nervous little jump. "What do you mean?" I thought my little tape recorder game was up.

"That bit about Tiffany sneezing yesterday. I guess I do overreact when something happens to the kids. Funny, I never did that before. When they'd fall and skin a knee, or get a cut, I'd usually try to tease them out of it. Now—" He shook his head. "Well, I'll try to watch it."

*So I did make a point,* I thought jubilantly. I crossed my fingers under the bedcovers. Now if the videos and tape recorders got their message across, maybe—maybe we'd be able to get some normalcy into our relationship with the children. *But I can bomb, too,* I thought, fear nibbling at me. Lenny might get angry that I dared to try something like that, or even fail to see what a fool he made of himself with the kids. *But when you're fighting for something precious—your marriage to the man you love— you have to take desperate measures,* I thought.

The next Saturday, Lenny saw the kids alone. He took them to the zoo, and I knew he'd be pooped when he got home. Which meant another Saturday shot for the two of us. But I went ahead with my plans, hoping if I caught him right after an afternoon with Tiffany and Sam, the impact of the tape recordings and videos would be stronger.

He came in, dragging, and saw me sitting by the VCR, tape in hand. "What's that for?" he asked, popping tiredly into a chair.

"The videos we took of you and the kids last

weekend," I said, my voice trembling slightly. I took a deep breath, trying to steady myself. "I think you'll find them interesting. I'll get you a nice cold beer first."

I hurried to the kitchen, heart pounding, and hurried back with Lenny's beer. "How'd they come out—did you look at them?" he asked.

"Yeah. They came out great. I got just what I wanted to get."

*Did I ever!* I thought. I'd reviewed the videos earlier that afternoon and Lenny came across just as I expected, spoiling and pampering the kids. And the kids were shown for the whining, demanding little brats Lenny had made them.

Lenny settled back in his chair, and I turned on the VCR. The video seemed to go on endlessly, showing Lenny frantically running around catering to his kids as if they were royalty and he was the court jester. He didn't say a word through the whole thing, and I couldn't see the expression on his face in the darkened room. My heart was beating so fast I thought maybe it would come popping out.

When the movie ended I turned on the lights. Lenny's face was twisted with so many emotions, I couldn't read it. Before he said a word, I quickly said, "There's something else I'd like you to hear, Lenny. I—well, just listen, huh?"

I brought out the tape recorder and turned it on. Lenny listened silently, to the kids' whining, complaining, demanding voices, and his meek acquiescence.

He put a finger over my lips. "I understand, baby. I began to get a little glimmer of light last weekend, when you pulled that bit about Tiffany's sneeze. Tonight I really got the picture. Man!" He ran fingers through his hair, standing it on end. "Now how the hell do I undo all the damage I've done? It's a lot harder to break bad habits than it is to start them."

We talked for a long time that night, and made plans. One thing we agreed was that we had to back each other up in whatever we told the kids to do.

Then I showed him another video I'd made. It was one of me, in a negligee, saying all kinds of seductive things. I'd set up the video recorded on a tripod, and I let it tape one in all kinds of X-rated poses. Maybe it sounds crazy, but I wanted to show my husband that I did love him—and remind him of how very good we were together. And it worked—our lovemaking that night was scorchingly hot. And also very sweet and tender.

Well, it's almost a year since that Saturday night, and it's been a hellish time undoing the damage. The kids fought like little demons to preserve their status. But we've finally got it licked. Oh, the kids aren't perfect, but then what kid is, or adult for that matter. But they no longer demand and order. And now they not only pitch in with cleaning up messes, but they also help with dinner.

Tiffany's showing an interest in cooking, and we're getting quite chummy as we talk while we bake cookies or make dinner. And sometimes Tiffany and I go shopping together or out to lunch on a Saturday. Sam and I don't have quite as much in common, but we can play a rousing game of checkers together, and share a few other activities.

The love between us is growing now that we can respect each other. And because of that, so is the love between Lenny and me. And, at last, I'm finally beginning to enjoy being a weekend mother.     THE END

# DIVORCE MADE ME A WILDCAT

The last person in the world I would have expected to deliver nightmare news to me was John Covington. John lived up the street from us, and he and his wife Sally and my husband, Charlie, and I had shared a casual friendship and a few friendly card games over the years. But then Sally had begun to seem distant, and the reason became all too obvious when suddenly she filed for a divorce last year and the moment it was final married another man.

I'd felt so sorry for John. He really loved Sally. I'd seen him a few times since it happened, when I made extra stew and brought it over to him for his dinner, but all I got for my trouble was a distracted, "Thanks, Allison."

He had grown thin, and his face wore a dark, brooding look all the time. The other neighbors had clucked about him for a while, saying, "Poor John. He's sure carrying a torch." But after awhile everyone forgot about him.

Now he stood on my front porch with the light

glinting off his police badge, and even though it was after eleven, I was glad to see him. The evening had been a boring one, with Charlie off on one of his endless business trips to help set up a new branch of the insurance firm he worked at.

"Come in!" I cried. "I'm glad to see you, John. I'm up the wall with TV tonight, and I just ran out of knitting yarn, and . . ."

"Allison," he said quietly.

"I'll put some coffee on," I babbled. I grabbed his hand and started tugging him through the door.

Then he said my name again, and I halted my excited speech in mid-breath. "What is it?" I exclaimed suddenly. "This isn't a social call, is it?"

"Allison, get your coat. Something's happened."

"To whom?" I cried. "Not to Heather or Brad?" My heart nearly stopped. Both my kids were attending college, but even with them far away, I worried sometimes. They were just babies, nineteen and eighteen, and I wanted them to have their independence, but I still fretted about things like car accidents. Kids these days thought they were so indestructible.

"Not Heather or Brad," John said quickly.

"Then . . ." I gasped. "Not Charlie—John! Is Charlie hurt?"

"There's been an accident," he said.

I reeled suddenly. The porch light wavered sickeningly in front of my eyes, and John reached out and grabbed my arm to steady me. "He isn't badly hurt," he said quickly. "Just a couple broken ribs, they think. But they're holding him overnight for observation."

A relieved breath eased out of me. "Oh, my God!"

I gasped. "John, I just came as close as a thirty-nine-year-old woman can to a heart attack."

"Get your coat," he said again. "I was going on duty, and when the call came and I got it and saw that it was Charlie, I knew I'd better be the one to tell you."

"But, John," I mumbled bewilderedly. "Albuquerque is over three hundred miles from here. Surely you don't want to drive me there. . . ."

"He isn't in Albuquerque, Allison," John said quietly. "He's out at Wayside Hospital."

"Here?" I gasped. "But, John, he can't be! He's in Albuquerque. He's not due home until tomorrow night."

Impatiently, John pushed right past me, opened the hall closet door, and tore out my coat and threw it around my shoulders. "Come on," he said. "I'm going to get you out of here, take you for a ride."

"A ride?" I muttered. Somehow I couldn't quite grasp what was going on. Charlie was hurt? And in a hospital here in town, not in Albuquerque? And instead of taking me to him, John was talking about going for a ride?

While all this was buzzing around in my head, I was starting to shake with the realization that Charlie had been in a wreck and might have been badly hurt, John was propelling me out to his car. Not a patrol car, I realized. But his own.

"I don't know what all this talk about a ride is," I said, irritated now. "But I want to go straight to the hospital. I've got to see for myself that Charlie's okay. My God, if anything happened to Charlie. . . ." For just an instant I tried to picture life without my husband of twenty years. I wouldn't have a life.

# DIVORCE MADE ME A WILDCAT

"I'll take you to the hospital after I've talked to you," John said. "For now, Allison, I want you to open that glove compartment. There's a fresh bottle of whiskey in there. I stopped and bought it on my way to you tonight because I knew you were going to need a good stiff belt of something. It doesn't solve anything," he said wryly. "I know from experience. But it'll help the shock."

"What in the world are you talking about?" I cried. "John, you know I rarely drink at all, much less straight whiskey from a bottle."

He grabbed at the bottle suddenly and savagely tore it open. "Take a swig," he ordered fiercely. "A big one, Allison. Take my word for it—you're going to need it."

Sudden terror started up in me. "It's worse than you let me think, isn't it?" I moaned. "He's badly hurt!" I did tip the bottle then. I swallowed hard and choked on the unaccustomed fire. Warmth flooded through me, and I began to cry.

"It is worse," John said, suddenly gentle. "But not the way you're thinking. His injuries aren't any worse than I told you. . . ."

His voice broke off. We'd been driving up a side street, but now he braked the car and turned off the motor. "God, Allison, I don't know how to tell you this. Charlie wasn't alone tonight. Someone was with him."

"I know," I cried. "Arthur Benton, one of his bosses."

"Arthur Benton didn't go to Albuquerque this weekend," John said. "Neither did Charlie. And they weren't together. The wreck happened in front of the Hide-a-way Motel out on Route 6. Charlie had

had a little too much to drink, and they decided to drive up the street and get a steak, and he backed out of the motel lot right into the path of a truck that was fortunately slowing up to pull into a diner."

"What would Charlie be doing at the Hide-a-way Motel?" I mumbled.

"What any man does at a motel with a beautiful young woman," John said miserably. "Allison, he was with a girl. Her name is Victoria Hobson. She's twenty-five, and she came to work for the insurance firm about six months ago. She told me that part. The rest—the motel part—I checked into myself after the ambulance took them away. Allison— Charlie and Victoria checked into that motel last night, and they paid till Sunday evening. It wasn't the first time, either. I talked to the manager. They were registered as Mr. and Mrs. Charlie Michaels, and this is the third weekend they've spent at the Hide-a-way."

Strange little stars were flashing around in my head. "This is a nightmare," I whispered. "I don't believe it, John."

"Neither did I," he said softly, "when it happened to me. Allison, I'm going to hang around to help you."

Hell is a mild word for what I went through that night and in the following weeks. I was still convinced when John and I reached the hospital that it was all some kind of mistake. I even fancied that John had mistaken somebody else for Charlie— until I saw my husband sitting up in that hospital bed with his ribs tightly taped. He was so serious now, and when I ran to take both his hands in mine, his eyes filled with tears.

"God, I'm sorry you had to find out this way," he mumbled. "I would have told you soon."

I burst into tears. "I don't care about anything," I sobbed. "Not any of it, Charlie. Just as long as you're all right. Whatever you've done, I can live with that. It's just that if anything happened to you, I'd die." I covered his hands with kisses.

"Don't, Allison," he said softly. "Please, don't. I didn't mean anything to happen. I wouldn't have hurt you. But something just hit me when Vicki came to work at our office."

Slowly I raised my eyes to his. "What are you talking about?" I whispered in terror.

"Allie, I would have told you tomorrow when I got home. I want a divorce. I'll see that you have everything you need."

"A divorce?" I gasped. "Everything I need? But, Charlie, you're what I need! Without you I wouldn't have anything. Life wouldn't be worth living. I just couldn't go on."

"Stop it," he said fiercely. "Things haven't been good for us for a long time, Allison. Our marriage is stagnating, dull."

What was he talking about? We had a good marriage. Maybe we'd been married young, when I was nineteen and he was barely twenty-two, but we'd made the years good. We'd raised two beautiful children. Maybe we'd had a more comfortable existence than wild and exciting, but it was still good.

"I know this is a shock. . . ." he was saying.

I gasped. "Charlie, this is something we can talk about. Whatever you've done—we can both survive that. You can't tell me you'd throw away twenty wonderful years for a . . . a . . ."

"For the woman I love," he said quietly. "I'm sorry, Allison. That's the way it is. I'm in love, and I want to marry her. I've been avoiding this confrontation with you, but when I caused that wreck tonight, when I saw Vicki all cut and bleeding. I thought I'd go crazy. I knew then I couldn't play games anymore. I want us to have the real thing."

I don't remember much of what happened that night. John was there constantly after I stumbled out of Charlie's room. He had waited down the hall, and he found me wandering dazedly through the halls. "I want to see her," I whispered.

"Allison, come on home," he said soothingly. "You've had a terrible shock. You need time to adjust. I'll stay with you. Only you've got to get away from this place."

"I want to see her!" I cried fiercely. "I want to get a look at the woman who's wrecked my home."

"Oh, Jesus!" he moaned. "She's in room 406. But if you make a scene. . . ."

"I won't make a scene," I whispered. And I didn't. She was asleep, with her hair flowing out over the hospital, pillow. She had two cuts on her forehead and one on her cheek that had been stitched, and the skin around them was discolored. But even then I could see how beautiful she was. I touched my own hair, drab suddenly, against that golden frame.

"It's the forties," John tried to tell me as he led me back down to his car. "It gets to men. Women it hits earlier. Sally was thirty. It's a sudden feeling that life is passing you by and you can save it all with a new partner."

But I was beyond reasoning with. In the car I grabbed up John's bottle and gulped down four or five swallows. I choked again, and the choking got all mixed up with wild sobbing.

"I'm going to go crazy," I cried.

"No, you're not," he said gently. "You'll survive. Like me. You'll never get over the pain of betrayal, but you'll survive."

When I couldn't stop crying, he pulled me into his arms and nestled my cheek against his rough uniform. His arms were the only real thing in the world to me. Everything else was a nightmare.

John stayed with me all that night. I was hardly aware of my surroundings. Suddenly my house looked bleak and cold, as if someone had died. Vaguely, I remember that John checked out my bathroom closets. "There aren't any pills," I said bitterly. But he was right to search. In my first shock, if I'd had any pills, I think I would have taken them. Instead I did something I had never done in my life. I got very, very drunk. That was only the beginning of the nightmare. In the morning I couldn't get out of bed. I could only lie there and cry. I cried all day. Sometime in the afternoon John came into the bedroom and thrust two pills into my mouth and held a glass of water to my lips.

"I called your doctor and he told me to get these," he said. "They're tranquilizers, Allison. But I'm keeping them in my pocket and doling them out to you when I see fit."

The pills didn't do any good. Nothing did any good. I wanted to die, was already dead, really. I just wanted my body to join the rest of me.

"I don't go back on duty till Tuesday," John said once. "I'm going to stay with you."

"Why are you doing all this for me?" I mumbled.

"Maybe because of a couple of pots of stew you were thoughtful enough to bring me when I was too hung up on myself to thank you properly," he said gently. "But mostly because I've been there, Allison. When Sally left me, it nearly destroyed me."

All that day he stayed beside me, dozing sometimes in a chair by my bed. In the evening Charlie came home, walking stiffly because of his sore ribs. For the first time I roused myself enough to begin pleading with him.

"This will pass," I moaned, while John sat silently in his chair beside my bed. "Charlie, please, please don't throw away what we've had!"

"I'm not throwing it away," he said quietly. "You're part of me, Allison. But I want something more."

"And that little girl can give it to you?" I shrieked. All control left me. I threw myself off the bed and would have pounded him with my fists, except that John grabbed me and held on tight.

"You're a bastard," John said to Charlie.

"I know that," Charlie said carefully. "But I can't help my feelings. I love you, Allison. But it's a quiet kind of love, the love a man has for a woman who's borne him two kids and shared all his struggles. There's just no excitement. . . ."

"Excitement!" I gasped. "What can she give you that I can't? What's the matter? Is my body too old for you?"

"Don't, Allison," John begged. "Can't you see it won't do any good?"

Charlie's voice still came dark with misery. "Do you want me to stay on a few days?" he asked. "Maybe get some things in order—the lawn, the garage. . . ."

# DIVORCE MADE ME A WILDCAT

My God, I couldn't believe what I was hearing! "Get out!" I shrieked wildly. "I never want to see you again!"

Charlie was throwing things into a bag. "I'll come back in a few days when we can talk rationally," he said. At the bedroom door, with his suitcase in hand, the very one he'd taken off to "Albuquerque" on Friday, he paused. "I didn't want it to end like this," he said.

"Why," John grated beside me, "don't you get out of here, before I blow my whole career by practicing a few karate chops on a civilian?" His voice was low, menacing. In a moment the door shut behind Charlie.

"I'm going to go insane!" I shrieked. "I'm going to die."

"You're not going to do either," John said gently. "I won't let you."

That easily, twenty years of marriage fell apart. I went around in such a daze I was hardly aware of my surroundings. I wrote my kids long letters that afterward I didn't remember mailing, letters in which I put all the blame on myself, without knowing quite what it was I was supposed to have done.

The kids called and wanted to leave college and come home to be with me, but I vaguely remember hanging onto my tears and telling them there wasn't anything they could do. After each call I went into the bathroom and threw up.

Charlie came back four days after he'd left. He tried to talk to me. "It wasn't anything you did, Allison," he said miserably. "It just happened. Things happen all the time. My God, look around you. People everywhere are making changes."

# DIVORCE MADE ME A WILDCAT

I remember looking at him blankly, wondering, "Who is this man? I thought I knew him. I thought I could trust him. But he's a stranger." The whole situation was unreal to me.

When Charlie said if I didn't see a lawyer he would, we went together to file for a divorce. It still seemed like a nightmare. It was as if I had died and didn't know it.

"Won't you consider a marriage counselor?" I remember the lawyer looking at my stricken face and asking that.

I remember looking with desperate hope at Charlie, but he had a young little sexpot on his brain. I had no idea how easy it is to get a divorce these days. Almost anything will do for grounds. Ours were incompatibility,

"Who'd incompatible?" I wanted to scream at Charlie. But it wouldn't have done any good.

"I'm sorry," he kept saying. "It kills me to hurt you, Allison. But I know what I want."

Only John held me to sanity. He worked different shifts, but whatever spare time he had he spent with me. Sometimes he took me to the zoo or to a little park a few blocks from our neighborhood. And always, wherever we were, he hung on tightly to my hand.

"You're going to be okay," he would say gently. "This is like any other shock of loss, Allison. What you're experiencing is grief, the same grief you would have gone through if Charlie had died."

"He's worse than dead to me," I said once, dully. "If he'd died, at least then I'd have memories to cherish. Now all the memories just seem fake."

Dimly I began to become aware that all my waking hours were spent waiting for the sound of John's footsteps out front, waiting to hear him say what had become his customary greeting. "Sergeant Covington to the rescue, ma'am." He was the rock I leaned on. Without him I think I would have wound up in a mental institution.

The Christmas holidays came, and again John saved me. The kids came home, all shook up when they saw how thin I had grown. It was John who took them aside and told them what I was going through was the natural course of things, that I would be okay eventually.

It was even John who stuffed the Christmas turkey, reading from a book how to do it. The day after New Year's he was on the swing shift at the police department and in the morning he drove the kids and me to the airport to see them off. The moment their plane left, I fell into hideous tears.

"They're all I have!" I sobbed as John led me through a curious crowd to the car. "I want them with me."

"No, you don't," he said. "You want to learn to be independent. You want to stop letting Charlie rule your emotions this way. Give yourself time, Allison. I'm still not over my own hurt, and I know how you feel."

I barely heard that. I was too busy feeling sorry for myself to think that John's divorce had only been final a few months, and that he was still in pain.

Then came the day when I knew the interlocutory decree had gone into effect, and I got off on a crying jag that wouldn't stop. John came off the day shift to find me nearly hysterical. "I can't survive this," I sobbed wildly.

# DIVORCE MADE ME A WILDCAT

"Get your coat and get in the car," he ordered. "I'm getting you out of this house."

We drove to our little park, where he wrapped me in his arms and just held onto me. He kept whispering, "Get it all out. I know how it is. I could have floated six battleships with my tears."

"Don't ever let me go," I moaned. "I need you."

In an hour he drove me home. I was so drained I couldn't lift my head from the back of the car seat. We were passing a pet shop when John suddenly braked the car.

"Where are you going?" I cried frantically.

"Right back," he said.

In a few moments he came out carrying a tiny, white puffball. "I don't know what it is, but it's friendly," he said. "And you need something around when I'm not there. Something you've got to take care of. You've got to start thinking outside yourself, Allison."

It was a puppy and when he placed it in my lap it fell all over me, licking my hands, and my face. My God, was John crazy? What was I going to do with a dog when I couldn't even take care of myself?

But it was such a wild, friendly little thing. And it kissed me and kissed me. "See?" John said happily. "It likes you."

And suddenly, to my own shock, I pulled the little fluff ball close and began to cry again. I hugged it and hugged it. All this affection it was giving me, and it didn't want a single thing in return.

"Hey," John said softly. "Hey, Allison, you're smiling a little." He leaned over and kissed my cheek.

Slowly I started to come back to life a little. I could take care of the puppy and even remember to comb my hair now. I started eating better and keeping the house picked up. And even though a lot of the time still seemed hazy to me and there were times I would watch a whole TV program without remembering a word, at least I was functioning. I even got so I could cook small meals for John sometimes, and I was starting to appreciate a little just how much he'd done for me.

Then the divorce became final, and I fell apart again. John was on swing shift that night, and he arrived at the house about eleven-thirty to find me a total mess.

"Oh, Allison. And you were doing so well. Get a jacket, honey. It's a little cool for April."

He drove me to our park again. Only this time nothing he said or did snapped me out of my crying jag. Until suddenly he pulled me roughly into his arms.

"I can't take seeing you so hurt!" He groaned. "Allison, you've come to mean something so special to me, so . . ." His voice broke off. I heard the moan low in his throat, and then suddenly his arms tightened around me. "I know what you need," he whispered.

Sex was the last thing that had been on my mind, these past months. How could a shell want sex? But John's hands were on me suddenly, everyplace. I felt them slipping underneath my clothes, and I was stunned to feel the wild excitement that started up in me. Somebody wanted me. After all the ugliness, somebody still found me attractive, desirable.

The kiss caught me wildly. When John's tongue parted my lips and I felt it against my own, I nearly went crazy with need. "Make love to me!" I moaned.

Oh God, the heat! My body was consumed. His frantic fingers probed everywhere, missing no spot that would send hot chills through me. I strained against him.

I don't know when John got the car door open, or when he was lifting me in his arms and carrying me behind a clump of bushes. He moaned. "All I need is to be caught here in this park and I'll be kicked off the force." But we couldn't stop what had begun any more than we could have held back a hurricane.

Never, never, had sex been like this before!

"Allison, I only meant to comfort you. What happened to us?" he said after it was over. He covered my face with kisses. "Is it love?" he whispered. "I sure feel something!"

I was too stunned and spent to even answer him. All the way back to the house John kept mumbling things in a bewildered voice like, "I can't believe it! I never dreamed we'd turn onto each other that way."

At the house he helped me out of the car. "I'm going to put you to bed," he murmured huskily.

I was fighting something strange inside me as he started switching on lights. It was a kind of guilt, as if I had somehow betrayed Charlie. *That's ridiculous!* I raged at myself. *How can you betray a man who's going to marry another woman in a few days?* But twenty years of living with only one man, of sharing my body only with him, couldn't be pushed aside so easily. It was silly, but I felt as if I'd just lost my virginity!

John was leading me toward the bathroom. "What are you going to do?" I muttered wearily.

"Give you a bath," he answered gently.

He was treating me tenderly, like a baby, and guilt or not, I didn't have the power to resist him. I didn't even want to. It was good to feel like a child, to have someone look after me. I wasn't even embarrassed when John got my clothes off and got me into the bathroom. Two minutes into the bath, though, I realized with shock that my body was starting to burn again with a slow, sensuous fire.

"I think—I think you'd better let me do this myself," I breathed.

But it was too late. John's eyes had gone dark. His hands were all soapy, and he smoothed them over my body. "Allison?" he mumbled distractedly.

I couldn't believe it was happening again! John lifted me out of the tub and wrapped me in a towel—but he didn't try to dry me off. He just carried me in to the bed and made love to me as if we hadn't already exhausted ourselves. This time when I hovered on that maddening crest of magnificent agony, I couldn't stop my moans. I was like an animal, completely abandoned. Nothing existed except the hot, violent thrusts of a male body throbbing inside mine.

After it was over, I lay there panting, my eyes on his hairy chest glistening with sweat, on his neck, his mouth, his dark, stunned eyes.

My God, what had happened to me? Wave after wave of emotion poured over me. I curled up in the crook of his arm, my cheek against his chest. If I were a cat, I would have been purring! I felt completely drained, but beautiful, too, soft and warm and wanted and beautiful. Never mind if a little fear hovered deep in my mind, a fear that said, "There's something wrong here, Allison. This isn't quite, right."

# DIVORCE MADE ME A WILDCAT

"I love you," John whispered, and I told him that I loved him too. Love and need—they're so very close.

John and I moved into a fool's paradise. Now when I was expecting him, my heart beat wildly with eagerness. I started to live again.

I went downtown and bought some new clothes, among them a black nightgown so sheer it was like a piece of black cloud. The first time I wore it, John's eyes misted. "You're the most beautiful thing I ever saw," he murmured huskily.

I got so consumed with the idea of sex, I bought a book on how to please a man and learned to do things I had never even known existed. I learned that a man likes to be made love to sometimes and nothing was more exciting to me than John's raspy breathing and narrowed eyes when I was practicing my newfound knowledge.

The weather turned warm and sunny, and that lifted my spirits. When John was off in the evening we would go places together, always wrapped up in each other's eyes, I had pushed my memories of Charlie far back inside me where I wouldn't let them hurt me anymore. I had a new love now, a better love than he had ever given me.

Then came the night when John and I went to dinner at Jason's, the flashiest restaurant in town. My mirror told me I had never looked better, I was wearing a long blue dress, with a shockingly low-cut top.

"Oh, wow!" John teased when he saw me. "I don't know if I can go out in public now. I'm not sure I want the whole world to see what you do to me."

I laughed softly. It was beautiful what we had together.

## DIVORCE MADE ME A WILDCAT

Until Charlie and Victoria walked into the restaurant. She was wearing a shimmering silver pantsuit, and I suddenly felt a hundred years old. I saw the men in the room turn to look at her, caught the gleam of wedding rings on her left hand, and I went a little faint.

Everything inside me crashed into blackness. I was terrified. I focused my eyes on John's face, trying to bring back all the feelings I had for him, but he looked like a stranger.

"Come on," he said gently. "They haven't seen us. We'll slip out the back way."

I was crying before we reached the car. "I'm sorry, I'm sorry," I moaned over and over. "I don't know what happened. I've been feeling so good, John."

In the car he held me close. "It's okay. I'd probably feel the same way if Sally came in with her husband."

When we reached home, we were both desperate to make love to each other. It was good—but deep in my mind a little voice seemed to be hissing: *You're just a couple of rejects, Allison, you and John. This isn't love. It's ego need.*

I pushed back the voice. It was love. It was even better than what Charlie and I had. We proved it. We both went clear out of our minds pleasing each other usually, and that night we slept the whole night together, something we rarely did because we didn't want the neighbors to talk.

In the morning John was up before six. "Sergeant Covington going on duty at seven," he said. "With what little strength he's got left. I hope I don't get any on chases today. Last time I had to climb an eight-foot fence, and if it happened today, I don't think I could even get my nose over!"

Dressed, he came to sit down beside me a moment. "I was awake half the night, thinking, and you know what I was thinking? I want to marry you, Allison."

I stared at him in shock. "Marry me?" I whispered.

"I don't just want to make love to you, Allison. I want to come home to you."

*Why not? I thought suddenly. We are something special together. And that business last night that was just the pain of too many memories surging up at once. This was today, not yesterday. And I was in love with John. I didn't question that.*

"When?" I whispered.

"Next week?" he said.

The week passed in a haze, like the haze I'd lived in for a long lime after Charlie left. Vaguely, I got it through my head that I needed a trousseau. John arranged to trade a week of his vacation with another man, so we could go away together.

I shopped, but I hardly knew what I was buying. Two different mornings I started out for a store and wound up walking in our little park, surprised to find myself there. What was wrong with me? I should be the happiest woman in the world. But something was nagging at my heart, something I couldn't pinpoint. Something was terribly, terribly wrong.

Two days before the big day John came over for dinner, as usual, I had made beef stroganoff, but he only picked at it. "Got the reservations for Tahoe," he said a little distantly. "And I've made arrangements with Reverend Tilson from that little church over on Harrison." We had both agreed the wedding would be no big fuss, with no guests. "Reverend Tilson's wife and son would be our witnesses," John said.

"That's fine," I murmured, but both our voices sounded far away.

That night we made love more fiercely than we ever had before. What are we proving? I wondered afterward, but I pushed the thought away.

In the morning both my kids called. I had sent them letters telling them about my marriage. "Be happy, Mom," Brad said gently.

But Heather knew me better than Brad did—better than I knew myself. "Mama, it's too soon," she said worriedly. "John is a sweet man—but you need more time. Won't you give it another six months?"

"We're being married tomorrow, darling," I said gently.

There was a long pause. "Okay," she said softly, and I thought I heard tears in her voice. "I just don't want you hurt anymore, Mom. And give John my best wishes, too. You both deserve happiness." Who could have told me why I cried an hour after that conversation?

John and I had agreed not to see each other the day or night before our wedding. Both of us had packing to do, and I had to find a kennel to board my dog in. And there was a nightgown I wanted to buy.

The day passed in a haze, but there was something mounting inside me, something that was very like a little frozen terror. I fought it back—but all day it grew. Buying my nightgown, it suddenly came to me that it was almost exactly like the one Charlie had given me our first Christmas together, and I let the thing drop from my fingers as if it had burned me.

"Is something wrong?" the saleswoman asked, but I stumbled out of the shop and was all the way home before I even realized it. I cried again, without knowing why.

John called that night. "All set?" he asked. I could hardly hear his voice, it sounded so faint.

"All set," I said.

"Then I'll pick you up at ten-thirty. Good night, darling." I started to hang up, but his voice called me back. "Allison?" he said. "I love you."

"I love you, too," I said, but my voice was shaking—like his.

I hardly slept all night because the terror inside me was swelling. *What's the matter?* I ranted in the dark hours. *You're getting a good man. You're right for each other.* But every time I dozed, it was Charlie I dreamed of, the same dreams I'd had when he first left me. Images of Charlie suddenly appearing at my door, saying, "I've come back to you, Allison."

Three times I came wildly awake, with tears of longing on my cheeks.

But in the morning I pulled myself together. I checked out my suitcase, made sure there were no gas jets burning and that everything was locked tightly, and at nine-forty-five, I got into my car and drove the dog downtown to the kennel. Before I got out of the car with him, I held him close and cried a little into his soft fur.

At ten o'clock I started back for my house. Only, I didn't wind up there. To my shock, I found myself at the little park. It was Sunday, and children were already swarming over the playground equipment.

# DIVORCE MADE ME A WILDCAT

"What are you doing here?" I whispered in horror. "John will be at the house in a few minutes. Get into that car and get home." But I couldn't. I began to walk around a small lake, listening to the sounds of the children playing.

Memories hurtled at me. Times when I'd brought my own children here when they were tiny. Pictures of Charlie and I sitting together on a bench watching them sail gleefully down a slide. Picnic lunches with bologna sandwiches because times had been hard for us then. I saw us at the zoo. Remembered the couple of times when the kids had been seriously ill. Heather once with pneumonia and Brad with scarlet fever. Charlie and I sitting at the hospital each time, holding tightly onto each other.

So many things. Charlie when he first got a job with the insurance firm, coming home with a bottle of champagne we couldn't afford to celebrate. Nights lying next to Charlie, feeling that no matter what else might be wrong in this world, this was right.

"Go home, Allison," I hissed. But I kept on walking. A young couple walked by me holding hands, their heads bent close together, and suddenly the terror that had only been threatening me broke loose.

I began to shake, and my whole body went icy cold. "You can't marry John!" I whispered. "Allison, you don't know if it's love. There's too much still there for Charlie. You're not over the pain. John's a defense for you—a protection. He makes you feel wanted, and you need that. But maybe that's not a healthy kind of need right now."

"Oh, God, he's waiting for me!" I moaned. But I

couldn't move. I could only sink down to the grass in a deserted spot beside the lake. I wasn't crying. I was too frightened for tears. "My God, how can I tell him?" I gasped.

"Allison!" a voice exclaimed suddenly above me. "Allison."

I stared up into John's stricken eyes. "You found me," I whispered.

"Found you?" he mumbled distractedly.

"Didn't you come looking for me?"

He shook his head dazedly. "I started out for your place, and God knows what came over me. I drove around the block four times, Allison, and I couldn't go in. The car wouldn't seem to stop. I drove over here to try and pull myself together."

"You feel it, too," I cried. "John, it's wrong, isn't it? We're not sure of ourselves, not sure why we're getting married."

He sank down to the grass beside me, not meeting my eyes. "I thought we were sure," he said. "But look at us. How come we're both here when we're due in precisely ten minutes at Reverend Tilson's?"

"John, I want to talk to you," I said. I told him about my dreams last night, about the memories. "I'm better," I said softly. "You made me better, John. But I'm not over him. Maybe I never will be. Twenty years. More than half my life."

"I know," he said gently. "All night I was fighting the old urges I used to get to go out and kill Sally's lover."

"Oh, John!" I whispered,

"Should we call it off?" he asked. "Maybe just for the time being? Maybe we shouldn't see each other for a while. Get our heads together. Date some other people. Allison, I've never told you, but you were the first woman since—I mean . . ."

I touched his hand, and tears streaked quickly down my cheeks. "I know," I said. "I understand. And, John . . . if we don't see each other anymore you know what I mean—the way we've been seeing each other . . . John, I do love you. You saved my sanity, my life." But he leaned over and touched my lips with his, and it was so sweet, for a moment I wanted to melt into his arms—but I caught myself.

John got to his feet. "So long, my almost bride," he said gently. I think we both smiled a little. "You going to be okay?" he said.

I nodded.

"Me, too," he murmured.

Weeks passed, then months. My kids came home for part of the summer and then went back again. They didn't question the called-off marriage. Brad was wrapped up in a girl he'd met on the bus coming home, and Heather seemed to understand everything about me instinctively, maybe because she was female, too.

Charlie came to the house a few times to see the kids. And after the first couple of times, it didn't bother me anymore, I couldn't hate him now. But I wasn't altogether sure I loved him either. It was a time of confusion, a time of searching.

I got a part-time job in the jewelry section of a department store. I didn't need the money—Charlie gave me plenty—but I found I liked being out with people. I began to make some new friends. All my old friends had been married, and though I still held on to a couple of those friendships, I was looking for new experiences. I even began to date.

Sex was a problem. Every man I went out with seemed to think I was desperate for sex, since I was no longer married. I learned to handle the situation with a sense of humor, and twice I did have sex. But each time I came home and cried, aware that something was missing—warmth. I saw John sometimes—driving up the street in his uniform, He always grinned and waved, and once he blew me a kiss.

*He looks fine,* I thought a little wistfully.

I missed John, missed his arms and his lips and his sweetness. But we were both discovering ourselves as single people. As time went on, I began to feel like a person in my own right, not just Charlie's rejected wife. But there was something lacking in my life.

Then, on a wintry evening when the wind was blustering around the house and the dog and I were snuggled up together watching TV, the phone rang. It was a woman's voice.

"Check your clock," she said. "In precisely ten minutes, open your front door. There'll be a surprise waiting for you.

"What kind of a new sales gimmick is this?" I cried, but she had already hung up. I couldn't help checking the clock. She'd intrigued me. I fully expected to open my door in ten minutes and find a vacuum cleaner sitting there with a salesman lurking behind it—but it wasn't a vacuum cleaner, and it wasn't a salesman.

"Surprise!" John cried.

I stared in shock at him, but the shock wasn't just because I hadn't expected to see him standing here in the glow of the porch light. My shock was at the little thrill of happiness that ran up my spine. "What in the world?" I cried.

"I had to share the new me!" he exclaimed. "See anything different?"

"You look like the same sweet John to me," I said, startled at myself.

"No, no, the uniform!" he moaned. "You are now looking at Lieutenant John Covington!"

"Oh, John!" I cried. "I'm so happy for you. A promotion!"

"Can I come in?" he asked. Suddenly he looked like a lost little boy. I grabbed his hand and pulled him through the door. "You look great," he said quietly.

"I'm making it," I said softly. "But it's good to see you, John."

"I miss you," he said suddenly. "When the word came through that I'd made lieutenant, I wanted to share it. Only there was only one person who meant anything to me. When I couldn't stay away any more, I had a secretary from the station call you. Sharing, Allison. That's important. We shared the bad. Now I want to share the good—with you."

For some reason tears were misting my eyes. It felt so good to have him in my house again. "I miss you too," I said softly.

I made us coffee and laced it with a little brandy for celebration. Somehow we got to talking a lot, about what we'd been doing. "I've been dating," he said. "Some fine chicks, as the guys at work put it. But I—" He looked at me helplessly. "Well, Allison," he said with a shaky little grin. "Those women aren't home with me. Could we try again, do you think? Start over again? Two people scarred maybe, but not bleeding anymore? Could we see each other—really get to know each other? Not as Sally's husband and Charlie's wife—but as us?"

"I—I'd like that," I murmured.

"Good." He let out a big sigh. And then suddenly he laughed, a big hearty, booming laugh.

"What's that for?" I cried. But I thought I knew. It was the release of all the past.

"I don't know," he said. "I just feel good." And it was the most natural thing in the world that he got up out of his chair and came to where I was sitting on the sofa and sat down with me and wrapped me in his arms. The smell of his uniform was the sweetest thing I had ever experienced. And suddenly I was laughing, too, laughing and crying a little.

"What's that for?" he demanded.

"I just feel good, too," I sobbed.

And right. Oh so right inside. We were both home in each other's arms, and we knew it.     THE END

# SEX JUNKIE

Brandon Myers leaned over my desk, his gold wedding band standing out all too obviously on his left hand. "Have lunch with me, Allie," he said softly.

I could have lost myself forever in the depths of his eyes. I'd been aware of them for all too long. I'd watched them change color with his moods.

"No, Brandon," I answered slowly, cursing the fact that all the exciting, interesting men were firmly attached to other women by the time they reached thirty.

"Allie." He leaned closer. "I really need someone to talk to. Someone who understands the personnel problems here. Please. If I can bounce my ideas off to you, then maybe I can get up enough nerve to talk to the boss." He nodded toward Mr. Conner's closed door.

I hesitated, torn. He made it sound so logical. "For the sake of business," I said lightly. I looked away from his face and rummaged in the bottom drawer of my desk. I'd had a yearning for Brandon

SEX JUNKIE

Myers since the first day I'd come to work there three months ago, but had managed to suppress it.

I'd done small favors for Brandon before. Like making sure he was the first to get the boss's attention when something came up. I'd never denied Brandon anything, except myself.

The spark was there. He'd tried to date me before. But his wife, Christine, also existed. I only knew her by reputation. The other girls in the office said she was the baby-doll type—a fluttery mass of beautiful hair and little-girl ways that included a soft, breathless voice.

I definitely wasn't the helpless type. I put in a day's work for a day's pay and was proud of being a good worker. I also managed my own life and paid my own bills. Frankly, it wasn't what I'd planned. I'd expected to be married and having babies by the time I was twenty-five.

When Brandon and I walked out of the office together at twelve, Joan Brady nearly fell out of her chair. I flashed her a look and shrugged to tell her it was just one of those things.

Well, it was one thing to tell myself that and quite another to feel it. Just walking beside Brandon without even touching him was doing things to my heart and my body. The zing running through me made me light-headed.

On the busy street outside, we passed up the usual delis and hamburger joints. Brandon led me around the corner and down the block to The Jolly Pub, a rustic, dimly lit restaurant. A hostess led us back to a reserved table in a corner.

We ordered immediately and I leaned toward Brandon. "What do you want to talk to me about?" I

308

asked him.

"Us," he said.

"Now, Brandon." I drew back, my pulse thundering in my ears.

"I haven't forgotten that kiss," he said. I shook my head, not wanting to remember.

"It was a silly thing," I made myself say aloud. "We were both a little tipsy and—" My voice trailed off. It had been a cocktail party for one of the office managers who was retiring. "It was just one of those things," I managed to get out.

"No, it wasn't, Allie. And we both know it." His eyes caught mine and held them and I went weak all over. "I want us to have a chance to find out about each other," he said slowly.

"Not while you're married," I said.

"I'm going to get out of that," he said. His intense eyes darkened into deep pools.

"You are?" I asked faintly.

"Yes." He nodded emphatically. "I'm trapped, Allie. And I'm desperate. Christine is so helpless. So dependent on me."

"And you want out of that situation," I said.

"Yes!" He leaned toward me. "I've got Christine enrolled in a business school. She's doing fine. As soon as she builds up her confidence a little more I'm leaving her. I'll support her until she's through school, of course. And after that she can make it on her own."

My head reeled. The shock of this conversation was almost more than I could take. Brandon Myers was no married man on the make. He was serious about the two of us being together.

I made myself sit still and tried to think. "How did

you end up married to Christine?" I asked him finally. "You must have had some idea what she was like before you married her."

Brandon sighed softly. He shook his head. "It's a long story. Christine was my mother's best friend's daughter. Her mother died and Christine was left completely alone. Totally lost. She was little more than a child, even though she was eighteen. Mom moved her in with us."

He paused, took a sip of water, and went on. "Christine and I had always been thrown together anyway. I took the easy way out. I wanted to sleep with her—and she boosted my ego. You know." He gave me a sheepish look. "Made me feel like the big man who would take care of her and protect her. It was the biggest mistake I ever made in my life."

He reached across the table and covered my hand with his. "And now there's you, Allie. You're the kind of woman a man can love on equal terms."

"Me?" My voice was a small squeak. "Wait." I pulled my hand away from his. "You're going too fast for me."

"Am I?" he asked slowly, his voice beating at my soul. "I've seen you every day for three months. I've kissed you. I want you, Allie."

The forcefulness of his tone left me spinning. No man had ever come on to me this way before. A soft warm feeling filled my body. Brandon was so strong, so confident. He knew what he wanted, and it was me.

"I'll be at your place tonight," he said. "Seven-thirty."

"I live at. . . ."

"I know where you live. I have your address memorized. And your phone number. I don't know how many times I've picked up the phone, dialed your number, and then hung up before it could ring. I've driven by your apartment and never stopped."

"Oh, Brandon. I had no idea," I whispered.

"You know now," he said and pulled back as the waitress brought our food.

I went back to work, breathless and totally disoriented. I'll never know how I got through the afternoon without blowing it.

It was almost quitting time when I remembered I had a date with Ernie Summers. Ernie was my age. He owned a small shoe store in a shopping center near my apartment.

We'd had a couple of dates before. Nothing big, just nice quiet dates with a nice, quiet man. I reached for the phone and dialed his work number. I couldn't hurt his feelings, so I just told him I felt like I was coming down with a virus and wanted to cancel our date.

"Gee, I'm sorry, Allie. Can I bring you anything?"

"No. No," I said as a surge of guilt shot through me. Why did Ernie have to be so concerned and so nice? "I just want to go home and sleep."

"Then I'll see you soon," he said and we hung up. I felt like a rat. I gritted my teeth, closed my eyes, and sank down in my chair. A real rat!

But by the time seven-thirty came I'd forgotten about Ernie Summers. I'd changed clothes three times and frantically wished I could do something new and exciting with my ho-hum hair.

I was glad I lived alone. I'd never been one of those girls who liked sharing an apartment. Not that I lived alone so men could come and go. I wasn't a bedroom hopper. I'd known exactly three men sexually in my whole life, and I'd loved each of them in a special and different way. Unfortunately I hadn't loved any of them enough to spend the rest of my life with them.

I surveyed myself in the full-length mirror on the bathroom door. I'd finally settled on a pair of leggings with an oversized sweater. It was a soft, pretty sweater, the kind men liked on a woman. The kind that made me feel totally feminine. It had been my private gift to myself for getting the job at my company.

My old job had grown boring and dull. I'd gone as far as I could. I knew all the people too well. So I'd gone job hunting and found myself a new one. I liked Mr. Conner, my boss. I liked the office. And I'd fallen in love with a married man with no hope of having that love returned until today.

I still felt awestruck by the suddenness of Brandon's words and plans. Though for him they hadn't been sudden. He'd wanted to call, wanted to come by. He'd been so near, yet so far away.

When he rang the doorbell I ran to answer it. Breathless, I opened the door. For a moment all we could do was stare at each other. Then he held out a small bouquet of wild flowers. "I saw these in an empty lot," he said. "I thought you'd like them."

"Wild flowers," I whispered. "Oh, Brandon!" For some crazy reason my eyes misted. It was such a sweet, tender thing to do.

I gently took the small collection of pretty flowers. He stepped inside and closed the door behind him. He opened his arms and I went into them. It was our first real embrace, yet the sensation was one of coming home after a long, long time.

Our lips met, touching tentatively at first, and then clinging as we discovered each other. The kiss deepened and his arms tightened around me. When we came apart I was trembling. "I—I'd better get these in water," I said, barely able to speak.

He nodded and followed me back to my tiny kitchen. I put the flowers in a vase and set them on the coffee table. "They are beautiful," I told him.

"So are you," he said, and my cheeks flushed with sheer happiness.

"Do you want to go out?" I asked him.

"I don't think we should date openly until I start divorce proceedings," he said. "I don't want to mess anything up."

"I see," I said as I licked my dry lips. Sneaking around had never been one of my strong points. Things like that made me uneasy and usually meant trouble. I'd just never done it before. But then, I'd never dated a married man before, either.

"Sure. I understand," I said slowly.

Brandon laid his hand on my waist. "It won't be for long," he said. "Just until I can get Christine's confidence built up. Once I start the divorce proceedings we can date openly."

He turned me around and I'd put my head on his shoulder. He massaged my back gently, comforting me. He was so dear and good, I realized. He knew what I was feeling and thinking without my having to explain.

I raised my face and he kissed me, and in that instant I knew we were going to go to bed. I wanted him as I'd never wanted another man before.

We kissed and caressed each other until I was aching with desire. I knew Brandon was, too. He was the one who stood back when we reached the bedroom. "I didn't mean for this to happen tonight, Allie," he said slowly. "Honest to God, that's not why I came here. I don't want to rush you."

"You aren't," I said and turned my back to him. His fingers lifted my sweater. His hands touched my naked flesh and the shock of it made me gasp. He kissed my shoulders and neck and I pressed backward against him, delighting in each caress that sent darts of fire through my body.

His eyes moved over my body, then up to my face and lingered there. "You are beautiful," he said. His hunger was so real I could feel it pulsating toward me.

I turned back the bed while he undressed. He stood before me, bare to the flesh, and I felt as if all my breath was knocked out of me. Trembling, I reached out one hand and he took it. Together we lay down on the bed on our sides, face to face. We explored each other's bodies, lingering here and there to caress, tease, tantalize.

When we could no longer prolong it, he drew me up close and we began to make love. Very slowly, at first, and gently. My hold on him tightened and my nails dug into his back. Our bodies began to move in the age-old rhythm of love.

"Brandon. Brandon," I whispered. He began a maddening new rhythm, so exquisite and sensual all I could do was lose myself in it. I could hear myself repeating his name over and over from a distance. Repeating it, clinging to it. I could feel myself moving into a new space, a new dimension.

I'd never known love to be so powerful, yet so tender. So blissful, yet tormenting at the same time. Then, all at once, he sent me crashing into eternity. Stilled, we laid together, barely touching, hearts pounding. Slowly, I opened my eyes and looked at him in awe. "I never knew it could be like this," I said.

"Me, either," he said gently. He reached over, touched my face, and pushed my hair back. He wound a tendril around a finger and loved me with his eyes. For what must have been the hundredth time I whispered his name softly, holding it on my tongue and lips to make it last forever. I traced the lines of his face with a fingertip, as if to memorize every feature. I felt as though I were seeing him for the first time. A tremendous feeling of love and gratitude welled up in me. I'd never dreamed any man could love me like this.

Tears flooded my eyes and I couldn't stop them as they slid down my cheeks. Brandon gasped. "Honey, don't," he whispered, all concern and gentle touches.

"It's all right," I said. "It's just that I love you so much."

"And I love you," he said. I held him, totally contented. I knew I could trust Brandon. I'd never meant for any of this to happen, but it had. He'd find a way to divorce Christine. Then we'd be together forever.

I wanted to stay in bed with him and never have to move again. But then Brandon was looking at his watch. "I have to get home," he said. "I told Christine I'd only be gone a couple of hours. She thinks I'm at the office."

I cringed at his words, at the age-old excuse men pawn off on unsuspecting wives. Desolation plunged down over me. But this was the way it had to be—for a while.

I pushed myself up from the bed and reluctantly watched Brandon hurry into his clothes. Our good-bye kiss at the door was rushed and wrong. I closed the door behind him and for a moment I felt like crying. But I firmly jerked myself away from that. Self-pity wasn't my style.

The next day at work it was all I could do to keep from grabbing Joan and telling her I was in love. I didn't, of course. It was a secret I had to hold close within myself.

When I saw Brandon he was all business. Of course, we carefully avoided any physical contact. At lunchtime I went to the deli with Joan. She wanted to know why I'd had lunch with Brandon the day before.

"He needed someone to talk to," I said. "Just business."

"Well, I should hope so," Joan said. "I got into that tangle with a married man once. Never again!"

I nodded, sympathizing with her, yet knowing in my heart that my case was different. Frankly, I'd always believed Joan was too quick to sleep with any good-looking man who came along. But it was her life and she could do as she pleased.

That night Ernie Summers called me. I answered the phone with a lilting voice. "Hey, you sound great," he said. "Guess you recovered."

My heart plunged. "I—I guess it was just an upset stomach," I lied. God, how I hated lying. It wasn't me. I felt so rotten about it I agreed to go out with Ernie that night to a movie.

It was a silly movie. A family-type comedy, full of slapstick and nutty people. Ernie laughed uproariously, and I couldn't help chuckling a little, too. It all seemed far removed from my kind of reality.

After the movie we had hamburgers and walked

back home because it was a lovely night. There was the smell of rain in the air and we held hands like a couple of kids. When he kissed me good night at the door it felt very quaint, like a page out of a high school dating book.

I drew back and looked up at Ernie. He was cute enough, with twinkling eyes, and a boyish grin. *Why do you have to be so darned nice?* I wondered. *You make it so hard to cut you out quickly.*

We said good night and I slipped inside, vowing to break it off with Ernie the next time he called. I would make some vague excuse and he'd get the message. I went to bed and closed my eyes, weaving fantasies about Brandon and how it would be after we were married.

During the next month Brandon and I were together whenever possible. Sometimes he'd phone and come over. Occasionally we'd know ahead of time when he could escape from Christine. I found myself becoming impatient.

"Have you said anything to Christine?" I asked him one night.

"Honey, not yet. She's having a hard time with the business classes she's taking. But she's going to make it. I just have to keep encouraging her. You do understand, don't you?"

What could I say? He looked so desperate and his eyes pleaded with me for patience. All I could do was nod and bury my head against his shoulder. I loved him so much. He did such wild, beautiful things to me in bed.

I'm sorry to say some nasty thoughts began to creep into my mind. Like how he'd learned to make love so perfectly although he and Christine didn't get along. From all I'd heard about her she wasn't the sort to enjoy a lot of wild bedroom antics. Had Brandon known other women? I began to feel jealous and possessive.

But each time, I'd force the nasty, doubting thoughts away. Brandon was my lover now. Not Christine's. It was like Brandon said, it was just a matter of time until he got the divorce.

In spite of my vows about Ernie, I still went out with him again. He was so boyish and eager. Hurting him would be like kicking an innocent puppy.

Besides, I'd had a couple of remarks from people about how I was glowing. "Bound to be love," Mr. Conner had teased. How could I tell him it was his prized Brandon Myers that I loved? I had to let people think it was Ernie Summers.

My office was big on company parties. A retirement always meant a cocktail party after work, and wives and dates were always invited, too. I invited Ernie to the one we were having on Friday.

I was glad I had when Brandon walked in with Christine on his arm. She was just like I'd been told. A petite, fluffy beauty that clung to Brandon's arm as they moved through the crowd to the bar.

I crowded back up against Ernie in the dimly-lit corner. I'd felt sure Brandon would bring her. Yet now that he had, I felt so utterly and totally betrayed I wanted to hide.

When Brandon asked her what she'd like to drink, a wistful little-girl tone came over her voice. "I don't know, darling. Whatever you say," she practically lisped. I felt sick to my stomach.

"Let's get out of here," I said to Ernie.

"Huh?" He looked surprised. "It just started."

"I don't feel good. Please, Ernie."

"Well, okay," he said reluctantly and put down his glass on a nearby table.

As we edged through the crowd toward the door, we had to pass by Brandon and Christine. His eyes caught mine and he frowned, but I looked away and hurried on. At home I practically pushed Ernie out the door. He was all worried, saying I looked pale.

"I'll get some sleep," I said. "Please, Ernie. I want to be alone." The words came out harsher than I'd meant them to be.

"Well, okay," he said, his tone hurt.

I closed the door and leaned against it, fighting tears. It had hurt so badly to see Brandon with his wife. It hurt right down to the center of my bones.

Saturday was just miserable. Normally I cleaned the apartment, did the laundry, my hair, and the ironing. All those working-girl things. I forced myself through the routine, doing it all haphazardly and fighting depression all the time.

By dark, I was so down I wanted to crawl off in a hole someplace and never come out. It was Saturday night. Fun night. Date night. Joan had a new guy she was dating regularly and I felt a certain envy. At least her guy was free.

When the doorbell rang, my heart nearly jumped out of my chest. *Brandon!* I thought and ran to open it. It was him.

He stepped in quickly and closed the door. "Why did you rush off from the party yesterday?"

"Why do you think?" I asked him. "I couldn't stand seeing you and Christine together."

"Honey, don't be angry," he coaxed.

"Why shouldn't I be? It hurt!"

"So how do you think I felt seeing you there with that shoe salesman? Huh?"

"He doesn't mean anything to me," I came back. "Just a date. Besides, if you loved me so much, you'd marry me."

"Honey. Baby." Brandon reached out and caressed my arm. "I do love you, and you know it." He led me to the sofa and pulled me down beside him. I sat stiffly in his arms.

"Christine is having a rough time. But she's trying at school. I have to make her independent and self-supporting or we'll have her on our backs for the rest of our lives. Now, you don't want that, do you?"

"No," I answered miserably. I didn't want that. The rest of our lives. Such beautiful words. I began to relax in Brandon's arms. I turned slightly and leaned against him. Giving a deep sigh, he cupped my face with one hand and kissed me hard on the lips.

"You're the one I love," he said. "That's the way it is, and don't you ever forget it. Do you understand?"

"Yes. Yes!" I cried, and kissed him back. I couldn't be angry when Brandon was holding me. He was so sweet, so tender. I hated the situation—the secrecy, the guilt. But when his arms were around me, when he was holding and kissing me, I could forget it all.

His hands, his mouth, the strength of his body pressed against mine—that's what I lived for. I felt him holding me, and we stretched out full-length together on the long, narrow sofa.

"Beautiful Allie," he whispered, caressing me. He kissed my ears, my throat, and my face. When he made love to me it was as if I were drugged, powerless to stop him from taking anything he wanted from me.

I closed my eyes and gave myself up to him, silencing the nagging, annoying voice of my conscience, cutting out the picture of Christine—Christine looking up helplessly at Brandon and waiting for him to make the simple decision about what she should drink. . . .

I let his kisses take my breath away. I could taste his breath, his skin, his lips. Magically, I was drinking him in, knowing all the ways of his body.

Every sense in me was sharpened as Brandon eased me out of my clothes, and then I from his. Every cell in my body was aroused and aware of every cell in his. He traced kisses, like gently falling leaves, over my eyelids.

*He can't be this way with any other woman,* I thought. *Not with Christine. No, it was me he loved! She was only a burden he must rid himself of. I loved him and he loved me. That made all things right. It must. It had to!*

We were still in each other's arms when the phone rang. "Don't answer it!" Brandon snapped.

But it went on ringing and ringing. I had to silence it. I got up and it was Ernie Summers. He wanted to know if I'd like to go for a late drive. "I'm sorry," I said. "I can't."

"I see. Good night for now, Allie. But we're going to have a talk soon."

I was trembling as I hung up the phone. Why did life have to be so complicated? Why couldn't two people just love each other and let it be at that.

I went back into Brandon's arms, but it wasn't the

same. "Who was that?" he asked me.

"Ernie," I said.

"I don't like you seeing him," Brandon said. "I wish you wouldn't."

"He's harmless. I don't sleep with him, you know."

Brandon stiffened. "What do you mean by that?"

"I mean, you go back and sleep in your wife's bed," I said, moving away from Brandon. I pulled on my blouse and slacks. I didn't want to be nude in front of him any longer.

"We don't have any kind of relationship," he said coldly, the words sounding almost prim.

"You mean you two don't have sex?"

"That's right. We don't!" He sounded furious with me.

"And what does Christine think of that? Doesn't she suspect something?"

"Of course she does. It's part of leading the way to separation. Besides, she never cared much for sex anyway."

"Then how did you get to be such a good lover?" I asked, my words dripping with sarcasm as my heart wrenched with pain.

"Allie!" He looked stunned, hurt. "How could you?" he asked. "Honey, I love you. You know that. My God, what does a man have to do to prove that he loves someone?"

I was immediately sorry. "I didn't mean it," I cried. "I didn't." Poor Brandon. He had so many problems. He was trying to rid himself of a clinging wife as best he could.

I forgave him and went into his arms. We made love again before he left.

True to his word, Ernie did talk to me. It was late Sunday afternoon and he didn't even bother to call. He just came over.

"Something is going on, and I have to know what it is," he said bluntly after he sat down on the sofa where Brandon and I had made love the night before.

I sat on the edge of a chair. "There's someone else," I admitted slowly.

"I thought so. Guess I'm what you'd call a slow mover. I thought something special might develop between you and me, Allie."

I looked at him. What could I do? He was a perfectly nice man, but I didn't love him. I felt a certain affection for him. I didn't want to hurt him. Yet in a curious way I could see he was exactly the sort of man a woman could marry and she'd know what to expect from life.

He was exactly the sort of man I'd once dreamed about finding. Only, love doesn't happen that way.

"I'm sorry," I murmured, unable to say anything more.

"This other man," Ernie said slowly. "He's married, isn't he?"

My heart jolted. "My God," I breathed. "How did you know?"

"You've been so secretive. Which isn't like you. If he was just another guy, you'd have told me. Instead you've kept on dating me. What am I, Allie? Some kind of cover for the two of you?"

"Oh, no, Ernie. It's never been like that. I swear it," I said, but my voice lacked conviction because I was lying.

Ernie stood up, his body rigid with anger. "Good-bye, Allie. I guess I read you all wrong."

I sat there and let him walk out without saying a word. I couldn't. He was right. I felt so ashamed. Hot tears burned my eyes. I sat there, my hands clasped together, and felt the tears run down my cheeks. They flooded faster and dripped down onto my clothes. There was nothing I could do to stop them.

I told myself it would be simpler with Ernie out of my life. And it should have been. Yet in a strange way I missed him, and the harmless fun we'd had together.

But there was still Brandon Myers and our love— what we could steal of it. I planned a small celebration for our three-month anniversary, fixing dinner at home, with candles and wine and all the corny stuff I'd once thought of in terms of married anniversaries. But all people in love have anniversaries, and they should be celebrated.

I begged Brandon to stay overnight, something he'd never done. I wanted just once to wake up and find him asleep beside me. I wanted to curl up against him and know he'd be there all night long.

He'd promised to try to work something out. Only it didn't come about. Christine was facing finals and was uptight over them. So we drank our wine and ate our food. I tried to be happy. I laughed, but it sounded hollow. I dressed in sexy, becoming clothes for Brandon and felt out of place in them. Only in bed was I able to blot out everything and lose myself in his lovemaking.

Sometimes I felt like a sex junkie. Like Brandon was the pusher and I the junkie, and without him I'd die. He knew more about pleasing a woman than any man should know.

Afterward he had to get up and dress. "But soon we'll do something special," Brandon promised me. "Look, there's Labor Day weekend coming up. I'll find some reason to go out of town. We'll make reservations at the lodge up in the mountains." He paused. "It'll be our time."

I wanted that. A three-day weekend alone, together. *Only it shouldn't be this way,* I thought. *It should be a honeymoon.* Still, I was excited and pleased. To have Brandon to myself for three days was a minor miracle in our situation. He made reservations and I was floating.

Then one week before Labor Day, Brandon told me the trip was off. "My mother is coming," he said. "She and Christine have made all sorts of plans."

"So let them do them alone," I said. "Business is business to them. If you say you have to go out of town, then you still have to go."

"Honey, I can't. This is my mother coming. I really do want to see her."

"Oh, Brandon!" I cried. "How could you?"

"Well." He shrugged. "What do you want me to do? Go announce to the two of them that I have a mistress and I'm going away with her."

"Mistress!" I yelled. "Mistress! Is that how you think of me?"

"No, honey. No." He grabbed me and actually shook me. "No, I don't. But they would. My God, I love you." He kissed me roughly.

It wasn't so easy to make up that time. I couldn't quite forgive Brandon for that episode. I spent a horrible, hot three days in the city, and Tuesday when I returned to work, Joan told me at lunch that

Mr. Myers had been talking about his weekend. "He took his wife and mother up to some lodge," she said. "He said it was great."

"His wife and mother?" I said and realized how angry I sounded. I swallowed hard and tried to ignore the puzzled look Joan was giving me.

"I thought you and I might go up there sometime," she said. "We might meet some new men. You haven't been the same girl since you and Ernie broke up. Honey, you need to spread yourself around and not sit home and brood. You can't meet a new guy without getting out and doing a little hunting."

"Maybe my hunting instinct isn't as strong as yours," I snapped.

Joan flushed. "What did I do?" she cried.

"Nothing. Nothing. I'm sorry." I pushed the rest of my lunch away and got out of there. It seemed as if I was fighting with everyone lately.

But the nerve of Brandon to take his mother and wife to the very place he'd made reservations for us! It was all too sick. I couldn't stand it anymore.

I marched back to work and straight to Brandon's office. He was in, munching on a sandwich, and still working. I closed the door behind me and ignored the startled look on his face. "I just found out you took your wife to our lodge," I flung at him.

"I took my mother, too," he hissed. "Lower your voice, Allie."

"I will not. I am sick of sharing you with her. This just can't go on, Brandon. You can't have us both."

"I don't want both of you. Only you, Allie." His voice was soft and pleading. Only this time he couldn't sway me. "Just give me a little more time, Allie. I have to arrange everything. I'll see a lawyer."

"Promise?" I asked him.

"I promise. Now give me a kiss and pop out of here before someone catches us."

Triumphant, I returned to work and nearly burned up my computer with my speed. It was all going to work out. Brandon and I were going to be together!

For one week I floated along on my little cloud of illusion. Then Brandon blew it apart. He was at my place after work. We'd made love, slowly, lazily, and then gotten dressed. I'd made us sandwiches and we were eating them when Brandon laid his plans down.

"Allie, I have to tell you something. That promise I made about seeing a lawyer. I can't just yet." A horrible silence spread over the room.

"Why?"

"Christine has dropped out of business school. She says she'll never be able to be a secretary. She's decided she wants to be a nurse now."

"A nurse?" A small laugh slipped from between my lips, then bubbled into hysteria. "A nurse." That bit of helpless fluff could never be a nurse. The idea was too ludicrous to even consider. Brandon and Christine both had to be out of their minds to even think such a thing could work.

"You're both crazy!" I told him.

"No. No." In all seriousness he shook his head. "She means this. She feels she has a calling. She wants to help people."

"Oh, Brandon," I whispered, going icy cold. I could see the years suddenly spread out in front of us. Christine would go from one career to another and always drop out, and Brandon would always drop in, to my place—but he'd never stay.

Maybe in some curious way Brandon did love us

both. I wasn't sure. I only knew it wasn't going to work. "I want you to leave," I said. "And don't ever come back."

"Allie!" He stood up so suddenly his chair fell over. "What's gotten into you?"

"Some sense, I hope. It's a dead end, Brandon. You and me. It's not going to happen."

"But I love you!"

"But you'll never leave her," I said.

"Sure, I will. I will!" His tone was desperate. But he was only kidding himself. Brandon hadn't deliberately set out to use me. He really thought he could change his wife and rid himself of her easily. Unfortunately, he was wrong, only he didn't know it yet.

Somehow, with a strength I didn't know I possessed, I got Brandon out of the apartment and out of my life. It wasn't easy. He telephoned—he cornered me at work. Finally I was left with no choice but to give up the job I loved and find another.

It's been two months now and Brandon has quit calling. In that time, I've learned a lot. I've learned I was wrong to try to find happiness at someone else's expense, and I'll never make that same mistake again.

I saw Ernie Summers recently. He was polite, friendly, and very much engaged. Though we were never in love, a part of me aches for what might have been between us if things had been different. Now all I can do is wish him happiness.

For me, there'll be another man in time, I hope. A man who is free to love. **THE END**

# *CARJACKED BY CONS ON THE LAM*

It was still raining outside the hospital as the paramedics pushed their stretcher in with a blanket-covered figure. Usually I was more than willing to help with every patient, but that Friday afternoon, I moved toward the group reluctantly.

Students are supposed to leave on time, and I was eager to get off duty because Darryl was driving to the lake with me to meet my parents and my son, Gabriel. We were going to celebrate his third birthday. But there had been more than the usual number of California traffic-accident victims that day. Rain had been falling intermittently for several days, and now it was fairly steady, slicking the freeways and limiting visibility.

I helped move the patient to a hospital stretcher and covered her shaking body with a blanket. A short distance away, a paramedic gave the oncoming nurse a brief report, and I heard enough to make me look at the distraught young woman again.

The patient's injury had little to do with the storm, he said. She'd been raped and then somehow got away from her attacker. In the struggle, she'd injured her ankle. As I was removing the young woman's wet shoes, one of the paramedics came back to speak to her.

"Sorry it took so long to get here," he said. "We had to detour twice. The roads were closed due to mudslides."

She blinked her eyes as if she was too exhausted to reply. Little wheels of worry began to move in my head. Resolutely I turned them off and went right on removing the soggy shoes. I was going to see Gabriel that weekend despite rain, rape victims, or mud-blocked roads. And Darryl was going with me. Suddenly my heart was lifting, despite the evidence of horror before me.

The patient groaned and I gave her my full attention. The doctor came then and examined her briefly, and the nurse gave her a shot.

"You can leave after you take Mrs. Hurston to X-ray, Carrie," the nurse said. She helped me position the pale young woman in a wheelchair. "Be careful going home," she added. "We don't need any more patients."

I pushed the wheelchair down the long hall to the radiology department and waited for an aide to take the patient into an X-ray room. She shifted in the wheelchair and closed her eyes. Her face tightened as she clamped her lips together.

"Does your ankle still hurt?" I asked, trying to keep my mind on the patient instead of the coming weekend.

She nodded. "But I bet it doesn't hurt as bad as that jerk's foot," she said with a show of anger.

"The man who attacked you?"

"Who *raped* me," she said. "And I took a rape-prevention class," she added wryly. "But at least I'm alive. Somehow I remembered the demonstration in class. I kicked his kneecap as hard as I could and stomped on his foot." She shivered violently. "I hope I broke every bone in his foot."

A radiology aide came and I left, telling her someone else would come after her and I hoped she'd feel better soon. Then I forgot her as I skipped around to the front desk, my heart fluttering again in anticipation of seeing Darryl. He didn't get off until five o'clock, so I'd have time to say hello and rush home for a quick shower at the apartment I shared with two other vocational nursing students.

"Hi!" I grinned broadly at the receptionist. "Think I could see Darryl for a sec?"

She nodded, scarcely looking up from the stack of reports in front of her, and I zipped around the desk and peeked in the first X-ray room. Darryl wasn't there, but one of the other radiology technicians recognized me.

"That pretty student is here, Darryl," he called into the adjoining room as he winked at me.

I smiled my thanks and waited for Darryl to finish his work.

"Hey, honey," he said when he came out to see me. "I'm not going to be able to go with you. Lipton called in sick, and with all the accidents, I'll have to take his weekend call."

My smile slipped right down to the toes of my shoes. "Can't you get someone else to do it?" I pleaded, knowing it was useless. Darryl was in charge of the department while his chief was on sick leave with an ailing gall bladder, and he took it very seriously.

"We can still see each other after the shift is over," he said, "if there aren't any more emergencies."

I sighed in defeat. "I have to go see Gabriel. It's his birthday tomorrow, remember?"

"Oh, Carrie, I'm sorry." Darryl's voice was leaden. "It's hard, having to disappoint a three-year-old."

"I'm *not* going to disappoint him," I said stubbornly.

"Carrie, I hate to see you start out alone for the lake in this weather. I hear that visibility is terrible, not to mention the condition of the roads."

"It's only an hour and a half. I've been driving it for eight months now. I could almost find my way in the dark." I struggled to keep my voice from wavering.

"I still think it would be wise to wait till morning. Call your mother and explain. Better to be safe than sorry." He smiled to take the sting from his words, and he reached for my hands. As his fingers closed over mine, I felt the warmth of his touch spread over my body. My heart did flip-flops as usual, thinking of seeing him when he finished work, and I thought seriously of waiting until morning to drive to the lake.

"I'll call Mom and see if it's raining as hard at the lake as it is in San Francisco," I said, pulling my hand reluctantly from Darryl's caressing fingers. I looked longingly at him, torn between seeing my son and staying here with Darryl. I wanted turn my lips up for the touch of his, even a hasty touch, but he was reserved and cautious. I stepped back, blew him a kiss behind the receptionist's back and hurried to the apartment to place a call.

I waited anxiously for Mom to answer the insistent ringing, wanting more to hear about my little son than whether or not it was raining. It was bad being away from Gabriel all week. I missed the feel of his arms around my neck, holding him on my lap as I read his favorite story for the thirtieth time, even watching ants cross the sidewalk with him. It had been two weeks since I'd seen him. I'd worked as an aid at the hospital last weekend to finish paying for the tricycle that was in the trunk of my car.

Gabriel had never known his father. Frank had been killed in a motorcycle accident the week we were to be married. I stayed home with my folks, working as a cashier at a gas station until Gabriel was born. Afterward I returned to the gas station, but when it closed I couldn't find another job.

Finally, an unemployment office worker suggested that I enroll in the vocational nurse's training program. The government program would assist me financially while I was getting the education that would allow me to get a job to support me and my son.

I was so happy, I felt I could touch the sky. That's what I wanted—to be able to take care of my son as Frank would have. The only problem was being away from Gabriel all day while I went to school. But I thought of the choices. Having loved Frank so dearly, I didn't think I could love anyone else enough to get married. And with Gabriel to take care of, I'd have to work or apply for welfare assistance.

I decided to go to school, and my parents offered to care for Gabriel. Then Dad had a heart attack, and they moved to the lake, a ninety-minute drive from San Francisco. Eight hours had lengthened into forty each week between my seeing my son.

Halfway through my training I met Darryl, who was an X-ray technician at the hospital. Because of him, I found I could love again. . . .

Mom finally answered the telephone. Gabriel's excited voice in the background dimmed my concern about the weather. I listened attentively as he told me about the cake Grandma and he were baking. A twinge tugged at my heart for a second, wishing I was the one helping him bake his birthday cake. Mom came back on the line to tell me she was glad the rain had let up, because the lake residents were worried about the rising water.

"It hasn't let up any in the city," I said.

"Maybe you shouldn't try to start for the lake tonight," Mom said anxiously. "We'll take care of Gabriel."

"I'll check the weather report," I promised. Then Gabriel had to say good-bye, and I forgot to tell my mother that Darryl couldn't come with me. I hung up with the sound of my son's voice haunting me.

I called X-ray, planning to tell Darryl about the danger of the lake rising and to discuss traveling on the freeway despite the storm. But the receptionist told me that they were swamped with a backlog of requests for X-ray examinations.

"I'll leave him a message if you like," she said. She seemed to be answering someone else at the same time. "But he's so tied up that it could be a while before he returns the call."

That settled it. I'd waited for Darryl's call before when he was on emergency. Sometimes it was three in the morning before things slowed enough for him to pick up the telephone, and he would be too tired and tense to talk long.

"Just leave a message that I'll call him on Saturday," I said.

It wasn't raining as I drove onto the freeway, but I wasn't lulled into a false sense of security by the rainless gloom. The sky was dark. Cars were lined up like boxcars on a freight train in every lane.

I crept along the crowded freeway behind a van. I tried not I think of the overload of traffic-accident victims, telling myself that if I kept alert it couldn't happen to me.

In a shutdown of traffic movement, I turned up the radio in search of a weather report or a report on road conditions on the way to the lake. "Mud-slides have closed many roads leaving the San Francisco area," a broadcaster's voice announced. He went on to list specific roads that were impassable. In addition, he warned of stalled cars and accidents blocking freeway travel.

His warning came none too soon. The rain started again with a rush of water that ran across the windshield like a released river. I strained to follow the minivan's taillights. Suddenly, they stopped moving. I slammed on my brakes. My front bumper touched the stalled minivan in front of me. I braced myself for a buffeting from the car behind me, but it didn't come. The van driver waved me around. I moved inches back, flicked the turn signal, and crawled into the next lane. I held my breath until I was around the stalled car.

By the time I reached the turnoff toward the small lake town where my parents had moved, I could feel the aching tenseness in my arms and shoulders. I shook my shoulders and unclenched numb fingers that clutched the steering wheel of my ancient car. Once I left the freeway traffic, it would be safer to drive, I told myself. There was little traffic on the road that led through the dairy lands. There was less chance of an accident. I breathed a sigh of relief.

Water poured across the road before me. I slowed the car, barely moving through the water, so the engine wouldn't stall. Minutes later, a wall of earth forced me to stop the car. I could see that a narrow section of the road was open. I switched on my bright lights, so a car coming from the other direction could see me, and shifted so I could back up and move around the mud hill.

Before the car had moved a foot, a traffic officer trotted around the barrier. "Better turn back, lady," he advised. "There's another slide behind me. It's no night for driving these roads."

# CARJACKED BY CONS ON THE LAM

He helped me turn around, and I drove back toward the freeway onramp. *Halfway to Mom's house,* I thought in exasperation. *And halfway back to the apartment in San Francisco.* I could hear Darryl, cautious Darryl: *You can go in the morning.*

I chewed my lower lip. Gabriel would be waiting up for my arrival. By the time I got back to the apartment and telephoned Mom, I could be holding Gabriel in my arms. I knew another route to the lake, past the prison, the county park, and the dam. It was nearly flat land—no mountains to loosen their layers of water-logged earth on the road and prevent my passage.

The rain was steady as I took the on-ramp leading away from San Francisco. I only had a few miles to travel on the freeway before I saw the sign for the new route to the lake.

There were no other cars and dusk was rapidly becoming darkness. Even though my headlights were bright, it was difficult to penetrate murky darkness. I crawled along, praying I wouldn't run off the road.

The prison lights, lifting upward into the wet sky, loomed to my left and faded as I moved past the towering fences. I rounded a curve and started down a long, narrow road guarded by columns of trees. The wind was rising, thrashing the wet branches into frenzied action. Water covered the road again, sucking at my tires and lapping at the fenders. I moved slower. I couldn't let the car stall here. Panic filled my chest. Why hadn't I returned to San Francisco?

As my foot hovered tensely over the gas pedal,

the car moved out of the path of the rushing water. Wet asphalt hissed beneath the tires with almost welcoming comfort. Even the wind-lashed rain that severed my sight two feet beyond the hood of the car didn't cancel my relieved sigh. The worst was over. I was on high-er ground now. I could stop and wait a few min-utes for my heart to settle back down in my chest. My foot pressed on the brake pedal.

Suddenly, the door opened on my side of the car. A harsh voice commanded me to move over as rough hands shoved me away from the steer-ing wheel. I was so startled, I couldn't speak.

A bare-headed, rain-drenched man plopped under the steering wheel and reached across me to unlock the passenger door. A second man slipped soggily into the seat beside me.

"What do you think you're doing?" I screamed when I found my voice.

"Shut up!" the man on my left snarled.

"Get out of my car!" I knew my demand was ridiculous, but I had to fill the silence with the sound of my voice. Otherwise, I'd panic.

"Lady, there's no buses going by, so we're going to let you be a Good Samaritan. A *live* Good Samaritan—if you play it smart," the man on my right muttered through clenched teeth.

The man in the driver's seat moved the car for-ward, seeming to pay little attention to me or his companion. It was too dark to see more than a dim outline of his face. His lips were clamped together in a straight line. His huge hands gripped the wheel inches below his chin as his eyes strained to see through the water sluicing over the windshield.

The car wiggled like a pollywog, inch by inch, traveling from one puddle to the next. I'd been as wrong about finding dry land as I had been about finding safety away from the crowded freeway.

I was stunned. My body shifted to a rigid, upright position, drawing in upon itself, straining to keep my skin from contact with the strangers on each side of me. The car swerved to avoid a falling branch. I lurched forward and kept my balance by catching the cracked cover of the dashboard. I continued to cling to the dash and felt the cracks in the vinyl cut into my fingers. The pain shocked me into reality. This wasn't a nightmare; I wasn't dreaming.

It seemed hours as I sat immobile between the two men. I didn't speak to them, and they didn't speak to me. The wind and the rain and the thrashing branches were the only sounds to break the silent terror in the car. Twice, headlights flushed the darkness ahead of us. The man at the wheel dimmed the light on my car and the two pairs of headlights sidled past each other. It was hopeless to try to attract the attention of the occupants of the other cars.

The man on my right leaned forward, gazing into the blackness, and I released my grip on the dash and settled back against the cushion. Turning my head slightly, I looked at him. He was older than the driver, and his hair was shorter. The dim outline of his face showed a humped nose protruding from a long, thin face. He had a toothpick or a twig in the left corner of his mouth. He moved back, and I kept my eyes straight ahead then.

I was afraid to look at the other man. Somehow, his harshness frightened me more.

Suddenly, I heard a muffled shot. The car jerked slightly before the driver could correct it. Then the flapping of a torn tire on the pavement added to the storm sounds.

The driver pressed his foot on the brake pedal and scanned the narrow road until he found enough space on the shoulder to pull off and park.

"You got a spare?" he growled.

"Yes, in the trunk," I said.

"Jake!" the driver snapped. He extended the car keys to his companion.

The man called Jake said nothing. He took the keys, opened the door, and slid out into the downpour.

"Stay put," the younger man said sharply to me. "It won't take long for Jake to change the tire."

He didn't have to tell me to stay out of the rain, but I didn't say so. I watched the water banging against the windshield as if it was determined to break through the glass, but I felt no pity for the man forced out in it to change a tire.

As time passed, the driver got edgy. "He ought to be through by now," he muttered. "Jake!" he yelled.

"Can't get to the tire," a muffled reply came back.

"Out!" the man in the seat beside me prodded me roughly with the heel of his hand. "This way." He motioned toward himself. "And stay near. I don't want to have to use this on you."

He pulled a knife from the waist of his trousers. Then he shoved it back and closed the car door, shutting off the light. I stumbled toward the back of the car, my feet catching on sodden weeds. Rain beat furiously against my light sweater.

Jake was struggling with Gabriel's tricycle.

"Help him get it out," the man with the knife ordered me.

Jake tugged relentlessly at the handlebars, but the tricycle seemed to be chained in place. Rain-blinded, I bent my head under the trunk lid, located the pedal caught under the latch of the lid, and released it. I stepped back, the rain drenching me again, and gasped for breath. Jake lifted the trike out and dropped it on the muddy earth.

I reached forward and flipped back a piece of canvas to reveal the tools needed to change the tire. Jake juggled the jack under the bumper of the car and stabilized it with rocks he had stacked nearby.

"Did you block the wheels?" the younger man asked.

"Done," Jake mumbled. He worked slowly but steadily until the damaged tire was replaced, and then he carried the jack and tools back to the trunk.

"The tricycle," I said hesitantly.

"What?"

"The tricycle. It's for my son's birthday tomorrow." The words came out jerkily. Fear threatened to trap each one in my throat.

"Leave it," the driver snapped. He grabbed my

arm violently and spun me around, shoving me toward the front seat of the car. Terrified, I slid under the wheel obediently and moved to the center.

A few moments later, I heard the trunk lid slam, and Jake joined us in the car. I pushed dripping hair away from my eyes and shuddered. And then my whole body began to shake with the cold. I clenched my teeth to try to control the shakes, but it didn't help.

The driver started the car again, then reached to switch on the heater. "It's broken," I said.

He turned on the headlights and guided the car back onto the asphalt. Minutes later, the tires made a different sound on the road as if the substance beneath them had changed to gravel. The car bounced as a tire found a pothole. There were few houses now, and their lights were faint and far away. Trees, too, were fewer, like lonely sentinels thrashing in protest at the savage, whipping wind. An occasional branch broke under the strain and skittered across the road.

For a moment I thought of the tricycle. How could I have been so foolish as to expect to save it? I'd be lucky to save my life to take to Gabriel, let alone a present!

"How old is your son?" Jake's voice startled me.

"Three tomorrow." I clamped my lips together. I didn't want to talk at all to these terrible men, especially about my son. Gabriel needed me to take care of him, and I was sure that my kidnappers cared little about that. Maybe less if they knew how important it was to me.

"I hope he likes the tricycle."

I darted a glance at the man.

"Only took a second to toss it in." His words were indistinct, muffled by lips clamped over the ever-present twig. "My son wanted a bicycle. I never got him one."

The driver snorted and reached over to turn up the radio. It crackled noisily and he turned it off. The sound of the storm poured into the car, and the driver braked suddenly.

Headlights struggled through the darkness, searching out a mass of shattered tree limbs and shuddering leaves blocking the path of the car. For a moment the rain lifted, as if to let the light illuminate the tower of broken branches. It looked like half the tree had split, toppling the severed section across the roadway in a barricade.

"I can't get around it, and I can't go over it," the driver snapped.

Jake moved out of the car without comment. The rain started again, filtering the light that clung to she tangled mass. The straining figure of Jake bobbed up and down amid the branches.

"I need some help, Ken." His voice came over the wind.

"Out." Ken prodded me. "We'll both help."

Jake latched onto a branch that looked as big as a telephone post and indicated a smaller one for me to grasp. Ken moved about three feet in front of us, moving his body in among the branches to gain a grip on a sizable surface of wood. Together, the three of us strained and pulled, and the mass began to move inch by inch until a narrow opening appeared on the roadway.

"One big pull might do it," Jake said. "On the count of three!"

I planted my feet as firmly as I could in the soggy earth and, on the third count, pulled until my chest screamed for relief. I felt the branches move. Suddenly, a loud crack thundered over the sound of the storm. The branch Ken held had snapped and he fell back with the crash into the wet, tangled mass. He lay there gasping for breath. When he found enough air, he began to curse and to claw at the branches to gain his footing.

For a moment I was dazed. I glanced at Jake. He leaned on the broken tree, breathing heavily. My mind jerked alert. This was my chance to escape!

I spun around and ran into the darkness. That is, my mind said I was running, but I was struggling, my lungs screaming for more air. The soggy soil was like glue, gripping my shoes. I strained to release them, and the sound of the released suction increased my fear. I was scarcely moving. I didn't dare look around to see how far I'd come. And then I felt a jerk as a powerful hand clutched my sweater.

I was caught, a captive again. Numbing terror struck me, freezing me into a drenched statue. Ken swung me around violently and hit my head so hard that I spun around and fell face forward. I fell sharp rock cutting into my cheek. I heard the man behind me breathing heavily and then someone moving toward me. I twisted on my side, trying to move away, all the time watching the menacing figure getting nearer. In the faint light of the headlight, I could see it was Ken. He was pulling a long, thin knife from his waistband.

"No!" Jake's shout didn't stop Ken. "She knows the roads. She can show us how to get to a highway."

He lunged at Ken, striking at the descending blade. The knife fell from Ken's hand. Jake straightened up, balancing himself awkwardly. But before he gained his balance, Ken lashed out at him viciously with a closed fist. He went down, his head making a dull sound as he struck the ground. I lay there, terrified.

"Maybe you're right," Ken snarled at the fallen body. He scooped up the knife. "You do know the way out of here, don't you?" He leaned over me. I nodded, not looking at him.

He grasped my arm and pulled me to sitting position. I struggled upright. "Let's go, Jake," he said as he pushed me ahead. There was no sound from Jake. Ken pushed me toward him. "Help him up."

I bent over Jake. Hysteria touched my voice. "He isn't moving." My finger touched his head and felt its dampness. I pulled them away, and in the filtered light of the headlights, I saw the rain wash away the pink stain on my hands.

Ken prodded Jake in the side with his shoe. "Come on, Jake. Let's get moving. The breakout will be discovered by now."

Jake lay limp. Ken pushed the body again with his foot. Jake's head moved off the rock it had struck. His mouth hung open as if it was trying to catch some rain.

Ken clamped his hand on my arm and dragged me back to the car, throwing me in the front seat. He never released his grip as his foot pounded the gas pedal. He shifted with his left hand.

I was still too scared even to notice the chill of my drenched clothes. One time, I stared at the gas gauge and saw the needle swing into the red zone. I just looked away into the darkness. What difference did it make if we walked? Walking would take longer to get to the highway. I'd have longer to live.

The car jogged along, hitting potholes with regularity. Far ahead, a yellow ball bobbled in the rain. Ken slowed to a stop before the yellow sawhorse that indicated a detour. Beyond the warning sign, the road dipped and disappeared under the cascading, angry water.

"I'm going to see how deep it looks," Ken said. "Come on." His hand crushed my wrist, cutting my metal watchband into the skin. I clenched my lips together and tried to unstick my wet clothes from the seat so I could move.

Impatiently, he dragged me toward the raging water. Farther down, the water leaked out over the low land, but a car couldn't get off the road and hope to travel through the shrub-thick terrain.

I figured Ken was thinking the same thing I was. Either we go through the water in the dip, or we go back down the potholed road. We stood on the edge and looked across.

Far away, a chain of lights indicated a highway. We could be saved if we could find a way to it. There was enough gas to get that far, and someone would help us. Suddenly panic gripped me in a tight vise. I dug my fingernails into my palms hard enough to draw blood.

*Saved!* But no way did Ken plan for *me* to be saved. If he tried to drive through the rising water, and if he made it to the other side, he had no further use for me.

I moved involuntarily, and he jerked me close to his body, keeping his hand clamped around my wrist. The knife in his waistband dug into my back. I knew then that I *had* to get away.

Somewhere in the back of my mind, I knew there was a way to stop him from running after me. The angry voice of the rape victim in the emergency wasn't even a conscious thought, but her words had stayed in my mind.

Without thinking twice, I leaned heavily on my left foot until I felt sure of my balance. Then I raised my raised my right foot, bent my knee and, with all the force I could gather, rammed my foot where I thought his kneecap should be. I didn't hesitate as his hand twisted my wrist. I brought my heel down on his foot as if I meant to grind it into the ground. Then I jerked my wrist free and ran.

I ran as far as the thick shrubs would allow, and when it was nearly impossible to move through them, I waded into the rushing water. I fell again and again. I felt my strength slipping into the seething water and washing away with it. Finally I stayed where I had fallen, lying half-submerged in the water, clinging to the branch of a fallen tree. I was exhausted, so exhausted that I scarcely felt the pelting rain.

At last it slowed to a drizzle, and in the direction of the road, I heard the wracking cough of a motor. It coughed again, then stopped, and I heard the engine running and saw the headlights flare.

The lights moved slowly toward the raging water where I lay. Then they turned. The car moved toward the water-filled dip in the road and disappeared. I strained to see the headlights emerge on the other side.

I filled my lungs with air. A traveling tree limb swept past me, touching my face with sharpened talons. I ducked my head toward the shelter of the fallen tree.

When I raised my head again, there were still no lights. Not even a taillight moving away from the dip. I lay there longer, afraid Ken had stopped the car on the other side and turned off the lights, waiting for me to walk back to the road.

At last, I struggled across the stream and into marshy land. I must have plodded two miles before I saw the light of a house. In the darkness, I voiced a prayer to God and started to run.

An elderly couple took me in. They wrapped me in a blanket and spooned hot coffee into me before they asked any questions. When I could explain my horrifying journey, the husband telephoned the sheriff's office. I wanted to call my mom, but I was so tired that I kept closing my eyes and drifting off.

When an officer arrived and heard my story, he suggested I go to the local hospital to have my scratches and bruises attended to. There, the doctor felt I should stay in the hospital overnight for observation.

I was given something to make me sleep, but before it took effect I called Mom. And then, torn between wanting to hear Darryl's voice and dreading to admit to him how foolish I'd been, I called him at the San Francisco hospital.

His voice held only concern and love. And he was sitting by my bedside when I awoke the next morning. I was too happy to ask how he'd gotten there, or who had taken over for him at the hospital. But late that afternoon, when I was safe at Mom's house, I did ask.

"I explained your ordeal to one of the other techs. He took over for me, and I got up here by taking the long way around." Darryl grinned at me. "Everyone's talking about my brave girl."

My heart swelled with love. Kind, cautious Darryl. Not one word about my lack of caution.

We learned later that both men were dead. Jake was found where he had fallen, and Ken's body was found days later when the water receded. My car was still in the dip when the water went down. The tricycle was somewhat the worse for wear. Nevertheless, we restored it to good enough shape for it to delight Gabriel. That was one birthday present that was a big hit, no matter how belated it was!

Darryl and I are married now. I'm taking care of Gabriel, and Darryl is taking care of both of us. We're living in an apartment near the hospital. I work as a licensed vocational nurse two days a week, but I will have to "retire" soon. With Gabriel and the new baby—who should arrive in

# CARJACKED BY CONS ON THE LAM

the fall—to take care of, I'll have enough nursing
to keep me busy!                    **THE END**